NIGHTMARE

Ernest Saunders joined the ~~the~~ Guinness Company in 1981 and 5 years turned it into one of the world's great companies. Then in 1986 after Guinness ~~takeover~~ battle for Distillers, d~~~~ ~~t~~he Government with an ~~election looming~~, launched an inquiry.

After 3 years of hell, entrapped in the legal system, he faces a fourth in court in 1990. Written by his son, *Nightmare* is a riveting business exposé, a legal drama, a family tragedy and a terrifying cautionary tale.

'a fascinating and enlightening read.'
Sunday Times

NIGHTMARE

Ernest Saunders
and the Guinness Affair

James Saunders

ARROW BOOKS

Arrow Books Limited
20 Vauxhall Bridge Road, London SW1V 2SA

An imprint of Random Century Group

London Melbourne Sydney Auckland Johannesburg
and agencies throughout the world

First published in Great Britain
by Hutchinson 1988
Arrow edition 1990

Printed and bound in Great Britain by
Courier International Ltd, Tiptree, Essex

ISBN 0 09 974480 5

CONTENTS

*This book is dedicated to all the friends who have stood by my family,
offering love, shelter and support over the last two years*

LIST OF ILLUSTRATIONS

Thomas Ward
Arthur Furer
Roger Seelig
Gerald Ronson
Lord Spens
Knoll House, Penn
Joanna and the author
Ernest after the Bow Street hearing of November 1988

Line Illustrations

Illustration Credits

Our thanks are due to the following: Photo Compeer, Klosters; *Evening News*; Camarascope Ltd; The Press Association; Mail on Sunday *You* Magazine; Universal Pictorial Press and Agency Ltd; The Scotsman Publications Ltd; Camera Press; Vickers plc; The *Financial Times*; Popperfoto/Reuter; Rex Features; The *Daily Telegraph*; *Punch*; The *Daily Express*; The *Standard*; Marc Boxer; The *Guardian*; The *Observer*.

ACKNOWLEDGMENTS

I would like to thank William Kay, former city editor of *The Times*, who helped me in the writing of this book and without whose invaluable guidance and assistance there would be no book at all.

Also, Norman Turner and everyone at Landau & Landau, who have worked with such dedication on my family's behalf.

Finally, my thanks to Nigel Urwin, Gill Coleridge, Richard Cohen and Peter Roche for bearing with me, and to Century Hutchinson for giving me the chance to tell my father's and my family's story.

PROLOGUE

For more than two years my father and our family have been living a nightmare. My father has been sacked, his reputation has been severely damaged, we have lost our home and used up all our savings in legal fees. At times throughout this period my father has been smeared by sections of the media that have been fed false information.

My father, Ernest Saunders, came to Britain at the age of two. He was a refugee from Hitler's invasion of Austria. His parents saved enough to send him to a good school and university, and when he graduated he took up a career in marketing. That was his life for the next quarter of a century. He married, raised a family and, like many other executives, jetted round the world on behalf of his employers.

In 1981 Ernest was approached by a firm of headhunters who wanted to know if he was interested in a senior management job with a major UK consumer goods company. This position turned out to be the managing directorship of Guinness, the brewers.

Once he and my mother were installed in a small flat over the head office in Mayfair, he quickly discovered the full extent of the job he had taken on. He waded into the task of salvaging the company and then built Guinness up with a series of successively bigger acquisitions, creating a world-class portfolio of quality brands.

When he participated in the Guinness takeover of Arthur Bell and Sons, the whisky group, in 1985, Ernest first encountered the nationalistic pride behind the so-called 'Scottish ringed fence'. But it was not until the next year that he was subjected to the full blast of the mistrust and resentment which appears to lurk north of the border when outsiders dare to intrude.

The battle for Distillers was one of the largest and most notorious corporate struggles Britain has ever witnessed. And as it ended, our family's nightmare began.

Two years ago, when my father was dismissed by his employers in a blaze of publicity, I was shocked and outraged by the amount of false and misleading information about his personal and professional life that was circulating in the public domain.

Last summer I decided that I had a unique opportunity to put the record straight and felt that I owed a duty to my family and to our loyal friends, if no one else, to do just that. I sat my father down and over the course of many weeks made him take me through the events of his life and business career. Many of the episodes he recounted were new even to me. I would like to apologise in advance to any readers who find the 'Ernest:' device for quoting my father irritating. I can only say that I found it most appropriate of the various options available.

When I turned to more recent events I found I could write much from my own memory as I have been intimately involved in the horrors that have engulfed my family and attended court on countless occasions.

Although I have been unconstrained in the writing of a large part of this biography, since a trial involving my father is pending I have been forced to omit any evidence which may be produced in court or discuss any matters with which a jury might be concerned. I can only hope that the remainder of the story will emerge at the conclusion of the trial.

Having said that, I have had the benefit of unlimited access to my father and, most importantly, his trust. I am writing his story in as full a form as I can at the moment. I hope it will serve as useful background for everyone interested in the current situation which, it is clear, involves matters of public importance.

James Saunders, 1989

FAMILY, CHILDHOOD AND UPBRINGING

My father's parents came from the Schleyer and David families of Czernowitz, a town which before the First World War was part of the Austro-Hungarian Empire, near the Rumanian border, and is now within the borders of the USSR. Michael and Melanie David had two children: Eric, who was born in 1903, and Joanna, known to everyone as Hanni, born in 1907. Michael David was a judge in Czernowitz, but when war broke out in 1914 he gave up his position and moved his family to Vienna, where he felt they would be safer from the advancing Russians.

Michael got a job as manager of a well-known Viennese aluminium company called Feischer-Magnesite, roughly equivalent to British Aluminium. At the end of the war, he was asked to stay on as the firm's legal representative. The family briefly returned to Czernowitz, by then part of Rumania, to organise their permanent move to Vienna, and to do this Michael had to become a Rumanian citizen, but he managed to retain his Austrian citizenship also. This was not difficult at that time: the Austrian Empire was disintegrating, and the borders of many states were changing. But having dual nationality was to prove a vital asset.

The David family settled in Vienna, and Hanni eventually went to the Les Allières finishing school in Lausanne, Switzerland. Her brother Eric qualified as a chemist at Prague University, and established his own chemical business in Vienna.

Emanuel Schleyer, known as Uly, came from a farming family in Czernowitz. He went to study medicine in Vienna in about 1920, when the Viennese School of Medicine was one of the most celebrated in the world. At an early age he had developed an interest in medical research, and later developed many new approaches to operating techniques and post-operative care. His father had died young, leaving Uly as the family breadwinner. Throughout his life he sent money to his family in various parts of the world, even when this involved considerable personal hardship.

On December 21 1933, Uly Schleyer married Hanni David. They continued to live in Vienna, where Uly was establishing his medical practice. In October 1935 their first son was born, my father, and they called him Ernest. He was followed in December 1937 by another son, Peter.

My great-grandfather, Michael David, was a man of foresight. He viewed the rise of Hitler during the 1930s with acute alarm, since both the David and Schleyer families were of Jewish origin. He had no doubt that anti-semitism would flourish in Austria, and he urged the family, including Hanni and Uly, to leave Austria for England as soon as possible.

Michael chose England because he believed in the basic freedoms and democratic processes which prevailed there. He and Melanie planned to leave first, and once they were established in England they would arrange Hanni and her family's entry as refugees. But in March 1938 Hitler annexed Austria, and it quickly became very difficult for Austrians to emigrate under the new regime, so in May Michael and Melanie travelled to England, using their Rumanian passports. Hitler had no jurisdiction over Rumanian citizens. Michael had moved my grandparents' most treasured possessions to his flat, and they were sent to England among his and Melanie's belongings.

Uly Schleyer was understandably reluctant to leave Vienna. By this time he was 40 years old and had established a growing reputation as a gynaecologist. Even so, it was soon obvious that to stay would risk the lives of himself and his young family. Neither he nor Hanni was religious, but they decided that, since their sons were going to be brought up as English boys, they should enter the Anglican Church before emigrating to Britain. In May 1938 my father, Ernest, and my uncle, Peter, were baptised in the English Church in Vienna.

Uly waited as long as he dared. By September 1938 he decided he could delay no longer. Taking with them what possessions they could, the Schleyer family were fortunately able to board a KLM plane in Vienna and arrived at London's Northolt Airport. When they quit Austria, Uly's brother Moritz also left and settled in Israel. One of his sisters, Sidy, stayed in Vienna, and another, Julie, went to the US after a spell in Shanghai.

Michael and Melanie David had been in England for some months and, after an initial stay at the Regent Palace Hotel off Piccadilly

Circus, they had moved into a furnished flat in Hodford Road, Golders Green, north London. Here the Schleyers made their first temporary home in England before moving to a rented house around the corner in Wycombe Gardens.

Ernest has vivid memories from this period: walking around Golders Green in a yellow gas mask, and speaking English at a local nursery school. He recalls my grandfather spending day and night at home, studying for medical exams. No matter how successful Uly Schleyer had been in Austria, the British Medical Association did not recognise his qualifications, and he had to retrain. Ernest: 'This was a difficult task for him. Although my mother spoke excellent English, my father had great problems with the language and of course the exams were all in English.' Nevertheless, Uly eventually sat his exams in Edinburgh, and, to his great relief, he passed and could start trying to build a practice.

When the London Blitz began, the Schleyer family moved to a flat lent by a friend of Michael's in a block on Berkeley Square, because they thought the four-storey building was bound to be sturdier than their small family house in Golders Green. But it was also nearer the Luftwaffe's favoured flight path. Ernest: 'I saw a red double-decker bus get knocked down by a bomb in Berkeley Square. I also remember one of the buildings in the square actually crumbling before my eyes during a raid. I couldn't understand why it was falling down.' Shortly afterwards they moved again, to Connaught Street, near Marble Arch, where Uly's temporary secretary owned a flat. Then, a few months later, Hanni and the two boys were evacuated to Oxford and went to live in a small house on Lathbury Road.

Ernest: 'This was one of the few occasions in the first ten years that my grandmother and grandfather did not actually live with my mother and the children. For years Grandmother, who in Austria had employed domestic staff, did all the cooking and most of the housework. Grandfather never spent a penny on himself, so that my brother and I could be properly clothed and fed. It is one of the memories of real decency etched in my mind, for here was a Czernowitz judge reduced to menial circumstances, never being able to do more than clerical work once he came to Britain, yet still making sure that whatever he had went to his daughter and her children.'

Ernest's memories of Oxford centre on air-raid warnings. He remembers spending most nights in an Anderson shelter erected under the dining-room table in Lathbury Road. Hanni, despite the fact that she had a young family, did voluntary work as a nurse at the Radcliffe Infirmary.

My grandfather did not go to Oxford, other than at weekends, and then only when his obstetrics practice permitted, because he felt it was important for him to establish himself in London. He rented a room at 56 Wimpole Street, where he set up his consulting room, at first on a shared basis since he did not have enough work to occupy it full-time. While the rest of the family was in Oxford, Uly lived in a bedsit in Westbourne Terrace, and Ernest particularly remembers one night he spent there: 'A bomb exploded right outside the building, the windows all shattered and the ceiling fell down. It was horrific.' After that incident, Hanni never brought the children to London again until the end of the war.

In 1941 my great-grandfather and -grandmother David decided that they were going to emigrate once more – this time to America. But emigration to the US had become very difficult as the list of applicants grew. The US authorities dealt with the problem by demanding ever higher financial guarantees, and finally the Davids were forced to give up the idea altogether. They went to Oxford instead.

Ernest was sent to New College School, a local pre-prep school. His only memory of it is not pleasant. 'I almost lost my eye when a gang of boys pushed me up against the wire of a tennis court and taunted me for being a foreigner,' he says. He still bears the scar on his face. By all accounts my father was a shy, reserved boy, and the taunts did not make it easy for him to make friends. At the age of six and a half, he was dispatched to Caldicott School in Farnham Royal, Buckinghamshire. He says: 'The sole reason for being sent there, instead of one of the many prep schools in Oxford, was that my father was terribly influenced by whatever his patients would say about life in England. My parents were keen to bring us up as proper English children, and my father had been told that English boys should go away to boarding school.'

For the first two years Ernest was at Caldicott, the family remained in Oxford. After that they moved to a rented house on Acacia Road in St John's Wood, back in north London, as the war was clearly coming to an end. Uly could now walk from his home across Regent's Park to his surgery in Wimpole Street. By this time the practice was beginning to flourish. Two-thirds of his patients were English. People wanted to come to him because of his Viennese training, as they had heard of the famous Viennese School of Medicine, and also because of his reputation for patient care. Uly never contemplated having an assistant, even when he could afford one, but would always visit in person. Ernest: 'That was how he developed his practice, as someone who really cared about his patients. He would not just deliver the babies, but would go and see the mothers once, twice or even three times a day for the time they were in the clinic.'

During the early days, my grandfather could not afford a car, so he used to cycle through London on his rounds with his doctor's brown gladstone bag on the back. Eventually he bought a secondhand Wolseley 10. He was always, according to Ernest, the most atrocious driver. I myself remember sitting in the back of a car which my grandfather was driving when he was in his seventies. My sister and I would hide behind the seats and close our eyes when he failed to notice red lights or avoided crashes only by inches. As my mother puts it diplomatically, 'He always had his mind on his work instead of on his driving.' There was one famous story my grandfather would tell of how he was simply driving slowly along when a bollard 'jumped' under his car!

Ernest was very unhappy boarding at Caldicott. Though he was in beautiful surroundings with magnificent sports facilities, he hated being away from home. Also, the war had unpleasant repercussions. 'Other children were incredibly cruel towards me, simply because I had a German-sounding name and parents with foreign accents. Of course, boys of that age couldn't distinguish between an Austrian refugee and a Nazi sympathiser, but things weren't made any better by searches in the school grounds for spies who were believed to have parachuted in from German planes.' Every week a battered envelope would arrive at school addressed to Ernest from his grandfather. It was no secret what was in it, since pieces of chocolate were either falling out of the inadequate wrapping or oozing half-melted out of the corners, condemning Ernest to another bout of leg-pulling.

The matron was a very ample woman called Miss Elgar. Ernest: 'She used to own an old-style Austin 7, from which she bulged out of all four open windows. She was incredibly tough at bath time. Twice a week we were submerged under oceans of Lifebuoy suds, which went up our noses and half-drowned us, while she scrubbed vigorously.'

Ernest's progress at Caldicott was moderate. His father never visited him – he always happened to have a case to attend to whenever there was a school function. There was no question: patients came before family. 'My mother, on the other hand, used to try and turn

up for everything,' Ernest recalls. 'She didn't drive, so she'd come
by train, and I remember one occasion when to get to Caldicott on
time she had to leave London so early that the police stopped her in
the street because they could not understand what she was doing
walking from St John's Wood in the small hours. They then gave
her a lift to Paddington Station.'

Ernest's dislike of boarding made him determined to go to a day
school in London, and his parents said that they would agree if he
passed his Common Entrance examination. Ernest studied hard and
well, and got into St Paul's, the school recommended as the best
London day school by one of his father's patients.

My grandmother, Hanni, felt that her two sons were somehow
very different from each other. Ernest was allegedly more sensitive,
Peter allegedly more sporty, and since she did not want them to
compete with one another, from the earliest days they were separated
at school, had different friends, and really only saw each other in the
holidays. Ernest: 'This was in fact not a very sensible thing to do. I
never had a natural relationship with my brother because I scarcely
ever saw him.' While Ernest went to St Paul's School, therefore,
Peter went to Westminster. And although both schools were in
London, Ernest went as a day boy and Peter as a weekly boarder.
Peter also was sent off to holiday camps for much of his holidays,
which did not help their relationship.

Before he joined St Paul's, Ernest's parents decided that a change
of surname would make life easier for him with other children. Since
the two brothers were in every way British, other than by birth, the
family simply went through the London phone book until they found
a suitable English name. Saunders was a name they all liked, and
seemed to go well with Schleyer. For professional reasons, Uly
wanted to keep his Viennese association, so he became Schleyer-
Saunders, while Ernest and Peter became simply Saunders. It was
a solution that worked. The persecution of Ernest stopped and Uly
was able to retain his Viennese links. Hanni, Ernest and Peter had
become regular Church of England members in London. Uly, by
contrast, never went anywhere near a church for the rest of his life,
unless it was to attend the christening of one of 'his' babies.

The family was still living in Acacia Road, but shortly afterwards
moved to the first house they bought in England, in Springfield
Road, a little further north. Ernest's grandfather had died in 1947, so
his grandmother again came to live with them. Despite his unpleasant
experiences at boarding school, she would insist that Ernest spoke

German to her at least some of the time. So it was that my father reluctantly acquired his knowledge of German, which has subsequently been so very useful to him.

My father went to St Paul's, in Hammersmith, at the age of twelve. 'It was a tough but not unpleasant school,' he recalls. 'My foreign background was really of no concern from then on.' It was at St Paul's that he started rowing. The school had a good coach, the much revered Freddie Page, a leading figure at the Thames Rowing Club and a steward at the Henley Regatta. Ernest raced in the junior eights, successfully competing in several school regattas. 'I was already very tall,' he says, 'but I was far too light for my height, despite all attempts by my mother to feed me up. Because of this I never made a regular place in the first eight, but I was nevertheless a member of the squad that would train every weekday after school and on Saturdays in all conditions, rowing to Putney or Mortlake, and even as far as Westminster and back.' The highlight of the rowing year was the series of regattas on the Thames, starting with the Head of the River race around Boat Race time, and ending at Henley in July. It was the most enjoyable period of Ernest's school life.

However, the rowing regime meant that there was not much time left for work. Uly would worry about this and make unannounced visits to the High Master, Dr Robert James, to ask how his son could spend so much time at the boathouse and still expect to pass exams. Dr James tried to reassure him by admitting that Ernest would probably never meet his father's exacting academic requirements, but would probably pass the exams necessary to get to university – which he did.

By now my grandfather had established a successful practice in Wimpole Street. He was recognised as one of the leading foreign gynaecologists and obstetricians in London. Uly read every medical magazine available, both at the BMA library and at home. He knew about every new technique in obstetrics and gynaecology worldwide, and pioneered many himself.

Ernest's special holiday treat was to wait in the car for his father outside clinics and then return to the surgery in Wimpole Street for a glass of squash and maybe a sweet while Uly went through his post. On the way home there would also often be a patient to visit in a nursing home. Years later my sister, Joanna, and I spent many hours in the same fashion. There were advantages, though – on one occasion in the surgery Uly cut off my warts and then sewed my

teddy's arm back on, and all the while Jo stuffed me with sweets! I
can also thank my grandfather for teaching me at a very early age
about taxi fares. Once, when Uly was inside on a call, I sat in a taxi
outside the London Clinic for two hours with the meter running,
watching the fare mount higher and higher. I've watched taxi meters
very carefully ever since to try to keep the fare to a minimum.

My grandfather had only one real disappointment, which was that
he could not get the British medical establishment to give him a
hospital appointment, even on an honorary basis. It seemed such
appointments were rarely, if ever, given to foreigners. Eventually,
on account of his work for the Italian community in London, he was
given an honorary post at the Italian Hospital in Queen Square,
Bloomsbury, where he was also a significant fundraiser. In 1962 the
Italian government recognised his contribution by making him a
Commandatore at a ceremony at the Italian Embassy in Grosvenor
Square.

As well as rowing, Ernest was also active in the school cadet force.
Earl Montgomery of Alamein had been a pupil at St Paul's, and had
made the school his headquarters for the D-Day landings. Ernest:
'There used to be a ceremony on the parade ground whenever Monty
visited. The cadet force used to spend weeks preparing. We polished
our boots and brasses until they gleamed, and before the great man
arrived we were issued with a stern warning that he was likely to ask
one of us at random what our rifle number was and we should be
ready with a reply – any number would do if we had forgotten – or
else he would not be satisfied. Luckily Monty didn't pick on me, but
shortly afterwards my mother took me to Switzerland for my first
ski holiday. We arrived at the hotel in Gstaad – and to my amazement
there he was. He obviously didn't remember me from the parade,
but when he discovered that I was at St Paul's he began to take an
interest in my progress on skis. Often he would turn up to watch
because his ADC was in the same class. I was terrified of meeting
him after skiing. He would call me over and ask, "Well, Saunders,
what did you learn today?", and then comment that my arms had
been in the wrong position, or my skis too far apart. I lived in fear
that he would send a report back to the High Master regarding the
incompetence of my skiing. I decided that I liked skiing, but I
never went back to Gstaad until I lived in Switzerland: military
commanders were not necessarily the best ski instructors.'

When Ernest started at St Paul's he often travelled to school by
bus with Jonathan Miller, whose father was also a doctor. 'Jonathan

looked like and was infatuated with Danny Kaye, then the most famous comedian in the world,' he says. 'At school, and even on the bus, his impressions of Kaye were hilarious and probably the beginning of his remarkable artistic career. He was a great travelling companion, and frequently had everyone on the bus in hysterics.' Another contemporary who rose to prominence was a spotty, hard-working and very bright boy called Kenneth Baker. 'We also had an eccentric geography master who used to grade essays purely according to length,' my father recalls. 'I proved this was true by including a nonsensical page about fish and chips in a twenty-page essay on geology. I got top marks.'

Whilst at St Paul's he began to travel through war-torn Europe on school trips and holidays with parents. 'The most powerful memories I have were of the devastated areas of northern France that we had to pass through if we were going anywhere in Europe by car,' says Ernest. 'There were acres of war graves in the same region. I also recall my first visit to Switzerland, where I met my mother's former headmistress from Les Allières, Emy Zorn, who had been such a strong influence on her. I also remember visits to Italy and Spain, but never to Germany. My mother would never go there, nor to Austria until I was really much older.'

In 1954 Ernest left St Paul's. He had won a place at Emmanuel College, Cambridge, but first had to face two years' National Service. He was told to report to the Labour Office nearest the school in Hammersmith. From there he was referred across the other side of London to Red Lion Square in Holborn. When he arrived there it was suggested that, since he was interested in cars, he should think about joining the Royal Army Service Corps, now the Royal Corps of Transport. Ernest: 'I had no military friends to ask, and the RASC didn't seem like a bad idea, especially if more driving meant less marching. I later learnt that the RASC had no "class", and that I should have tried for some posh Guards regiment, but luckily I've never attached any importance to that sort of thing.'

Some of Ernest's school friends had tried to get friendly doctors to certify that they were not fit for National Service. Some claimed flat feet to gain exemption: he really did have flat feet, but he was resigned to his fate. Eventually, just before his nineteenth birthday, he received orders to go to Buller Barracks in Aldershot, the then headquarters of the RASC, for basic training. Ernest: 'We were a motley crew. We came from all sorts of backgrounds, from all over the country. The first few weeks were awful: my cadet training counted for nothing when it came to the incessant marching, loo-cleaning, and the dubious task when generals were visiting of painting worn-out patches of grass green. Two years of this, I thought, would be no fun at all, so I decided I had better try to become an officer as soon as I could.'

It was during officer cadet training that Ernest first met Gerald Landau of Landau and Landau, the small firm of London solicitors that was going to be so important to him from 1988 onwards. Gerald had already qualified as a solicitor before doing National Service. To Ernest he seemed much older and more sophisticated. 'I much admired Gerry's management of the system. He got leave when he wanted and, unlike the rest of us, generally appeared to be in total control. Gerald either controlled the military machine or ignored it.'

After passing out of Aldershot, my father was initially posted to Warley Barracks in Essex. It gave him his first taste of responsibility – and his first decent pay packet. There he met Michael Bonallack, now Secretary of the Royal and Ancient Golf Club at St Andrew's. He was a fellow officer, but was usually away on special duties, playing golf for the Army. He was the Army golf champion, and played in the British Amateur championship which he was later to win five times. The Army was obviously pleased to have Bonallack's services for two years. Ernest: 'Since that time I have always thought that anyone who is good at sport had an enormous advantage in this country. I also recall hearing of how the top oarsmen at St Paul's spent their National Service: they joined the Royal Air Force base at Benson in Oxfordshire, formed a boat club and devoted themselves to international regattas. I don't suppose they did any traditional RAF duties at all.'

As in most Army barracks, the food at Warley was awful, but occasionally Ernest was able to supplement his diet. His mother was worried about his weight, and when Ernest was alone as duty officer at the weekend she would turn up by train with Pyrex dishes full of home cooking: traditional Austrian wiener schnitzel and cakes!

Ernest was later posted to another RASC unit at Stansted, also in Essex, where he was to spend the rest of his National Service. Here he also had his first experience of criminal law, as one of his duties was to represent soldiers who had committed offences outside barracks, and were therefore subject to the discipline of civil courts. One of his 'briefs' was to defend a drunken young soldier accused of biting a man who had kicked him on a bus. The *Saffron Walden Weekly News* reported: 'Second Lieutenant E. W. Saunders RASC told magistrates that since April of this year the company of which the accused was a member had been on rigorous exercises with little sleep. The visit to Bishop's Stortford (where the fight occurred) was his first night out for some time – and as you can imagine tempers were liable to become slightly frayed.' That was apparently eloquent enough to get his charge off with a caution.

The Suez crisis erupted at the very end of Ernest's National Service. He was invited to extend his two years' service to go to Egypt with the unit, but Cambridge beckoned and he declined. His service ended with the responsible job of locking the barracks behind the departing convoys and dropping the key off at the War Office.

My father went up to Cambridge in October 1956 to read law, but found it difficult to settle. 'The most positive aspect of National Service for me was the responsibility of being an officer and having charge of men and equipment. I was also earning from the age of nineteen until I went to university. So returning to student life was a problem. In addition, my father by this time was worried about his heart, and also about money. Although he was a successful surgeon, he was not earning a great deal of money, and he had no savings at all. This was partly because his interest lay in patients and not in money. He simply didn't charge enough. And since my brother was studying medicine in order to become his successor, that meant years of yet more fees for my father to pay.'

Ernest decided to go through the minimum three years' study, gain a basic law degree and then try to get some sort of job. 'I didn't enjoy legal studies,' he admits. 'I found the subject dull, dry and academic. The most enjoyable part of my legal studies was my involvement in the College Law Society, of which I became Secretary and then President. Our dinners were splendid seven-course extravaganzas. I struggled on with the law Tripos and eventually passed, thanks to excellent pre-examination tutorials from our college law tutor, Freddie Odgers, and the study of *Nutshells*, the idiot's guide to law which reduces 500 pages of text to 50 pages of notes.'

Ernest dabbled socially in a wide range of sports at Cambridge, but found he had to spend most of his time working because he had such a basic lack of interest in the subject that he would have failed otherwise. 'I obviously outgrew my strength while I was at Cambridge, because I got 'flu every year and several viruses including jaundice.' This last illness has made him wary of alcohol ever since.

During vacations my father travelled a great deal in Europe, improving his languages. This planted in his mind the idea of working on the Continent. In his final year, having determined that he was not going to be a lawyer, Ernest started actively to look for an alternative career. 'I attended presentations from prospective employers in various fields, and came to the conclusion that industry offered the most interesting prospects. But I found it difficult to know where to start, as my family had always been in the professions. Eventually I decided that instead of getting involved in a training course, with yet more studying, I wanted a job where I could learn by *doing*.'

2

THE MAKING OF A MARKETING MAN

My father's approach to work has hardly varied throughout his career. Since his formal training effectively ended the day he left Cambridge, from then on he taught himself the disciplines needed to take him through a progression of increasingly responsible jobs, largely with well-known international companies based in Britain and Switzerland.

Like thousands of other graduates, his choice of career owed more than little to chance. His father kept impressing on him the need to consider the duties he would owe to any prospective employer who would be 'good enough' to pay him for his work. This would involve a fundamental change in Ernest's attitude, which until then had been that he needed to do only just enough to scrape by. Uly impressed on Ernest the concept of always doing one's very best, and that involved dedication, hard work and pride in a job well done. As in his own practice, he stressed that it was not material success or personal ambition that mattered, it was the satisfaction of having done a thoroughly professional job. This outlook has stayed with Ernest ever since.

He had begun to hear the word 'marketing' used at interviews during his last year at university. It seemed to be used interchangeably with 'selling', 'advertising' and 'market research', and he was not at all clear what it meant; but it seemed to be very much a coming area, combining an aura of excitement in a field that required above all practical common sense.

Ernest's parents were pushing him to get a job that paid well, as his brother Peter's medical studies were eating into the family's funds. So Ernest first went to work for the American company 3M, in a clerical job with what they described as their marketing services department.

He had never heard of 3M, which was then largely making copying products, photocopying machines, industrial abrasives and Scotch Tape for industrial use, but he was hired by a dynamic personality called Les Young, who had previously worked for Procter & Gamble, which was regarded as the mecca of marketing. Les was proud of having worked there, although nobody knew how long he had been on the P & G staff, or exactly what he had been doing. He was so keen on the cachet of marketing that he introduced the word into his 3M job title, even though he was only a clerical administrator. In fact his department merely serviced the sales force. Ernest started, aged 24, on £600 a year.

Although Young's team was not in marketing, Ernest soon found that 3M was a fine company with a reputation for product quality, research-based innovations (from the headquarters in St Paul, Minnesota) and good after-sales service. The most profitable part of the business was the sale of copying machines and copying paper. Salesmen were on commission, and Ernest recalls one of them earning enough to buy and run a Rolls-Royce. 'We were all very impressed. The key to such success lay in the training, which taught the salesmen to develop a long-term relationship with clients.' It was a lesson Ernest took note of.

He gained no experience of marketing goods for the man or woman in the street at this stage, since the day of Scotch Tape and magnetic recording tapes as everyday household items had not yet arrived, and 3M dealt solely with industrial customers. However, after a year or so, during which he had been rewarded with regular small promotions, Ernest asked to be moved to a new department that seemed to him to be getting involved in consumer marketing. It was a small sales promotion unit working on Scotch Tape development for domestic customers, and also testing the possible introduction of synthetic ribbons for gift-wrapping. Ernest was sent out on his first fieldwork projects, a crude form of market research, and he had to come up with sales promotion ideas. 'This was much more to my liking,' he says. 'I began to feel what the focus of my career should be.'

At this time Ernest was still living at home with his parents in Hampstead, and travelling in to work by bus. He started reading about his new area of work in his spare time, particularly *Marketing* by Colin McIver. It is only about 200 pages long, but it spells out the basic principles of the subject: the process of meeting consumer needs with the best product at the right price. McIver's book, which

Ernest reread many times, convinced him that he should move into consumer marketing proper, and that few companies really practised consumer marketing as McIver described it. 'I realised that to master all the skills described in the book I would have to put myself through various marketing jobs in different companies.' He decided to look for a consumer marketing job outside 3M.

In contemplating how he might get the most rapid and widespread exposure to consumer marketing in the UK he noticed that marketing was still very much an American concept, and that the large advertising agencies, especially those that were American owned and had big US clients, had departments that did much of the marketing thinking on their clients' behalf. Since advertising was in any case one of the most exciting of marketing's tools, Ernest decided to look for a marketing position within an advertising agency. That was how he came to walk through the front door of J. Walter Thompson in Berkeley Square, then the largest agency in Britain.

The agency's managing director was Tom Sutton, while the marketing department was led by Dr John Treasure, with a team of executives who were assigned to account teams to provide the marketing strategy, planning input and statistical discipline to guide the creative staff. They performed many of the analytical functions that are today handled by what are known as strategy consultants. Ernest: 'I was lucky to be taken on there. Although I never felt up to the standard of the majority of the rest of the group intellectually, the work was stimulating and just what I needed to get an understanding of marketing in all its aspects. It was my marketing "university".'

Among the outstanding brains in Treasure's department was Stephen King, then a guru of marketing philosophy in JWT. King was heavily involved in a document which was known internally as the Thompson 'T-Plan'. It set out the basic JWT principles for the advertising framework. This analytical plan struck Ernest as the ideal way to create relevant advertising, provided that everyone recognised that it was only a framework, and that the team's account director should allow the creative group to develop advertising freely within it. Ernest believed completely in the T-Plan and has had it in the back of his mind whenever it has been his turn, much later, to approve advertising in which he or his company was involved.

JWT had some enormous clients while Ernest worked there, including Lever Brothers, Kraft, Bowater-Scott, Kellogg's, RHM and Oxo. Famous campaigns were being produced, including 'Persil washes whiter', 'Oxo with Katie', 'Gives a meal man appeal' and the introduction of Mr Kipling cakes. Ernest worked on a number of accounts, most notably Kraft and Lever Brothers.

Kraft, for example, had been with JWT's London office for many years. Ernest: 'The chairman of Kraft UK, Frank Frost, whom one practically never saw, had a reputation for regularly following the 73 bus route through London in his car so that he could personally inspect poster sites for his products and stop off at shops to see how they were displayed. If he didn't like the poster sites, or they were damaged, or if the products were not displayed properly, the sales force and the agency would get hell.' The agency team was in this way closely involved in all aspects of the brand's performance, good and bad.

The JWT account team was headed by John Humphries, whose success came partly from his ability to take care of the Kraft top management's weakness for golf and good food. Humphries's wife was a bright American who excelled at getting on with Kraft's visiting American chiefs. Under Humphries was Bobby Bovill, one of advertising's vivid characters. My father's first project on Kraft, organised by Bovill, was a 'store-check', which involved visiting shops to check on product availability, display and pricing. On one occasion my father was sent to Bath in a hired car to check on the presence of a test-market product made of frozen dough called Kraft Cookies. It was a product ahead of its time, but it was designed to enable people to make biscuits at home.

My father was supposed to find out how many shops were stocking it. It turned out to be in only one or two tiny shops, and instead of being displayed along with ice cream in a freezer the mushy cardboard remains of packages wallowed in buckets of melting ice. Ernest was very disappointed. His research pad was full of 'No's', and against 'Condition of Product' the word 'awful'. Then he discovered the second purpose of the outing: to have an excellent hotel lunch and a lavish evening 'debriefing' with the product manager back in London in the May Fair Hotel, off Piccadilly, to discuss the 'findings' over a magnificent dinner. The entertainment programme for Kraft senior management was evidently as important a planning function as was the marketing plan for the products themselves. However, the client seemed happy, billings improved and the account grew, so my father saw no reason to rock the boat.

Working with Lever Brothers on Persil was quite different. Here was a highly sophisticated client, with a history of consistent and successful advertising from JWT. Together advertiser and producer had kept Persil at the top of the washing-powder market despite all the push from synthetic detergents. Whereas Kraft at that time could have done with marketing help, Lever Brothers had their own excellent marketing and research teams in house. The challenge to JWT was to provide a significant contribution when the client already had most of the marketing skills he needed, a task that involved keeping the creative group stimulated with marketing ideas and analysis that would satisfy Lever's people that the agency was always thinking of what to do next to keep ahead of the competition – the formidable Procter & Gamble.

It was an excellent training, which Ernest later brought to bear at Guinness. He learned the value of campaign consistency, and he could see at work on one huge brand all the components of marketing: advertising, sales promotion, merchandising, market research and packaging. He began to appreciate the value of *qualitative* market research, as opposed to mere number crunching – of asking consumers why or how they like or dislike a product, rather than just analysing sales trends or playing around with percentages. The ideal was to use a combination of both approaches and thus give a rounded picture of the market for a product. Ernest also met some of the finest marketing brains of the time at JWT and Lever Brothers, including a Persil product manager called Alan Toop, who subsequently set up one of the first specialist sales promotion consultancies – the Sales Machine – which Ernest was to use at Nestlé and Guinness.

Ernest: 'One of the most exciting tasks I got involved in consisted of new business pitches – the delicate art of pitching for new client accounts against competition from other agencies. As a marketing executive I had to provide the data around which the creative people would work to produce winning advertising for JWT's formal presentation to a potential client. The tension preceding these pitches was extraordinary, because in the nature of things only one agency could win the new business even though half a dozen might be shortlisted.

'An unforgettable episode at JWT was a brainstorming session which involved the marketing department and creative groups getting together to think up new ideas for products for the client, which in this case was Lever. Two extraordinary concepts were actually given serious consideration. The first was 'spray-on' socks and the other was an aerosol spray to produce 'self-folding handkerchiefs'. I was so amused by these that I actually laughed aloud and was severely reprimanded for taking too narrow a view of product development. On another occasion, after a boozy lunch, an account director started his presentation about a product whose sales were declining with the sales chart upside down, apparently indicating that sales were rising instead of falling. As the client too was suffering from the after-effects of his lunch, nobody seemed to notice.'

At JWT Ernest read all the marketing books he could lay his hands on, and the company produced outstanding booklets on all sorts of marketing subjects. They developed a concept called 'the dynamic difference'. This was a mathematical formula involving Unilever, whereby it seemed possible to prove that sales would go up as a result of spending a lot more on advertising. Ernest was always sceptical about this, and does not think there was ever a case where the concept was actually followed. In later years, however, when he was responsible for allocating advertising budgets in client companies, there were several occasions when agencies presented him with proposals for a radical increase, quoting some mathematical formula they had developed. Ernest never approved them.

A marketing executive at JWT could always be recognised by the portfolio of superbly produced charts he or she carried around, but in fact a marketing executive's function there was extremely varied. Above all, it required a high degree of flexibility in order to cope with several bosses: John Treasure, the marketing director, the account director for the particular account, and of course the client. But it was also frustrating, since it was often possible for the agency to work through the night on planning and creative work, only for a quite junior representative of the client to reject the lot. It was this that finally made Ernest decide to move to a position where the authority for advertising decision-making really lay – with the client company.

Ernest met my mother, Carole Stephings, as she was then, when he was taken to a party one Saturday night in his early days at the company by a JWT colleague. She was then 19 years old, working in the exchange control department of the Bank of England, and about to go abroad to work as an *au pair*, before starting a course to become a radiographer. Ernest always tells the rest of us in the family that it was love at first sight.

In their early days together Carole used to accompany Ernest on store checks – taking picnics rather than eating hotel lunches – in his first car, a yellow and white Triumph Herald coupé, bought at a discount from a garage across Berkeley Square from JWT. It was his pride and joy. Carole inevitably picked up an understanding of marketing from these and other working trips, and Ernest has always valued her common-sense views. Carole: 'When I met Ernest, he was extremely shy and rather thin. From the start we could talk about anything, and our different family backgrounds were never an issue. I adored his parents from the minute I met them, and his mother was a special friend to me for seventeen years until she died. Ernest has never found socialising easy and has always tried to compensate for his shyness by working harder. And, of course, his father was the only role model he knew.' They married in September 1963, a week after Carole's 21st birthday.

During Ernest's third year at JWT he was beginning to get offers to join marketing companies on the product management side, and had discussions with a number of large companies. He went to Banbury to see General Foods about Maxwell House coffee, but was not keen on moving house there. Eventually he accepted an invitation from a London-based JWT client, Schweppes, to become what was described as marketing manager. Unfortunately he had forgotten his determination to be careful about definitions of 'marketing', and the job in fact never materialised in the way either side had intended. Shortly afterwards Ernest accepted an offer from the Beecham Group to join its food and drink division, and this led to nine years of real marketing work and one of the most interesting periods in his business life.

At that time Beecham was headed by Henry Lazell, renowned as one of the great practitioners of modern marketing techniques. Ernest: 'Although trained as an accountant, Lazell saw the importance of the marketing potential in products, insisted on a marketing orientation throughout the group, and took a personal interest in the marketing and advertising of certain products, notably Macleans toothpaste, Brylcreem, Lucozade and Silvikrin shampoo on the consumer side, and Penbritin, the great pharmaceutical moneyspinner that he had nurtured from the research stage. He had thoughts daily on how a product could be developed and how the advertising should be changed. He would appear at agency presentations to approve the copy, and God help any agency with one of his pet accounts that did not have the product in the washroom if it was a toiletry or served at lunch if it was a drink.

'This attitude stemmed from the old-fashioned belief that dedication to the product should start at the top, and if client service companies were not sufficiently keen on the product to take care of such niceties then they should be sacked. There were even occasions when all the agency's staff had to use the latest products for their own hair care, involving a strict regime of Brylcreem and Pure Silvikrin! But Lazell's tirelessness paid off. When Brylcreem sales were fading in the US because it was unfashionable, it was Lazell who hired the baseball star Joe DiMaggio to front the slogan "I came back to Brylcreem". Sales turned around for a time purely because of Lazell's input.'

Fundamentally the Beecham Group was divided into two parts, pharmaceuticals and consumer products. At the time Ernest joined the company the consumer side was itself split into three: toiletries, such as Brylcreem, Macleans, Silvikrin and Body Mist, proprietary medicines like Phensic, Eno, Beecham's Powders and Phospherine, and the food and drink division, which ranged from Lucozade, Ribena and PLJ through Corona, Tango and Quosh to Morton's peas and pie fillings.

The original core of the group was Beecham of St Helens, founded by distant relatives of the conductor Sir Thomas Beecham, which was responsible for Beecham's Pills and, later, Powders. Lazell had built the consumer products side largely by acquiring smallish companies owning well-known brands where he saw potential which could be realised by better marketing and advertising and the economies gained by bulk distribution. Beecham was in fact one of the first of Britain's acquisition-orientated companies, and the portfolio of consumer product brands that Lazell and his successors put together proved to be enormously successful. The toiletries business was based on the acquisition of the Macleans company, just a few yards away from the London headquarters of Beecham on the Great West Road. Lucozade had been a one-man band operation in Newcastle, and Carters of Coleford in Gloucester made Ribena and Quosh. County Laboratories, on the North Circular Road, had developed Brylcreem and Silvikrin.

Ernest and Carole set up home in a small thatched cottage in Loudwater near Rickmansworth in Hertfordshire. They could afford the house only because it had no road access and everything had to be carried up some sixty steps.

While Ernest took the train to work, Carole ran the household, to which in 1965 was added Joanna and in 1966 me. My mother looked after us and everything to do with the house which, apart from mowing the lawn, my father was not much good at. He hated washing up, and so ours was the first household in the road to own a dishwasher.

Ernest was never interested in money, and did not know what bills Carole was paying, or how much was in their bank account. Friends would remark how nice it was that he was so unmaterialistic. He and my more practical mother therefore formed an excellent working partnership.

For relaxation, Ernest used to play squash and golf. He also enjoyed long walks in the countryside with his dog – both for the exercise and for the thinking time it gave him. Skiing was a favourite holiday pastime, and it became an important part of all our lives in later years when my father was working in Switzerland.

Ernest's arrival at Beecham's food and drink division coincided with the return to the UK from the US of Ron Halstead, now Sir Ronald. Although he was under 40 he was already one of Lazell's protégés, had successfully relaunched Macleans toothpaste in the US, and now came back to shake up Beecham's UK food and drink division, with a seat on the main board, replacing a director who had been opposed to his rapid promotion. Halstead arrived with a fearsome reputation for toughness. American techniques, he said, were what it was all about, and the soft English approach would not do. Ernest: 'Ron made it clear from the outset that he would only tolerate success, and excuses such as bad weather affecting soft-drink sales, or lack of 'flu affecting Lucozade sales, were not acceptable.'

Initially Halstead had a marketing director, Don Campbell, reporting to him, but Campbell soon left, after which the marketing managers (which included my father) reported direct. The division had been stagnating, and Ernest's first six months under Halstead were demanding but exhilarating. 'Ron set tough budgets, and like Lazell wanted to see all aspects of the consumer programme for each brand, notably the advertising. He put the sales force under intense pressure.'

Although Halstead, in his capacity as divisional chairman, was responsible for all aspects of the business, his main thrust was in marketing matters, and Ernest was to follow this style of management at Guinness, where his focus was always on the marketing side. He recalls: 'Ron would not accept inadequate distribution or lack of progress in brand share, and he backed this up with personal store checks on Saturday mornings – although we eventually got to know where he usually did his shopping, and someone was dispatched to rearrange the shelves at Safeway in Kensington High Street on

Fridays. But there were often complaints on Mondays all the same, when Ron had been away for the weekend. On top of this, Henry Lazell himself could be relied upon to send Micky, his chauffeur, with a dented can of Tango or a badly labelled bottle of Ribena, to the agitated product manager, demanding an immediate explanation.

Halstead also believed in pragmatic action over theory. When Quosh sales were not going well he simply instructed Ernest and others to 'get off your arses, get into the field and stay there until we know how to sort out the problem'. During one of these blitzes, for two weeks on end Ernest kept tabs on the rest of his work only by going into the office very early or very late. But the end justified the means: the exercise helped pinpoint Quosh's problems.

A number of Ernest's fellow executives left. Campbell, the marketing director, went to GEC. Glyn Williams, the managing director of Corona, moved on, as did Mike Brady, who became a founder member of the advertising agency Allen Brady and Marsh. Others escaped to less demanding jobs elsewhere. The sales manager and research director both had heart attacks. But Halstead was not just clever and tough – he was lucky. After years of 'flulessness in the crucial season, his first year brought an epidemic with the resulting surge in profits at the right time to meet the budget. And then, after a series of wet summers, the sun shone for Ron and for soft-drink sales.

By this stage Ernest was already working very long hours. From boyhood he had had my grandfather's philosophy drummed into him: 'do everything to the best of your ability.' Recently, critics have accused my father of 'vaulting ambition', but they have mis-understood his driving force. He has never been personally ambitious, but ambitious rather for his account group or team. To begin with he wanted the team he was working with to be the best in the department, and he carried this competitive approach right through the years that followed, until he reached the point where his 'team' was the whole company.

It was at this time that Halstead decided that the soft-drinks range was missing a mixer component, which should include tonic water and fruit juices. The supermarket sector was growing fast. Beecham had a strong position in supermarkets, so Halstead could not see why Schweppes should have all the business. He bought a small company, Hunts of Yarmouth, for the name and formula, and instructed Ernest to create and launch a range of Hunts mixers. During the development of this project Halstead was often away in the US and elsewhere, so Ernest was left almost entirely alone. That enabled him to learn by trial and error what it took to co-ordinate the many departments of Beecham that were involved, from production to distribution and sales, so that a launch of this scale could take place.

The division had no marketing director then, so Ernest being a new boy lacking long-term relationships to help him, had to achieve results largely by persuasion, or even by Japanese-style consensus. The Hunts range was duly launched, and Lazell's then favourite advertising agency – London Press Exchange – developed a campaign around the slogan 'Call for Hunts'. Ernest: 'Carole helped to devise the "H" logo with the jumping horse for the Hunts label, but what struck me was the focus on marketing that existed throughout Beecham, backed up in all other areas, such as technical and finance.'

Beecham's basic philosophy, which Ernest later adopted, was that from the earliest planning days there had to be 'an adequate marketing profit margin' to cover advertising and other marketing expenses. This was a percentage figure, and getting this percentage right from the outset enabled the management to concentrate on marketing and sales, safe in the knowledge that there would always be the required profit. There was a simple document known as the 'working outline', which was the means for committing all relevant departments to any proposal and co-ordinating their activities. Much though he admired this tool, Ernest would not be able to get it introduced at Guinness until he had imported several managers from Beecham.

Halstead was evidently satisfied with the Hunts launch, and although a marketing director, Geoff Darby, arrived to whom Ernest then reported, Halstead took an obvious interest in Ernest's progress. He would see him twice a day, early in the morning to check on the previous day's sales, then again in the early evening. 'Halstead was always available if one needed him, but he was a tremendous delegator to people who worked hard and produced results. He didn't want to know everything, only about the things that interested him, and that were important. I always knew where I stood.' Ernest was to adopt this same practical approach at Guinness.

With Geoff Darby's appointment, the Beecham sales force was strengthened just at the time when important changes were happening in retailing, as wholesale buying power became concentrated into fewer large groups such as J. Sainsbury, Tesco and Boots, and new merchandising techniques had to be developed. Lunch guests at the Beecham boardroom, to which Ernest was occasionally invited, started to include personalities like Daisy Hyams, the legendary Tesco buying director.

There were vital relationships to be built with the large retailers. Beecham was one of the first companies to recognise the fact that, whereas media advertising was crucial in image terms, constant attention to the retail marketing aspect was mandatory. However, the ever-increasing demand for larger trade discounts was already becoming a problem. The marketing manager's allocation of funds within his budget, as between image and the discounts he could offer in order to achieve store presence, became an issue of major significance.

After Hunts, Ernest was asked to handle other projects, including the entire soft-drinks range, as marketing manager. In early 1967 Halstead and Lazell thought that Ernest should get some theoretical business knowledge by attending the Harvard MBA programme. This was a considerable honour, and he was naturally excited. However, just as he was about to pack his bags, a new management study by the consultancy firm of Booz Allen was accepted by the board.

This report recommended merging all the consumer products activities into one division, to be known as Beecham Products, with Halstead as chairman. A general management position was created covering the overseas territories controlled by London, which was eventually to be called Beecham Products International. At the age of 32 Ernest was asked to take this on. Jack Smartt, the group personnel director, urged him to take it.

My parents discussed the proposition that weekend. They had spent several happy years in their first home at Loudwater. My sister, Joanna, was two years old and I was one. Although he did not fully appreciate quite how much there would have to be, Ernest realised that the new job would involve a great deal of travelling to Asia, Africa and elsewhere. Nevertheless it was a great opportunity, and on the Monday my father told Halstead he would accept the new job.

The territories for which he was to become responsible largely represented the traditional British Empire, the Far East, Middle East, India, Africa and the Republic of Ireland. Without any real management supervision these countries had been a handy source of profit over the years, but Halstead felt that a more dynamic marketing-led approach could develop them dramatically. Ernest's brief was to get on with this, leaving Halstead free to concentrate on the

UK and his wider group responsibilities. Ernest's task was to be accomplished with the minimum necessary additional load on Beecham's UK management, but he could draw on technical advice from Beecham Products, including the production division, headed by a no-nonsense character called Jim Sullivan, to whom the production people worldwide seemed to owe an extraordinary loyalty.

Even so, my father was very much on his own in the early stages, with no staff at headquarters, and no real idea of what was facing him in the world beyond. The businesses for which he was responsible had previously been loosely supervised by individual executives at Beecham, whom he was now supposed to weld into a cohesive international division. The difficulties were soon apparent. Each unit was managed by a local 'baron' who for many years had had almost total freedom of operation. They were much older than Ernest, and inevitably his appointment was not particularly welcome to them, especially since his job was to shift the emphasis from a cosy increase in profit by an annual price increase to the revamping of existing brands and the introduction of new brands – a demanding process almost totally foreign to those out in the field.

Ernest's first visit was to South Africa, seeing the desert and Victoria Falls from the air and stopping off at Nairobi on the way. 'I recall the excitement of crossing the Equator for the first time, and receiving the first of many certificates from British Overseas Airways Corporation, the forerunner of British Airways, testifying to the achievement. I also remember sending postcards home from this very first stopover, a practice I was to continue throughout my life of travel.'

Any travel-induced intoxication he might have had ended abruptly on arrival at his destination. He was met at Johannesburg Airport by Fred Campbell, the local Beecham 'baron', complete with safari suit. Ernest: 'In his hand Fred held the plane timetable and a proposed itinerary for my stay. He made it clear that he considered the visit solely for my benefit and entirely irrelevant to him and so he didn't want to complete the itinerary until he knew precisely when I wanted to leave. I explained that this depended on how long it took to find out what I had come to learn. He said flights were heavily booked, but there would be a seat available in about a week's time. I was not impressed by this attitude, but it was to be repeated in many other parts of the world. I told Fred that he should assume I would be around for at least a week, probably longer.

'I was taken to a delightful hotel, the Balalaika, consisting of individual thatched-roof cottages, and was then subjected to the routine I came to know as "let's wear out the visiting executive". From morning to night I was kept busy with entertainments of a very high standard, presumably so that I wouldn't be able to concentrate too much on business. Unfortunately for them, I have never been keen on alcohol, and the local soft drink, Appletizer, kept me pretty alert. In fact it was *they* who had the problem of keeping awake as I pounded them with questions. After all, this was my first overseas visit in my new job, and I was determined to report back to London not merely with criticism, but also with ideas.'

It has always been Ernest's belief that information is not an end in itself but a means to other ends. So he set about learning as much as he could about the brands being marketed, then about the competition, gaps in the market and ways of improving Beecham's performance. It was clear that, although the local company had a competent marketing director, decision-making was in the hands of the managing director and his number two, an elderly finance man of the old school who knew nothing about marketing and would oppose any development which put at risk the comfortable ten per cent profit increase that could be achieved by putting up prices to counteract static or declining sales. The South African operation had had important successes. Brylcreem had huge sales – and not exclusively for use on the head: it was known as the best sexual lubricant in the business! Eno Fruit Salts had very large sales too, mainly as a hangover cure. And the hot weather created a steady demand for Body Mist deodorant.

There was no television in South Africa at that time, so all advertising was on posters, radio, press and cinema. It was on this first visit that Ernest encountered the 'not invented here' syndrome, which used what little market research there was to prove that any approach developed locally had to be right, and anything from London had to be wrong. So Ernest laid down an important principle that he stuck to from then on: any local deviation from successful London-developed advertising had to be justified by research honestly structured and objectively analysed. The non-European market had enormous potential, but only careful adaptation of international advertising techniques would work. Wherever he went, therefore, he introduced competent research specialists and demanded the use of the best local research companies. Whenever an important decision was due, involving the launch of a new product or a change to an existing advertising campaign, he tried to be present at the research briefing. He felt, and still does, that there is no substitute for being able to question the research executive directly, rather than relying on a summary from a brand manager with his ego to protect. So Ernest was personally involved in advertising or packaging decisions from the earliest days in his new job.

This led to a revolution in the overseas companies' entire marketing ethos, and to a shake-up in the marketing teams. Eventually my father established an effective internationally-orientated marketing operation, but it took time and consumed much nervous energy. 'I never felt secure that the situation would not rapidly deteriorate in the absence of a marketing-trained general manager who could be held responsible at headquarters.'

The South African company grew to be one of the most successful overseas businesses in the Beecham group. South Africa also gave Ernest his first experience of being directly involved in an acquisition. A major local headache remedy was Grandpa Headache Powders, which was backed by one of the most famous advertising campaigns in the area. It had huge sales to non-whites and it became possible to acquire the business due to the extraordinary negotiating abilities of a senior Beecham executive, Tom Scrutton, who simply charmed the people he dealt with. Taking over 'Grandpa' gave the local Beecham management a considerable boost in morale, and within South Africa the sales potential of what may have seemed an outworn product turned out to be tremendous. Another business Ernest tried but failed to get hold of was Appletizer, a fascinating example of an apple drink positioned as a sophisticated adult soft drink. But he was right to spot the potential: about twenty years later Appletize was successfully introduced on a franchise basis in to the UK.

Local South African executives lived in glorious homes and in a manner reminiscent of England in the 1930s. Although the political situation was always in their minds, there was a feeling that any real problems were a long way off.

Fred Campbell was by then over retiring age, and a successor had been recommended by an executive search company. Unfortunately the new appointment did not last long.

Ernest: 'This was a reminder to me of the need to look carefully into the glowing assessments of headhunters, and even the references produced by them in support of a candidate, for there were no guarantees. My discussions with colleagues in other companies confirmed the scale of the problem, so I became extremely careful about external recruitment. But I was on the horns of a dilemma. In the event I had to use headhunters on a large scale, not only at Beecham, but subsequently at Nestlé and Guinness, because I had to improve the management of these companies, and quickly. Having good ideas is one thing, having them implemented still requires the right people on the ground.'

On the whole, Ernest had more successful recruits than failures. Obviously it was easier to find good management material in countries where living conditions were attractive. But there was at that time a nagging fear in many people's minds that an overseas posting would lead to being forgotten by head office, and if not forgotten then typecast as an 'overseas person', which to a young marketeer was a major disincentive.

It had also become obvious that Ernest needed to set up a small but highly competent headquarters team to help him manage the development of the business and to plan strategic marketing. A combination of internal Beecham people and outsiders was put together, and this group ensured the long-term success of the division. Central to this success was the role played by John Davies, the financial controller. His grip of financial matters enabled Ernest to concentrate on marketing and development.

For the rest of Africa and the Middle East, my father saw as his principal objective the recruitment of competent executives, able to obtain local import licences and overcome the many other hurdles in trying and unreliable trading conditions. Some companies simply did not bother with such countries. Beecham's view was that they should try to obtain business from them, but not rely on them for regular income. Ernest: 'It was impossible just to add ten per cent to the profit every year from countries where one never knew if one was going to get an import licence or not.'

Beecham had a large business in Nigeria, based on Phensic, Macleans and later Lucozade. It had a sizeable operation in Kenya and good but irregular business in the Middle East. Logistics and the uncertainty of these markets meant that finding good managers was very difficult, and getting them to stay was even harder. If they were any good they would want promotion to a more sophisticated territory where more interesting marketing tools would be available. They would also be on the shortlist for other companies' headhunters.

Ernest devised a way of supervising such territories over the years, by adapting his flight schedules to include stopovers in hotels nearby or at airports where the local executives, sales agents and sometimes advertising agents could make marketing presentations to him. It was amazing what could be achieved in even a very short space of time.

Beecham's largest overseas manufacturing plant outside South Africa was in Petalying Jaya near Kuala Lumpur, Malaysia. Here the business was initially based on two products: Brylcreem and Ribena. Brylcreem was going through a rough patch in Western societies, where the natural look was replacing the Denis Compton look. In Asia the trend was almost the opposite. The Japanese had come up with a very sticky product called Tancho – a predecessor to today's male hair-gels. Tancho was catching on and Brylcreem had to counter-attack, which it did by ignoring 'not invented here' and using a new red plastic pack developed in the UK, which instantly gave the brand a modern image. This was backed up by completely new advertising featuring pop stars and other folk heroes of Chinese and Malay consumers. The cinema advertisements were spectacular, since local audiences seemed to be impressed by commercials only if they lasted at least two minutes and included stunning action shots, dashing men laden with hairfuls of Brylcreem, fast cars and sexy girls.

Brylcreem was supposed to be a classic example of the 'product life cycle' theory, the proposition that brands had only a limited life, and after a certain number of years would inevitably decline and not be worth supporting further. Ernest believed that brands were too valuable just to be dropped after years of advertising investment. In his view products could be modified both physically and in their presentation to maintain an up-to-date market profile. He felt that a brand like Brylcreem, in particular, should be capable of some form of line extension into other related products, to balance the huge cost of advertising that had gone into it. In Malaysia a range of Brylcreem accessories and line extensions was successfully introduced, including an anti-dandruff version. And the base product continued to attract consumer support.

Ribena had developed as the blackcurrant health drink that good mothers gave their children, who loved it. With consistent advertising the product's sales grew and grew. The secret of its success lay in the campaign's emotional appeal to mothers. The advertising in the Far East was so effective that similar local blackcurrant drinks hardly sold at all, despite every attempt to copy Ribena's packaging and at a far lower price. 'Ribena mothers' felt it was worth spending the extra to obtain the 'real thing'.

Ernest learned to be careful about colours, brand names and

symbols. A good colour for a product in the UK could represent death overseas. A UK name could have a totally inappropriate interpretation for the Chinese, who lay great store by a product's symbol or 'chop' as they call it. Brash new marketing managers who thought that certain symbols on packaging got in the way of clean design found that if they removed, changed or reduced those symbols they could kill a product that might have been selling well for generations. Chinese consumers are intensely suspicious of change of any sort. The automatic assumption is that any change, however minor, results in an inferior or even a counterfeit product.

The importance of understanding local psychology was underlined by the huge success of a new approach for Eno, the fruit salt. It had been a slow seller for years among the Chinese until Ernest became aware that the Chinese regarded products in terms of the way they were 'heaty' or 'cooling'. Beecham then developed a campaign showing how a body lit like a furnace could be cool as a gentle spring after Eno had passed through it – sales were incredible.

Ernest also became aware of the huge sales of Horlicks in the Far East, and of so-called energy products in general, which included Nestlé's Milo. He reported this situation back to Halstead, who later bought Horlicks in the face of fierce competition from Sir James Goldsmith.

The Far East grew rapidly as a market for Beecham consumer products. Malaysia became the management headquarters for the Far East, covering Singapore, Hong Kong and Thailand. The product range was considerably widened over the years. Ernest: 'There was a real excitement about marketing in the Far East. The population was huge, even before the opening of mainland China, and increasingly prosperous. Promises of health, sex and success could seemingly sell most products at a premium price, so business was extremely profitable.' It all helped to produce a high standard of marketing and management, and Beecham was able to recruit go-ahead managers, at least to stay for a while. Indeed John Robb, who stepped down as chief executive in 1988, was recruited by Ernest and sent to Malaysia. Advertising agencies, market research companies and other support groups also saw the opportunities and were prepared to invest in good people in the region, eventually enabling the proprietors of some of those businesses to sell out and make fortunes.

Whilst Malaysia became the regional headquarters, largely because the management infrastructure existed in Petalying Jaya, this was in spite of some extremely unpleasant episodes, including riots, caused by the volatile political situation.

Then there was Thailand. From a business point of view the dominance of the Swiss-owned Diethelm distribution company was total. They even controlled the media. Going it alone was destined to failure, and going to a local distributor other than Diethelm was also useless. The major brand owners of the world would compete for the time of Diethelm executives, the senior of whom were always Swiss, under 40, and not allowed to marry without consent from headquarters – although Ernest discovered from visiting many of their homes that there were undoubtedly attractive local compensations!

While there was a lot of smuggling in the Far East, as well as counterfeit production, Ernest felt that it was an area with tremendous business potential, so he fell in with local custom and sold through the all-powerful Diethelm.

India was another matter. Ernest: 'I will never forget my arrival at Bombay Airport on my first visit. The BOAC plane touched down late at night, and at once I was struck by the extraordinary poverty. Apart from the primitive facilities at the airport, the whole stretch of road to the centre of Bombay was jammed with bodies lying in the street amid tremendous stench. The Beecham business was based on Brylcreem and a little Macleans toothpaste. The market was run for the company by a loyal and hard-working Indian called Shri Gupta, who did his very best in difficult circumstances. He had continual problems with raw materials and little support capability from service companies, and this at a time of maximum indigenisation and pressure on foreign companies to reduce their equity holdings below forty per cent.

'Sir David Orr, who became chairman of Unilever, told me that he had started his management career in India and had found this enormously useful. Experience of extraordinary difficulties could not be picked up by managers who worked only in the sophisticated markets. I believe Sir David was the first marketing man to become chairman of a leading public company. He told me I was the second.'

During my father's tenure a massive change took place in the importance of India as far as Beecham was concerned, largely because of the acquisition of Horlicks, which already had a major Indian operation called Hindustan Milk-Food Manufacturers, run from Delhi by a very able man called John Pountney and his team. Demand for Horlicks was insatiable there: they could sell as much as they could make. Pountney's team had to build production capacity while giving away the minimum required amount of equity to the Indian government each time additional factory space was approved. India was by far the largest Horlicks business outside the UK, and the supply problem meant that advertising in India was hardly an issue. But elsewhere in the Far East careful marketing attention was needed to make the most of Horlicks' potential.

There was a fundamental difference between advertising Horlicks in the UK and in the Far East. For years the British image of Horlicks had been as a nightcap, featuring the famous campaign about 'night starvation'. The graph on the back label in the UK was depicted as a 'sleep-rhythm curve'. To Far Eastern markets the same product was promoted for active energy during the day, so the curve on the label was called an 'energy curve' instead.

Integrating Horlicks with the rest of Beecham Products International was a major exercise for Ernest. 'Much depended on the enthusiasm of the local manager. Head office could produce the most persuasive arguments and advertising concepts, set budgets, change managements and control development funds, but in each territory the job still had to be done on the ground. Nevertheless Horlicks progressed throughout the region, against tough competition from Nestlé's Milo, and remains one of Britain's most famous international brands.'

Beecham's most promising development market in the east was Japan. Some far-sighted companies such as Nestlé and Beecham Pharmaceuticals had got into that market many years previously and were in a strong position, but as far as consumer products were concerned Beecham had to find another way in. To get the business moving, Ernest encouraged Halstead to acquire a Japanese marketing company that happened to hold the rights to Tabasco, the American pepper sauce. In effect a charming American lady owned the Japanese company and Halstead, with Tom Scrutton, persuaded her to sell it to Beecham. And since Horlicks had an arrangement with the Louisana company that made the sauce to market it in many other countries, that gave Beecham a small but profitable base from which to start developing the group's consumer business in Japan.

Nearer to home, Ernest's main European responsibility lay in the Republic of Ireland. Although Beecham had a wide product range there, most of the sales came from Lucozade, Quosh soft drinks and Macleans toothpaste.

Ernest: 'The Irish business was very special to manage. Although there was a typical English gent in charge at the time, Cliff Baggott, his team was extremely adept at charmingly eliminating as much "UK interference" as possible. Local managers always regard head office help as "interference", but some, as in Ireland, are more polite about it than others.'

Beecham's Irish headquarters were in Dublin, while Northern Ireland marketing was run from London. It was difficult for Ernest to understand why, although Northern Ireland marketing campaigns – on identical lines to their English counterparts – appeared to work there, the Dublin management consistently felt that something entirely different was required in the south. 'To my mind, Dublin was and remains the king of the Not Invented Here syndrome. And this was particularly frustrating since the market, though small, was extremely competitive, and quality brand management was difficult to obtain – and yet there was often the basis of a proven campaign sitting unused in London.'

The one exception to all this lay in the success Beecham had with small bottles of Lucozade in the Republic, in contrast to the position in the UK. Ernest kept pushing his UK counterparts to take a greater interest in the potential for the small bottle, but it was not until the recent Daley Thompson advertising campaign that the small bottle suddenly began to establish itself in Britain.

Beecham International's concern with the rest of Europe was confined to exporting small lines that were not managed by local companies. In Germany the sales of Tabasco took off on the back of a minimal public relations budget consisting largely of recipe suggestions. It was a good example of how a product can be got off the ground without a massive advertising spend.

Ernest enjoyed travelling on the Continent, visiting distributors, and his minor involvement with European business gave him the thirst to manage a more substantial business there. Globe-trotting round South Africa, India and the Far East for several years had been physically draining and emotionally difficult. 'It was certainly not unabated tourism,' he insists. 'I don't remember seeing any of the tourist sights over that period. By now I had a family of three – Joanna, James and John – but I was seldom at home. These long-haul trips took at least two to three weeks, and with the work that had always piled up by the time I returned the job was turning into a killer. I had also noticed that more than seventy-five per cent of

the US executives I met with the title Vice-President International
had been divorced at least once.'

I have memories of a father who was away most of the time, but
who would send us postcards almost every day from far-off places,
and brought presents when he came back. On especially long trips
he would send us tape recordings. A 'message from Daddy' tape
would arrive, and the family would gather round the kitchen table
to listen to his news.

So in 1973, when he was 38, Ernest decided to put a stop to long
trips and seek a posting with Beecham in the UK or Europe. He had
by this time recruited an excellent team of managers, including a
ready-made successor. And the overseas territories were in good
shape. With Ron Halstead he had made a recent visit to all the
markets, and had also accompanied the new group chairman, Sir
Ronald Edwards, to various countries. They had both declared
themselves satisfied with business progress, and with the management that had been put in place. Ernest talked to Halstead about
his personal problems, but no suitable job appeared to be available
at Beecham at that time.

Coincidentally, Ernest's father had introduced him to the husband
of one of his patients, Sir Isaac Wolfson, chairman and effectively
the founder of Great Universal Stores, the retail and mail-order
giant. Sir Isaac fired Ernest's enthusiasm, predicting that a major
explosion was about to come in retailing, and in the mail-order
business. Ernest had hitherto regarded this last as a downmarket,
dying industry, but Sir Isaac, on the contrary, believed that marketing flair could make it into a very dynamic business.

Ernest met Leonard, now Lord, Wolfson, the managing director
and Sir Isaac's son. He eventually invited Ernest to join the board
of the mail-order company, British Mail Order Corporation, and to
become chairman of GUS's European mail-order subsidiaries. He
also intended, he said, to assign to Ernest's supervision other UK
retailing interests, and wished him to advise him personally on how
to improve the marketing orientation of the group.

Ernest discussed the opportunity with Carole, and with Ron
Halstead. It was a difficult decision. He had enjoyed his nine years
at Beecham and had learned an enormous amount. But the GUS
offer would give him the chance to broaden his marketing experience,
and to get involved with the entirely new world of retail and mail-
order marketing, particularly in Europe. He decided to accept the
offer.

Ernest maintains relations with former Beecham colleagues, including two ex-chairmen; but perhaps his regard for the company is to be seen best by the number of excellent Beecham executives he recruited to Guinness to help him fill the huge management gap that existed there.

Above all, who knows what might have been avoided had Ernest persuaded the excellent John Davies, who had taken care of finance for him throughout his period in charge of Beecham International, to become the finance director at Guinness, rather than the managing director of Guinness Overseas. But unfortunately, at the time Ernest felt that the profits from Guinness's overseas territories were so vital that Davies's experience in managing similar areas for Beecham's was best used there.

3

FROM CATALOGUES TO CUCKOO CLOCKS

The world of Great Universal Stores was centred upon a spartan building in the midst of the electronics and computer shops huddled in the shadow of the Centre Point office block near London's Oxford Street. But there was also the huge mail-order headquarters in Manchester, and the group was, in addition, stretching its tentacles on to the European mainland.

The operational boss of GUS was and is Leonard Wolfson, who learned at the foot of the acknowledged master of mail order, his father Sir Isaac. But whereas Sir Isaac had true entrepreneurial flair, Leonard was more sober, driven by figures and statistics. The headquarters staff was small, because operating subsidiaries were controlled largely through their financial performance. Unlike Beecham, where brands were all-important, GUS had only one brand of significance, Burberry, which the chairman looked after himself.

It was financial performance and merchandise that interested Leonard Wolfson. He knew all the numbers personally and watched them like a hawk. He would know the previous week's sales by the weekend, and if there was a shortfall anywhere the executive responsible could expect a chillingly brief note or phone call on the Monday. There was also a crude but effective one-sheet Monthly Financial Statement which, Ernest believes, Leonard developed himself. This gave Wolfson all the monthly numbers he wanted in a form convenient to him, and it haunted the rest of the management each Monday. It was a huge, unwieldy piece of paper, with the numbers and columns spread out in an unusual way, but that was how Leonard liked it.

Ernest had been used to an emphasis on margins to cover product marketing costs and profit derived from selling price. But at GUS the *buying* price of merchandise was what mattered, together with the selection of the merchandise itself. The buying and merchandise selection skills were key. Ernest quickly learned that marketing in the mail-order business was a very different affair from anything he had previously encountered: it was basically about getting new customers for the catalogues, including Kay's, Great Universal and Marshall Ward, and finding ways of increasing the order per customer. This in turn depended on the range and value of the catalogue selection. Most marketing was done by direct mail, and in the UK through thousands of agents.

Advertising in the sense Ernest had been used to, as an image-maker, was really only used as an announcement vehicle for new catalogues, which came out twice a year. Selecting merchandise, pricing and the layout of the catalogues, these were the crucial skills. Fashions were the image-maker: they had to be just right – up-to-the-minute but not too outlandish – because they set the style of the catalogue. But mail order's backbone was operational efficiency: computerised stock control and mailing lists, automated warehouses and continual investment in new delivery and mailing systems. It was and continues to be a very efficient and profitable operation. Whether, despite what Sir Isaac had suggested to Ernest, marketing flair was of any real importance in this business remains a moot point.

Ernest was directly responsible for the mail-order companies of Wehkamp in Holland, Sweden's Halens and Universal in Austria, and he was on the board of the British Mail Order Corporation, based in Manchester. His immediate boss was David, now Sir David, Wolfson, a charming and intelligent man who knows mail-order techniques backwards. David, a cousin of Leonard and therefore nephew of Sir Isaac, was always open to new ideas – but it was Leonard who took the decisions. Leonard's annual 'state' visits to the operating companies were, for them, a gruelling experience, involving much preparation, and the facilities had to be both spotless and economy-conscious. He could be as tough about unnecessary lighting and telephone extensions as he was with below-budget sales of ladies' underwear. But Ernest had to admire his grasp of detail.

This was in 1973, when the oil crisis was in full spate. Nevertheless, the mail-order business flourished consistently because of its convenience and the facility it offered for paying for everyday goods by instalments. Ernest visited the European companies regularly and, having understood the importance of merchandise and value, he set about gradually introducing the more conventional aspects of marketing into catalogue selection, presentation and advertising. Market research was introduced for the first time so as to understand better what customers and potential customers wanted, which led to better direction of the all-important buying directors, whose attitude shifted from offering what they wanted the customers to buy because they had bought it on good terms, to providing what the customers wanted – which had been bought from the manufacturers on equally good terms!

As the fashion element in mail order was the image-maker, Ernest was concerned to ensure that GUS catalogues were appropriately fashionable. On his desk there were usually the latest catalogues of the fashion-conscious French companies, such as La Redoute and Trois Suisses, and he endeavoured to develop relationships with other European companies to broaden GUS's European base.

Meanwhile, financial pressures were mounting at home. Carole and Ernest wanted the best education for their three children, and had real doubts about being able to afford this in the UK. They felt they had to consider moving abroad to improve the family's financial situation, even though it would involve leaving Loudwater, where they had spent their married life so far and had many friends.

Also, since wage freezes were in force in Britain, headhunters were working overtime to tempt executives overseas. So it was that my father left GUS in 1975 on amicable terms, and agreed to become head of European operations at Castolin, a private company based on the outskirts of Lausanne, Switzerland – a country he knew well, as his mother had gone to school there, the family had spent many holidays in the Swiss Alps, and they had friends there.

After Ernest had spent several months training with the company's New York subsidiary, the Saunders family settled in Préverenges, a small lakeside village about halfway along the lake from Geneva. It was a nondescript place, but I do remember a beautiful view of the lake and across to the French Alps on the other side. And it was only minutes from my father's office.

Castolin, an industrial marketing company, was owned and dominated by a dynamic if eccentric entrepreneur, Dr René Wasserman. He believed he needed a top marketing executive to plan the expansion he wanted from a highly profitable, traditional core business into more glamorous sectors of the engineering industry. However, although Castolin gave him valuable training in New York, once

Ernest got his feet firmly under the desk in Switzerland he realised that marketing industrial goods was too remote from what he really wanted to do – and he discovered that working closely with an eccentric genius could be difficult. Wasserman was a great motivator of salesmen, and had dreams of becoming the IBM of the engineering business; but he was also paranoid about the danger of nuclear war, disappeared to Brazil whenever he felt war was imminent, and lived when he was in Switzerland in a mansion overlooking Lake Geneva, surrounded by high walls and patrolled by Doberman Pinschers. After about twelve months they agreed to part company, and Ernest revived contacts he had made in the UK with Nestlé, the world's largest food company, which was based not far from Lausanne, in Vevey, further along the shore of Lake Geneva.

After a series of trips along the lakeside to meet Nestlé executives, he found himself working in one of the most beautiful office buildings in the world, right on Lake Geneva. Nestlé's headquarters, known locally as The Centre or Bergère, housed some 2,000 people and had outstanding facilities for working, training, conferences and entertaining. Most of those who worked at head office lived a few minutes away: the Swiss regard even a half-hour car journey to work as a stupidity. We ourselves moved closer to the office, to St Légier. Although there were flexible office hours, most people arrived very early – even if, according to a well-worn local joke, they only 'woke up' later. Everyone had to clock in and out with a special computer card, and a print-out arrived with the salary cheque indicating how many hours had been spent at work. Ernest: 'There was unspoken rivalry for the title of being the person to put in the most extra hours (without extra pay, of course). And even though the computer would cut off after a certain number of extra hours had been exceeded, this did not stop the contest. A special machine in the entrance hall could tell you at any time how you were doing in the "hours" contest, and most people wanted to know their position.'

Despite the fact that there was a magnificent staff restaurant, many continued the traditional Swiss habit of going home to lunch. This was often hard on the wives who, after taking children to school, had everyone back at midday and again in the late afternoon. There was a remarkable difference, however, between those wives who had lived abroad and those who had not: the former demanded a more emancipated, modern way of life, and would actually tell their husbands *not* to come home for lunch, while the latter continued in the old servile ways. After all, in some cantons women had only relatively recently even been given the right to vote.

Nestlé employees received a good salary, but none of the traditional perks, bonuses or stock options associated with British executive life. So they had to buy their own car – or go by public transport. As a product director and member of the management committee, Ernest ran a little second-hand VW Polo, and nobody thought anything of it. Cars were not a status symbol. Even top executives lived modestly by comparison with the style in which they live in the UK: Ernest was earning less than he had at Castolin, but considerably more than he would have been paid in England, and he felt he had far more promising career prospects. Prices were high, but taxes were lower at the time. At weekends most people would have somewhere in the mountains to go, often a shared apartment for the summer or skiing in winter. But it would not be unusual for a Swiss manager, on holiday, to return to the office if the weather forecast was unfavour-able.

A pleasing distinction between working for the Swiss and working in England, Ernest found, was the apparent absence of the 'Estab-lishment' factor that seems to be woven into British society. At Nestlé's head office there was only one front entrance, one garage, and promotion was based solely on merit and service. Having been at the same school as a colleague made for friendship, but there was no 'right' or 'wrong' school – in any case, they were all State-run.

There was a considerable difference too between working inter-nationally from a Swiss base as opposed to a British one. From Vevey Ernest now had to view the world through central European eyes. To Beecham and GUS, the UK market had been big enough for them to live on, and overseas business was a bonus. But not to Nestlé: the domestic market for their products was comparatively very small, so the overseas markets were crucial. Head office was the nerve centre, providing expertise for operations that extended to every country on earth, and Ernest's previous international experience suddenly appeared insignificant.

The driving force in Nestlé's relatively recent conversion to modern sophisticated marketing was Dr Max Gloor, a giant *bon viveur* (he was always allocated two first-class airline seats to himself on account of his size) who told Ernest that if he were eating in a restaurant and discovered that the chef was thin he would instantly walk out, on the grounds that the food could not possibly be any good. It was Dr Gloor who had brought Ernest into his group of directors responsible for the strategic marketing of Nestlé products throughout the world.

Nestlé's product portfolio was immensely impressive. Whereas in Britain people think of 'Nestles' making chocolate for slot machines on railway platforms, and perhaps make the link with Nescafé, in fact the range includes some of the best-known food brands in the world. The instant drinks group includes Nesquick chocolate drink mix and Milo energy drink as well as Nescafé. A large percentage of the group's profits had always come from this sector. Packaged foods include Maggi soups and sauces, Crosse & Blackwell, Findus frozen foods and Chambourcy yoghurts. The chocolate products group has of course been strengthened by the acquisition of Rowntree, but has traditionally had a strong base in Europe, notably Switzerland itself and France. The origins of the whole business lay in the various milk products, including baby foods. Nestlé also owned a sizeable percentage of the L'Oréal cosmetics business and had an optical products pharmaceutical business, Alcon.

Ernest: 'The attention paid to excellence in product quality was legendary, and a dedicated technical freemasonry existed throughout the world, dominated by Dr Carl Angst, a tough but fair-minded Swiss who had spent years in the US, and had a phenomenal grasp of the products and production processes. His influence was such that he was a man not to cross under any circumstances, but was often too busy to talk. Nevertheless, provided one was around in the car park at 7 a.m. or 7 p.m. to catch him on his way to and from home, even the most complex matter could be taken care of.'

The great strength of Nestlé's position in so many countries around the world stemmed from the skill with which local managements, backed by the immense resources of the centre at Vevey, had established long-term relationships with the governments of the respective countries. Nestlé's overseas managers were respected everywhere. Ernest: 'They were also very much God in their territories, none more so than Helmut Maucher, then head of the huge German market. Woe betide a visitor to Germany from head office who did not know his stuff or, more importantly, did not bring some worthwhile and concrete new thinking or product ideas with him.'

So, although the Vevey headquarters housed expertise in every conceivable discipline, from marketing to production and research, the degree to which this expertise was put into practice, especially in marketing, depended largely on the personal relationships between the man from Vevey and local management. Inevitably this led to 'not invented here' conflicts in the marketing area, particularly in countries like France, for example, where the calibre of marketeers on the ground was outstanding.

Nestlé had an international training centre near Vevey, called Rive-Reine, where executives from all over the world would learn about all aspects of the Nestlé way of doing things. Most important of all was the Nestlé 'spirit', which transcended nationalities and nationalism in a most remarkable way. Therein, Ernest felt, lay the terrific strength and continuity of what was a huge and far-flung business.

Also, since financial control was administered with an iron discipline throughout the world, product directors and those involved in the various specialist marketing areas – such as packaging, advertising, market research and sales promotion – could concentrate on their tasks, knowing that financial and technical matters were totally taken care of. That enabled them to develop their side of the business and start to catch up on the more established operations. Dr Gloor reckoned that Ernest's wide experience of marketing across a variety of products and companies would be especially useful to Nestlé at that time, because its importance had yet to be instilled into the corporate consciousness there. And the group lacked a senior Englishman at headquarters, a considerable shortcoming when so much business was conducted in the English language.

Ernest was to assist Dr Gloor in the development of marketing structures, and to support him in introducing to Nestlé such concepts as the use of the same advertising to promote specific products on a worldwide basis, with packaging of a particular product consistent throughout the world. The chairman, Pierre Liotard-Vogt, would also frequently ask Ernest to help him with issues raised in English-speaking markets, and with correcting the English translations of speeches or reports that had originated in French.

Dr Gloor felt that the world's largest food company needed to take a lead in the opportunities provided by the developing interest by health authorities and consumers worldwide in nutrition and health. He believed that this could pave the way for the development of improved and new products with nutritional benefits – thus revolutionising the traditional food business in which taste had been all that mattered – and my father was asked to manage a programme across all product groups along these lines. He was allocated one assistant, the multi-lingual Angelo Husler, and a multi-lingual secretary, Wendy Boyle, an Englishwoman who had been working in Switzerland for several years.

Ernest; 'Wendy could take dictation in one language and produce a document in another. The language problem loomed large in my early days at Nestlé. Although the company allowed groups of individuals to meet and speak in their own preferred language out of English, French and German, French was still the principal tongue. Even though I had believed that my French and German were pretty good for an Englishman, I soon found out that there was a world of difference between coping socially and working professionally.'

Ernest and his assistant, Husler, were both convinced that a programme for healthier and lighter eating had enormous potential. Their task was to change fundamental eating habits, and their research served only to back their feeling that the key lay in marketing. But the marketing battle had first to be waged inside Nestlé, to convince the top management that it was the right thing to do. Ernest coined the phrase 'nutritional marketing' to describe the all-purpose programme that would cover all product groups.

Having reviewed the programme initially with Dr Gloor and the product directors, Ernest spent considerable time with Dr Angst to ensure that he would be willing to endorse the technical work involved. An outline was accepted by Nestlé's Corporate Management Committee, and on the basis of that they set to work examining the nutritional aspects of existing and new products, and developing new marketing concepts with the co-operation of product directors, local marketing companies and the Vevey technical staff. The canvas was global. Inevitably it took time to fill in, and is still being filled in. But the principles Ernest and his assistant worked to then are now accepted as common practice by food companies, restaurants and consumers throughout the developed world.

It was a long road from the printing of a product's nutritional composition on its packaging to a mass acceptance of 'lighter eating'. Above all, this involved a long-term education programme, starting with product groups and technicians not only at Vevey but throughout the Nestlé world. Ernest and Husler adapted locally relevant programmes whenever possible, and spent a great deal of time either addressing groups of area managers at Rive-Reine or visiting the markets, giving presentations, and setting up project teams to work with them on specific products and programmes.

Ernest: 'It was a time-consuming and somewhat frustrating

process, but the required degree of consensus to get things moving always took time at Nestlé, partly because of the innate conservatism of the Swiss and partly because of the standards of excellence against which every new product was considered.'

The biggest hurdle was a deep-rooted fear that to improve the nutritional content of food would necessarily harm its taste, which of course would have been a sure road to marketing failure. Equally feared was the possibility that a nutritional improvement might mean a product being taken from the mainstream shelves of a supermarket into the 'ghetto' of so-called 'dietetic products'. So the nutritional marketing programme had three main aims: to improve the nutritional value of existing products without affecting taste, to extend existing products with 'light/lighter' versions, and to develop entirely new products.

In the first category, a comprehensive analysis of all products was carried out, with the intention of cutting sugar, fat, salt and additives, and/or replacing them with other more nutritious ingredients. This was backed by extensive consumer research, and took a long time. It was relatively easy to produce 'light' versions of products that were ordinarily high in sugar and fat, and Nestlé did well with Crosse & Blackwell's Waistline range of salad dressings, Libby's canned fruit packed only in its own juice, Thomy's 'light' mayonnaise and Chambourcy Sveltesse yoghurts. Frisco ice lollies and Disch sweets were also successfully marketed without sugar.

The booming frozen food business was given some entirely new thinking by Michel Guérard, the famous chef associated with the origins of *nouvelle cuisine*. He introduced alternative ingredients to 'lighten' recipes without damaging taste, such a the substitution of *fromage blanc* for cream. But his most significant contribution was to the evolutionary thinking that led the American Stouffer subsidiary to develop its Lean Cuisine range of frozen foods, subsequently sold under the Findus label in the UK and elsewhere.

An entirely new range of nutritionally improved breakfast cereals was developed and marketed initially in France – and all this activity was in fact only the beginning of a process that would turn Nestlé into a leader in today's vast range of food and drink products sold in supermarkets and restaurants all round the world, and enjoyed by many millions of people who want healthier eating and drinking as well as good taste. Ernest: 'This trend was part of a new lifestyle that good marketing and good products were able to exploit, and at the same time was entirely in keeping with the nutritional recommendations of national and international health authorities.'

However, Ernest's growing success with the nutritional marketing programme was about to open the door to problems of a quite different nature. He was asked, in addition to his current responsibilities, to take over from Dr Alfred Keller, who was retiring as worldwide product director of Nestlé's Specialist Nutrition and Infant Products Group. These were already the company's most nutritionally excellent products, but had not previously been thought of in that light.

The product group's task was to improve and broaden the range of nutritional products for the so-called vulnerable groups within the population – babies, the elderly and those with specific nutritional deficiencies. Most sensitive among these was the range of products which came under the heading of infant formulae. These included all commercial supplements and substitutes for breast-milk. There have always been mothers who were unable or unwilling to breast-feed their babies, and even breast-fed babies often need extra food to make sure they grow strong and healthy.

The technical quality of commercial infant formula products has been above reproach, but marketing them became increasingly difficult as Nestlé, with the other infant formula manufacturers, was criticised for what were seen as aggressive selling methods in developing countries. Pressure groups claimed that mothers were encouraged to give up breast-feeding unnecessarily, and infant formula was promoted in areas where, since the water it had to be mixed with was of varying quality, hygenic preparation could not be guaranteed.

Although Nestlé had already been shifting its sales methods towards those prevailing in pharmaceutical and para-medical products, and consumer advertising had been discontinued, every time the company thought the issue was settled there would be another outbreak of criticism. This had led to low morale within Keller's product group, as more and more time was devoted to political and public relations questions rather than to scientific or marketing research. Ernest: 'Whereas on most other matters within Nestlé, so far as I could see, there appeared to be consensus as to how to deal with things, on this subject there were different voices throughout the company.'

They ranged from outright indignation by the late chairman, Pierre Liotard-Vogt, and Dr Furer, the managing director, that Nestlé of all people should be criticised at all, to the hawks among the most powerful individual country managers who wanted the company to fight back hard, and to those who thought Nestlé should just ignore the critics, because answering them was not worth the hassle.

Ernest: 'It was extremely difficult for a product director, supposedly concerned with nutritional product development, to have to deal with political issues that clearly involved many different personalities, opinions and areas of responsibility within the company, both at Vevey and in the markets. Moreover, there was a great deal of personal involvement from right at the top; after all, this was a company that had traditionally kept a very low profile, but now found itself in the public spotlight. But on one point we were all united: the infant nutritional products met a real need, and whatever the grounds might be for attacks on our selling methods, the scientific development and availability of the products had to be continued.'

Within Dr Keller's product group, known internally as P.I.D., there was an expert on the controversy, Geoffrey Fookes, a knowledgeable and deeply religious man who took the attacks much to heart. Fookes educated Ernest on the history of the issue, and on how he believed the situation should be managed; without a more determined approach he thought the political argument would absorb far too much of the company's time and effort. He had a strong belief in providing the facts so that responsible research institutions could study the subject for themselves. He believed totally in what he was doing, and successfully argued that even though Nestlé, as the largest producer of infant formula, had been principally selected by pressure groups for attack, the problem in fact belonged to the industry as a whole, and Nestlé should work more closely through ICIFI, the International Council of Infant Food Industries, the industry's self-regulatory organisation. A move had recently been initiated by ICIFI, involving Senator Edward Kennedy of the US, to encourage all concerned to work with the World Health Organisation in Geneva towards creating a code of practice for the marketing of infant formula. This made sense, and Nestlé's first meeting with the WHO was held in October 1979.

However, across the Atlantic, where a number of major companies were involved in the industry, the critics had become vocal. They instituted a boycott campaign against Nestlé in the US, even though the company only made coffee and chocolate products there, not infant formula. Dave Guerrant, head of Nestlé's US operating subsidiary at White Plains, was irritated and uncomfortable at being dragged into an issue that seemed to him totally irrelevant to his business. But no Nestlé manager ever relinquished control over what went on on his patch, and Guerrant had his own views as to how the matter should be dealt with in the US. These involved large-scale direct mail shots to explain to thinking people why the boycott attempts should not continue.

Guerrant used Hank Ciocca, Nestlé's assistant legal director, as his principal aide in the matter, and Hank brought in Tom Ward, a long-standing external legal consultant to Nestlé's White Plains office.

Ward had, according to Ciocca, strong political connections in Washington, and a skill for negotiating difficult political issues. That was how Ernest first met Ward, who was also working closely with Dr Furer, the managing director, on Washington-related matters.

Geoffrey Fookes meanwhile was working in Switzerland on his own solution. He thought the only way to get people to understand the problem would be to have independent studies, and the facts presented to the public in an intelligible form. But in the early days, when studies favouring the industry had appeared, activists tried to rubbish them as propaganda.

Fookes and Ernest had many discussions with Dave Guerrant about the boycott problem, reporting back to the chairman and managing director in Vevey. Ernest: 'Eventually I won agreement for my suggestion that, since the boycott campaign and seemingly the overall campaign of criticism against Nestlé and the industry was now co-ordinated from Washington, Nestlé should itself set up a specialist unit in Washington to deal with the issue in the US.' This led to the establishment of the Nestlé Co-ordination Center for Nutrition, and to Ernest's recruitment of Ray Pagan, an experienced manager of political issues, to run it. In the event NCCN devised and implemented a strategy that was to end the boycott campaign in 1984. 'The essential first step in resolving the infant feeding dilemma,' said Pagan in 1983, 'was for Nestlé to recognise that it was a political as well as a nutritional issue.'

Meanwhile, in Geneva, the tortuous process of drawing up a code of conduct dragged on through many drafts, with the posturing, polemic and political compromises that such multi-party negotiations seem to demand. Eventually in May 1981 the WHO produced a draft that provided the basis for an agreement that, although workable, still involved significant differences between what the industry thought responsible marketing required and what the most extreme opponents of any marketing at all would have liked.

However, the industry had the endorsement it needed to justify the continued marketing of infant formula in developing countries, and Nestlé, whilst having reservations about the code's provisions, was quick to accept the document. It instructed all its subsidiaries to co-operate with governments in developing appropriate national codes which would implement the WHO recommendations.

Ernest had been elected to the presidency of ICIFI, and Ciocca and Guerrant had recommended to Ernest and Dr Furer that Ward be involved in the WHO negotiating process for Nestlé, particularly since the American manufacturers were very heavily concerned, with lawyers abounding, partly to avoid anti-trust problems. Ward continued to work with Pagan after Ernest had left Nestlé.

Pagan was to say: 'The fact that Nestlé risked its reputation on what was a small part of its overall business indicated that its motives were based on more than just profit.' Douglas Johnson, National Chairperson of the activist Infant Formula Action Coalition, said: 'Nestlé has moved forward to become a model for the whole industry, a model which created a new standard of corporate behaviour.'

Although it was not until 1984 that the US boycott of Nestlé products officially came to an end, Ernest had helped to start the ball rolling in the right direction. His principal contribution was the appointment of Pagan and the NCCN operation.

In 1980 Nestlé was visited by the proprietor of the US Beechnut baby-food business, offering the Swiss company a product entry into the largest infant products market of all. Despite the boycott problems, Nestlé's chairman decided to buy the business, since he wanted to be represented in the category in the US for future development, and to start from scratch was unthinkable. Ernest: 'It was, at that time, seen as a bold decision, but Liotard-Vogt was known for his courage.'

Despite the distractions of the infant formula issue, which was at times most unpleasant, Ernest continued to develop the company's position in the field of specialist nutrition. A number of key managerial appointments were made. An experienced French medical director was recruited to set the tone for a science-based initiative. Under the direction of Dr Angst, a Nutrition Council was established, bringing in some of the top names from the various schools of nutritional thinking. Ernest: 'It was informative to see at first hand how the French, English and other countries' professors had quite different views and ways of expressing themselves from one another, even though they were talking about the same subject. But this para-pharmaceutical attitude to the business was not only the correct way to go forward, it actually took Nestlé much closer to its original marketing approach applied to infant formula products.'

During the years the family lived in Switzerland, Jo and I were at boarding school in the UK. We normally saw our parents and our brother John, who went to school in Lausanne, only in the holidays, but my father would sometimes appear at school functions or would fly in for the odd fathers' and sons' cricket match.

At the beginning of each school holiday we would spend a few days in St Légier before heading into the mountains. As children we found it very difficult to amuse ourselves down by the lake. We did not have many friends there so we either swam or played tennis or ended up going to the shops. Then we would set off for the mountains. We would take the motorway to Aigle, at the eastern end of Lake Geneva, and then the mountain road to Les Diablerets. You climb steeply for almost an hour, passing through centuries-old villages and hamlets. The grey Swiss architecture of the valleys gives way to picturesque chalets, and you go up through the cloud level, often into brilliant sunshine.

Les Diablerets is still a small, unfashionable farming village, nestling in the shadow of the Les Diablerets glacier, with mountains on all sides and views back down the valley towards Geneva. The weather is invariably better than down by the lake, where the climate is like England – grey, foggy and rainy! After sunny days in the mountains, in the late afternoon a blanket of fog often rolls up the valley from the lake and engulfs the village and the ski slopes. One minute you are skiing along and can see every bump: the next you are immersed in grey soup and have to rely on your knowledge of the trees to get down safely.

The village has few hotels, and most chalets have been owned by the same families for years. We all have friends in the village and still look forward to each visit. It is not the most exciting place on earth, but it is beautifully peaceful and detached from the outside world.

4

THE CALL FROM GUINNESS

During the years in Switzerland, Christmas holidays were a time when the Saunders family got together in Les Diablerets. Our parents would ski together and talk in detail about we children, of whom they saw so little. At the end of the Christmas holidays they would invariably come round to the same question: we were a true family only at holiday time, we children were growing fast, and was my father's Nestlé job really worth the sacrifice?

The Swiss life also involved considerable loneliness for my mother, since women played no role in Swiss business life. Wives never travelled with their husbands on business trips, nor were they even invited to attend dinners for foreign visitors in Vevey. And it was not customary to invite business acquaintants home. Ernest was again travelling a great deal and needed to attend a lot of business functions when he was in Vevey, so Carole had a pretty unsocial time. Furthermore, the expatriate community was very transient.

Carole: 'I always looked on England as my home, and I wanted to return so that I could play more of a part in my children's lives. I didn't just want to come to England to visit – I wanted a home there.'

So Carole and Ernest fell to musing about the sort of job that could be attractive in England. It was possible that Nestlé might offer my father the UK market to look after, but the UK managing director, Tug Wilson, was not due to retire for some time and undoubtedly had his own succession plans. Thus they were always left with the same list of ideal priorities: the position should be with a blue-chip consumer goods company which could be developed around its brands by using Ernest's marketing experience. Ideally, he would want to make the leap to managing director, even though he had had no financial training, because he needed the authority in order to ensure that the company would be marketing-led. He would prefer to be dealing with a number of brand names, and with a company that required revitalisation.

In the early months of 1981, not long after the family's annual post-Christmas holiday blues, Ernest received a call from a London headhunter, asking if he would be interested in returning to the UK. There was a possible senior management position available that they would like to discuss with him. Ernest went down his checklist. Was it a blue-chip company? Yes. Was it operating in consumer goods? Yes. Were the brands in good shape? No. Was the job senior enough to give him authority? Yes. The company was Guinness.

It was a business Ernest knew little about at the time, beyond the famous advertising slogan 'Guinness is good for you', promoting a thick black beer that he had never tasted. And he remembered seeing *The Guinness Book of Records* in the bookshops when he was looking for Christmas presents. But the opportunity seemed in line with what he had been mulling over. Ernest told the headhunters he would like to discuss the job, and would let them know when he was next in London. He did not mention the approach to Carole, as previous experience had taught him that the vast majority of such calls led to nothing.

In March that year Ernest had to go to London on business. He arranged to meet the headhunters at their office for a preliminary chat, but before he drove to Geneva Airport he visited the Nestlé central library to see what he could learn about Guinness. Understandably the alcoholic drinks industry was not well documented there – nor were British companies in general – but he established that Guinness advertising was known throughout the world for its wit and originality. The Guinness board was packed with personalities from the pages of Debrett's *Peerage* ... but the company's performance, which involved many businesses other than just brewing, was at best stagnant: press comment on recent results had been less than kind.

The first meeting with the executive search company in London left Ernest with the impression that the Guinness board and family genuinely recognised the need for a more professional marketing approach. Sales of Guinness stout were not growing, lager performance was patchy and the company clearly needed some sort of marketing review. On top of that, a large number of unrelated companies had been acquired in the previous twenty years: they and their brands, such as Callard & Bowser, appeared to be going nowhere. Even so it sounded to Ernest as if what they thought they wanted was a high-powered marketing director, not a new managing director, which was the level he was now aiming at.

That initial meeting was also memorable for the apparent lack of company concern about Guinness's profit performance, and a similar lack of urgency to have the post filled. Ernest went away feeling that the company was not yet ready to make any radical management changes. And when the search agency asked him to think seriously about the opportunity, he in turn asked them to consider whether they did not in fact need a marketing-orientated general manager, possibly with a brief to sort out operations as well as marketing, to get the company moving again.

Ernest returned to Switzerland. A few weeks later he received a call asking him to meet the current managing director of Guinness, Tony Purssell, who was on his way to a brewers' conference in Copenhagen and could stop off in Zurich for a chat. Their conversation confirmed Ernest's impression that the company needed a thorough management overhaul led by strong marketing. But what they appeared to want was a senior marketing manager who would bring fresh ideas to the company for consideration but not necessarily for implementation. Ernest repeated his position, saying that if he were to leave Nestlé and return to the UK it had to be for a managing director's post with genuine responsiblity for operational leadership. As Purssell was already managing director, Ernest did not see how that could be arranged. The two men agreed to keep in touch.

In the early summer the headhunting firm called Ernest again. The forthcoming Guinness results were apparently not going to please the stock market, and the board's thinking had shifted. They would now like to discuss a position much closer to the one Ernest had outlined: could he come to London to meet Purssell and others as soon as possible? One of the Guinness family, Peter Guinness, was eventually delegated to see if a compromise could be agreed. Events slowly evolved to the point where Ernest was to be offered the job of managing director, responsible for day-to-day operations, and Purssell was to find himself a new title, concern himself with the longer-term strategy and continue with his outside interests until he retired. Ernest: 'The process leading to the ultimate offer had been incredibly tortuous and frustrating, but I now had in my sights the sort of job that justified a move.'

He talked the job over with Carole, who was enthusiastic. I remember my father broaching the subject to Jo and I when I was rowing for my school at Reading Regatta. We too were both very excited at the prospect of having the whole family back in the UK again.

Ernest's final interview was with the Earl of Iveagh, the chairman and head of the Guinness family. Ireland was seen as the Mecca of Guinness brewing, and Lord Iveagh invited my father to lunch at his magnificent home, Farmleigh, in Phoenix Park, Dublin. Ernest: 'It was a huge empty stately home, with an enormous entrance hall lined with dozens and dozens of wellington boots.' The butler took him to meet Lord Iveagh in a huge, draughty dining room that could have seated fifty, but on this occasion was set for just the two of them at a small table in the middle of the room. They drank water, and the conversation was punctuated by the sound of the butler padding sedately to and fro between their table and the kitchen. Ernest: 'Lord Iveagh, who had recently returned from hospital, and looked much older than his then 44 years, was charming and diffident. He thanked me profusely for coming to see him.'

Ernest (by now 46 – two years older than his prospective employer) found himself outlining the job he was expecting to be offered – and which Iveagh subsequently offered him. 'My other recollections of that meeting are to do with animals. First there was a cat who jumped on to the dining-room table and walked through the butter. I shooed the cat off the table, but Iveagh frowned, mouthing "Don't do that!" I could see the job vanishing out of the door with the cat. Second, we were accompanied into his lordship's study by one of his dogs. With the doors and windows closed, there was no escaping the tremendous impact of the animal's farts. Despite the provocation I kept my nose tightly closed and my mouth shut.'

On returning to Switzerland Ernest told his immediate boss at Nestlé, Dr Von Reding, who had replaced Dr Gloor, that he had been approached by a famous British company to be managing director. He said that if he received a firm offer – and given the leisurely way Guinness had behaved so far there was no guarantee of this – he would probably accept. Von Reding told him he had a promising future at Nestlé, but his colleagues had been aware of Ernest's doubts regarding his family situation and there was in any case no chance of an Englishman becoming head of the company. 'The money may well be better for you with Nestlé,' said Von Reding, 'and certainly the skiing too, but never that kind of job status and challenge.'

By this stage Ernest was naturally anxious to know for certain whether or not he was going to receive a definite offer from Guinness. But protracted negotiations ensued. He visited London to agree terms at the offices of Guinness's solicitors, Travers Smith Braithwaite & Co. Ernest was accompanied by Henry King of Denton Hall and Burgin, as the firm was then known, and he had to return to Switzerland before they had concluded a deal, which was to be based on a salary of about £73,000 a year (which matched his Nestlé pay). This was finally agreed by telephone, and the contract sent to Ernest by courier. He arranged to be at the airport office of DHL, the courier company, to receive and sign it, along with the rest of the Saunders family, as we were all on holiday. We hung around Geneva Airport all day, waiting for the document to clear customs. The reason for the delay soon became clear: Guinness had sent the contract in a suitcase full of company papers which they thought Ernest might like to look at on holiday. He extracted the contract and leaned on the bonnet of Carole's Volvo estate to sign it so that it could be returned straight back to London. Then we all drove off in search of a bottle of Guinness to toast his new appointment. We could not find a single bottle anywhere in Geneva. Distribution in Europe was obviously a problem!

My father had planned to have a decent three-week holiday for once, knowing the challenge of the new job would inevitably mean a period of intense activity when he started. For a few days the Guinness suitcase remained unopened, as did his battered briefcase containing a few Peter Drucker paperbacks on management theory. But these good intentions were abandoned after he had read the opinion of the British financial press on the latest Guinness interim results. Certainly the board had announced figures which showed profits down by thirteen per cent. But the real problem was that Lord Iveagh had made a brief comment to the effect that the dividend could not be guaranteed at its present level. Now the UK stock market had become used to mundane profits from Guinness, but even so the dividend had always been reliable enough to form the backbone of thousands of investment portfolios, including those of many small investors. Not the least of these portfolios were the far-flung Guinness family holdings, amounting to something over twenty per cent of the total. Suddenly a prime reason for investing in Guinness shares was under threat, and the share prices started to tumble.

Each day Ernest tried to get hold of an English paper. Although it was not possible to buy the *Financial Times* every day, the *Daily*

Mail, *Daily Express* and *The Times* all told the same story: Guinness shares dropping steadily. My father calculated at one stage that if the rate of fall continued, the price would be down to zero even before his three weeks were up and he arrived at the company. He had to be prepared for instant action. Out came the Guinness suitcase and the reading began.

The documents turned out to be a mish-mash of unrelated material, ranging from a history of the Dublin brewery since the early years of the century to a philosophical treatise by Tony Purssell on possible ways for the company to move forward in the 1980s. What was missing was any factual data on how the group was doing now. This was Ernest's first experience of the Guinness information vacuum that was to cause so many problems in future. There was no such vacuum, however, in the wealth of scathing City stockbrokers' analyses sent over by friends. Ernest read and reread a thick report produced by David Campbell, then the drinks analyst at Wood Mackenzie, who followed the sector closely. His firm subsequently became one of Guinness's brokers. His fact-laden thesis on the company's past performance and apparent lack of coherent strategy left Ernest horrified, quite apart from Campbell's heavy innuendoes about lack of management ability. Colin Mitchell of Buckmaster and Moore, considered at that time to be the guru among drinks industry analysts, was no more charitable, nor was Colin Humphries of Scrimgeour.

Ernest learned that Guinness had a market capitalisation of £90 million, and was still regarded as essentially a family business. In 1981 the brewing division accounted for the bulk of trading profits. A ragbag of non-brewing subsidiaries had been spawned, apparently the result of a boardroom belief that, if the company had enough activities, some were bound to succeed. However, group profits had been falling, and the City was worried about a lack of management direction. In 1981, even the ruling family had become concerned: their own dividends were in danger.

Apart from spelling out in blunt terms the underlying reasons for the share-price weakness, the brokers' work did provide Ernest with an initial assessment of Guinness's product portfolio. It was centred on stout, which seemed out of step with the growing fashion in developed countries for lighter drinks. Stout sales had particularly been declining in the UK and Ireland, and profits were strongly dependent on the Third World, with a frightening proportion flowing from the notoriously volatile economy of Nigeria. Harp lager was in grave difficulties in the UK and really only viable in Nigeria and Ireland. It was also clear that the company's non-brewing activities were problematical, to say the least.

Under the constant reminder of the daily share-price falls, Ernest began to formulate a list of first steps that, if the brokers' prognostications were anywhere near accurate, would have to be taken as soon as he arrived. He dug into Drucker to refresh his memory about basic management techniques. He had always regretted missing the opportunity to attend Harvard Business School when he was at Beecham. Now he was about to take the leap from marketing into full-blooded general management.

My father's copies of Drucker's books still have grains of sand between the pages as a memento of days on the beach in 1981. But the holiday was soon over, and he was back in Vevey standing in the office of Nestlé's deputy managing director, Dr Carl Angst, to confirm his resignation and to ask for an early release. In the light of the Guinness share-price performance and what he now knew about the company, he wanted to be in London in time for the start of Guinness's new financial year, 1 October.

Dr Angst was co-operative, and my father got his release, but he had apparently offended the top brass at Nestlé by wishing to leave. It was considered an honour to be asked to join the headquarters team at Vevey: asking to leave was therefore a sign of ingratitude. Ernest very much regretted this, and happily the mood had passed by the time he held his leaving party, which was attended by the chairman himself. Ernest made plain in his brief speech that the Nestlé experience had been extremely valuable for him, and he sincerely hoped that he had been able to bring some new thinking to Nestlé. Subsequently, the family's regular visits to Switzerland at Christmas have maintained the many friendships we made.

Ernest left Nestlé on the last Friday of September 1981, and Carole and he planned to drive to London, allowing themselves a night in France *en route*. They arrived in London at about 10 p.m. on Saturday night, and went straight to the Guinness head office.

The Guinness head office was then at 10 Albemarle Street in Mayfair, known in the company as 'No. 10'. It contained a small two-bedroom flat on the top floor, with an L-shaped sitting-cum-dining room cheaply furnished. It was normally used for directors' lunches. Ernest: 'We wondered whether they had ever served steak, since the forks bent completely the first time we ever tried to cut steak with them!' It was to be Ernest's and Carole's home for several months, while the children lived at boarding school. The building was badly designed, either as offices or a flat, for it consisted of six small floors linked by one tiny lift which must have ranked as one of the slowest in London. It took hours for them to get their luggage up to the flat that night, even though they had only the contents of one car. When they had finished, they found that the pile of luggage was matched by another pile – of documents laid out on the dining table, thoughtfully accompanied by a bottle of champagne.

On Sunday morning we children arrived from our various schools. A lunchtime family reunion with Ernest's elderly father had been arranged at nearby Brown's Hotel, but lunch ran into tea before Ernest felt obliged to return to the flat and the paper mountain on its dining-room table.

The biggest problem was that there was no logical sequence to the huge collection. There were files, reports and correspondence covering every conceivable aspect of the business, but only scraps of information were connected with one another. The one piece of paper that told a complete story was the agenda announcing that there was to be a board meeting on the Tuesday, at which Ernest would be formally installed as managing director. No one, however, had drawn up an introductory programme, and my father did not know where to begin. The next morning Ernest met his part-time secretary, Margaret McGrath, whom he then found he had to share with another director. He immediately sought out Tony Purssell to discuss a programme to get things moving, but Purssell was not in. Since Ernest still could make nothing of the papers in the flat he returned to the brokers' reports and studied their criticisms. He was beginning to get a nagging feeling that he must get round the company's operations himself as soon as possible, if he wanted to understand how things really were with the business.

His anxieties were increased by the first board meeting. He had met only a few of the directors before. 'The family behaved as if it was still their private business, rather than being a public company with a Stock Exchange listing.' Lord Iveagh was chairman. Simon Lennox-Boyd, later Lord Boyd, became vice-chairman after his mother retired from the board. Jonathan and Finn Guinness, two sons of Lord Moyne, a former vice-chairman, were directors. Edward and Peter Guinness, from different branches of the family, were also on the board, but were not considered full family members. This honour seems to have been confined to direct descendants of the Iveagh, Moyne and Boyd families. The Marchioness and Marquess of Dufferin and Ava were also on the board. (The Marchioness retired at the next annual meeting.) There were two non-executive directors who owed their position to family connections: Christopher Parsons was a former senior partner of Travers Smith Braithwaite & Co., the family's solicitors, and Ken Whittaker was an Irish associate of Lord Iveagh. All the Guinnesses except Peter were thought of as non-executive. Over the years the size of the family's combined shareholding had become dissipated and was something of a mystery. Estimates varied from twenty to thirty per cent. Purssell had no time for the family as directors, and said so. He was equally uncharitable about the outside non-executives.

Of the executive directors, Peter Guinness was in charge of the overseas brewing markets, known as Guinness Overseas. Michael Ogle ran the 'trading companies', including Morrison Son and Jones, which he had originally sold to Guinness for a fortune. Stanley Darmon was responsible for the plastics group and one or two other non-brewing activities. Michael Hatfield was managing director of the UK brewing group based at Park Royal in west London, and Mark Hely-Hutchinson ran Ireland. Edward Guinness, theoretically non-executive, was chairman of Harp and responsible for public relations. It turned out that the company secretary was responsible for an orchid business in Madeira, and Tony Spicer, the financial director, was in charge of one or two businesses, including Callard & Bowser. Ernest: 'It was perhaps significant that directors' responsibilities were often referred to as their "special interests" – hardly the description for executive responsibility.'

Ernest began to form the opinion that, if Purssell was right, then regardless of any change of operating strategy or marketing philosophy he might come up with, he did not have the management to make it happen. Purssell had another surprise. Having previously been managing director, he told Ernest that he had now decided to call himself chief executive, which opened countless avenues for confusion both inside and outside the company.

When Ernest's first Guinness board meeting began, he introduced himself to those directors he had not met before, and was allocated a seat next to the company secretary, Alan Scrine. Ernest's appointment was the first item on the agenda, and he was warmly welcomed by Lord Iveagh. Ernest: 'My clear impression was that from that moment the company's many problems had been pushed clearly and squarely on to my lap. I was surrounded by the representatives of the major shareholders, but it was up to me to sort out the mess.'

The other items on the agenda were dealt with swiftly and they moved on to lunch, to be served in the flat which was Ernest's and Carole's home. Carole had been asked to make herself scarce while the board had their meal, bent forks and all.

Ernest: 'What struck me most forcefully when I thought through that first meeting was the absence of any facts and any sense of urgency, despite the picture painted by the brokers' reports. There was lots of chat and many opinions on all sorts of subjects from a group of what seemed to be very pleasant people talking as if they were in a private club. But there was no real feeling of concern that they had to take a grip of the situation.'

However, the dining-room table in the flat was frequently to be littered with empty bottles of Guinness's most potent brew – Foreign Extra Stout, which possibly showed the directors' inner tension. 'It seemed that certain members of the board were used to slipping up for a quick one whenever the pressures got too much.'

After the meeting he and Purssell agreed that Ernest should visit the main brewing operations, UK and Overseas at Park Royal, then Dublin, and then 'chat' to the directors of the non-brewing activities with a view to visiting the main operating units, as necessary. The idea was to spend Monday and Friday in head office and the rest of the week out. Ernest felt that the question of his and Purssell's confusing roles could wait, and he set out right away on what became a four-week whistle-stop tour of the company. Every day that passed confirmed his initial fears that the calibre of the management was questionable, and that despite the famous Guinness advertising there was no marketing orientation anywhere. All the time he was nagged by the eerie absence of hard facts, which he later characterised as making him like a pilot trying to fly an aircraft through fog without any instruments. Ernest: 'There may not have been meaningful data, but I soon noticed that there was no shortage of executive toys. Mini computers and calculators were everywhere, but what were they being used for?'

However, one of the most significant discoveries from Ernest's visits highlighted a massive problem that he had not foreseen at all in considering the Guinness job. Unlike the position at Nestlé, GUS or Beecham, back-up resources were nil. 'There may have been accountants floating around, but no one was producing monthly management figures, overheads were not being properly allocated to subsidiaries, and when I asked the financial director about our debt position at a board meeting I was told that we were well within the arrangements agreed with our banks, who were willing to extend further facilities. I'll bet they were.' He soon learned that the company's debts were such that they could not afford to borrow any more.

Increasingly he felt that people either did not realise what bad shape the business was in or knew and simply did not care. The only progress report submitted to the board was based on chatty telephone conversations between Purssell's secretary and the secretaries of the directors with operating responsibilities. Ernest: 'It consisted of highly selective tit-bits, usually ending with the suggestion that since the year's forecast would not be met it should be reduced. No one was putting forward possible remedies – and this was at the start of the financial year. The brewers, notably in the UK, were convinced that the company's major brand, Guinness stout, was in a state varying from stagnation to terminal decline, even though it was the group's flagship and the basis of the stock market quotation. And the non-brewing activities included some extraordinary businesses with potentially enormous problems.

'Beyond a lack of financial expertise at headquarters, there wasn't a lawyer in the place. The personnel and secretarial functions were out of the way at Park Royal, and Edward Guinness sat alone in our Jermyn street office, looking after what was supposed to represent PR. A lean corporate head office may be okay if the expertise available is of a high order, and the management resources at operating level are competent. Neither was the case at Guinness at this time.'

He was beginning to wrestle with these structural worries when he received a call summoning him to meet major institutional investment managers who were large holders of Guinness stock, including Britannic Assurance and the Merchant Navy Pension Fund. He had never met institutional managers before, as his marketing career had not brought him into contact with the City, but their attitude left him in no doubts about the seriousness of the situation. They felt the company needed a total shake-up, and fast, if Ernest were to head off a major crisis of confidence.

Lack of both time and information became his recurring nightmares. As he worked on, sometimes through the night, at the Albemarle Street flat, he came to some basic conclusions. He needed to find some way of showing shareholders and employees that things were going to change. He had to overcome the lack of information. There was so much money being wasted that perhaps he could protect profits in the short term simply by turning off the expenditure tap.

So he produced a crude four-point plan of action. First, he decided to hire external resources to get him the facts about the group's performance and especially its bewildering array of businesses as quickly as possible. Second, he would have to order a spending freeze. Third, he would take personal charge of the Guinness advertising in the UK. Its high profile and huge budget had to be made to work for the brand. The name of the brand was the name of the company and the name of the family. Fresh confidence in the brand would help to rebuild confidence in the company. Finally, he would find a way to monitor the performance of the company regularly and effectively.

Ernest worked long and hard. It was eerie, living in what was effectively a non-residential part of London. After 7 p.m. and on weekends there was hardly anyone about. One night Ernest was burning the midnight oil in the flat when the burglar alarm went off. He rushed out into the street, where he was stopped by a policeman. 'Who are you?' the officer demanded. 'The managing director of Guinness – I was working late,' Ernest replied. The policeman looked at him curiously and said something that summed up Ernest's own impression of the company at that time: 'What on earth is going on at Guinness? No one works late there.'

5

THE FIGHT FOR SURVIVAL

The Guinness Company that my father inherited was like a large, genteel family mansion that had been allowed to decay through neglect. Contrary to the public's image of the company, it was near to collapse. Ernest could see that he was going to have to take some drastic steps before he could embark on any ambitious marketing-led developments. But before he could even take the steps essential for the group's survival, he had to map out some way of gathering the information on which those steps could be based.

Ernest: 'I felt that I had to have a resource from outside the company to get facts quickly that I could rely on, before I could take vital and long-overdue strategic decisions. The reporting system at Guinness, what there was of it, was entirely based on financial accounting and did not provide management information of anything like the quality I had been used to at Beecham or Nestlé. What is more, the finance department at head office could not cope with what I needed, and I frankly did not trust the figures I was getting from the operating companies, who seemed to see life through rose-tinted spectacles.'

Purssell and Hely-Hutchinson told Ernest that McKinsey, the American management consultants, had worked for Guinness Ireland, so he went to see Norman Sansom at McKinsey's smart offices in St James's. His views on what seemed to be necessary at Guinness coincided with Ernest's, but McKinsey had been working for another brewer and so was unable to take a commission from Guinness. Ernest asked him: 'On the assumption that McKinsey consider themselves to be No. 1 in consulting, who would you rate as No. 2?' Samson replied: 'Bain & Co. They are coming up fast.' Ernest had never heard of this firm, so he went to Boston Consulting Group, who had worked for Harp Lager, and asked them the same question. Again, they named Bain.

After some searching, Ernest tracked Bain to a building in Fitzhardinge Street, off Portman Square in London. There he met John Theroux, the firm's young American vice-president, who was initially concerned to assure himself that Guinness had the financial resources to underwrite the quality of work Bain provided. He also asked if Guinness had a management structure that would permit his company to work in the way they were used to and indeed insisted on, with direct access at all times to the managing director. Ernest was impressed: 'I decided that Bain would have a tremendous motivation to do an outstanding job for Guinness, since this would enable them to establish a significant base in the UK. This would cost money, but Bain prided themselves on providing a very high return for investment in their services. And I would not be committing the company to an overhead that I would eventually not need.'

He and Theroux later had a series of talks in the Albemarle Street flat, usually in the evening or at the weekend, during which Ernest outlined Guinness's problems as he saw them and what he might want from Bain. The first major requirement would almost certainly be for an analytical fact-gathering exercise concentrating on the non-brewing activities, so that Ernest could decide what to do with them. Then he would need an analysis of the brewing business to cut costs, improve efficiency and protect profits. However, they would have to agree to a flexible arrangement regarding priorities. Speed was critical. Ernest: 'While I was without facts I felt I was sitting on a time bomb. Bain had in mind more sophisticated strategic projects, but in my view these could be considered later. The immediate priority was a rapid cost freeze and cost reduction programme to stop profits from slipping further.'

Theroux and David Hoare, one of Bain's senior British managers, felt that they and Guinness could only find out if they could work together effectively by a practical experiment, so they agreed to start by collecting the facts needed to understand the scope of the planned cost freeze. Theroux had one other suggestion: in view of what Ernest had said about the state of the company's finances and its finance department, what Guinness needed was a controller, to act as focal point for the financial and operational data that would be generated. Bain could provide such a person, effectively on secondment. Ernest agreed. They sent a Frenchman in his early thirties called Olivier Roux.

On a freezing cold day in January 1982, Ernest called a conference at Park Royal of the top 100 managers of the whole group based in the UK and Ireland; some came from further afield. It had been snowing, and many turned up late with travelling tales of woe. Purssell, Ernest and representatives of Bain explained the need for what to their audience must have appeared to be a draconian series of spending cuts.

The need for such action had become even more urgent after a crude canvass of estimated results for the first half of the current financial year, and for the year as a whole, was conducted, partly by a telephone survey of Guinness executives round the world. Ernest made some calls himself from the flat one Sunday, just so that he could get a feel for the extent of the problem first-hand. The tally was alarming. From profits of £41 million in 1980–81, sales projections suggested as little as half that for the current year unless drastic steps were immediately taken. A sales improvement campaign could not realistically be organised in time, so the axe had to fall on costs.

Ernest: 'A pragmatic and arbitrary campaign was devised, to be implemented by Roux with help from two excellent Guinness executives, Phil Parnell and John Cleave, one for brewing and the other for covering the rest.' Each operating unit was to be given a cost reduction target for the first six months and the year as a whole, and would receive guidance as to where to find the savings. The emphasis was to fall on costs that were not sales related. It would have been easy simply to cut beer advertising, but over the years that area had already been dangerously eroded.

Ernest: 'I gave them a personal lecture on saving money, using the invaluable experience I had had with Leonard Wolfson and the Swiss. Ernest issued a series of detailed basic edicts to cut costs: 'I told the managers, "Walk into your warehouse and look around – if the height of the stacks on the pallets is reaching the ceiling, there must be too much stock, so reduce it. Cut down telephone extensions, and stocks of light bulbs and loo rolls. If in doubt, cut ten per cent all round."' He reduced travelling and entertainment allowances. Staff who left could not be replaced without written authority. 'We also explained that Bain executives would be evaluating data on the operating companies to help determine the necessary strategic decisions for the future.' He introduced the key Bain people, who then went right over his own head and the managers' with a catalogue of management consultancy theories. This was not in the script he had approved, and that was the last time they got away with such a manoeuvre.

By the time the meeting ended the atmosphere in the room at Park Royal was as chilly as it was outside, but Ernest was convinced that his cost reduction programme was fundamental to the company's survival. He hoped that if they could stabilise profits during the first six months they would be given the necessary breathing space to rebuild Guinness. If not, the company would be a sitting target for predators.

To monitor progress, weekly control meetings were introduced and became the crude but effective way in which Ernest kept a check on the entire group. He insisted on a simple weekly sales analysis, believing that this was ultimately the key, and since it provided fifty-two opportunities a year to put things right.

'The controllers', as Roux, Parnell and Cleave became known, worked frenetically with the operating companies, who on the whole responded reluctantly but positively. Ernest: 'Inevitably a few did not, and they received direct attention from me! It must be recognised that the managements of the operating companies had never been expected to provide the sort of performance details to head office that were now demanded, and they were irritated at having to do so. But it was my view that it was not only those of us at HQ who needed the figures. How could the operating companies themselves be properly managed if their executives didn't have this sort of data at their fingertips? The days were over when they could merely send a friendly message to Albemarle Street to the effect that the year's profits would be unlikely to hit budget – and not provide any plans to remedy the matter.' The control department was in effect to become the nucleus of a completely restructured finance head office.

By the time of the half-year results the cost freezes had begun to show up in improved figures. Profits for the first half-year were £20 million compared with £18.4 million in the same period of the previous year, which was regarded in the City and the financial press as satisfactory. Ernest had survived the first six months thanks both to the cost freeze and to a little help from the improved prospects of the UK stout business. These came entirely from the media impact provided by the change of advertising agency from JWT to Allen Brady & Marsh. Meanwhile Bain were on their second assignment, an analytical review of the non-brewing businesses.

In 1981 Guinness owned more than 150 non-brewing subsidiaries. These had been bought over the years because successive group managing directors, and the board, had no real confidence in the long-term future of the stout on its own, certainly not in the developed world. The introduction of Draught Guinness into the UK in 1969 had appeared to help sales grow until 1972, but part of that growth was really due to price increases, and in any case there was no denying the slide after 1972. In the traditional Irish market, where until recently the word "Guinness" had been synonymous with 'beer', business was still buoyant. Overseas, sales had undeniably progressed in the traditional former outposts of the British Empire like Malaysia, Nigeria, the Caribbean and other tropical countries with a stronger product known as F.E.S. (Foreign Extra Stout). But lager had not yet taken off in these territories, and Guinness was still seen as not just a beer but also as a tonic. Therefore, confronted with evidence of a worldwide shift towards lighter drinks, the board had accepted that stout was nearing the end of its natural cycle. As Purssell remarked in 1982: 'It has to be said that stout is unfashionable. We have lost a million barrels on our output over the past fifteen years. And it is the dearest beer in Britain.'

He and his board had no experience of how to rebuild images and turn round brands. Faced with such grim statistics and no internal product development marketing capability, they opted instead to use the cash-flow from Guinness to develop other profit streams by buying other businesses. But the process amounted to a higgledy-piggledy string of diversifications spread over as much as a quarter of a century. Ernest: 'In the earlier days there had been production-based rationale behind some of the diversification decisions. The fermentation part of the brewing process was thought to have a spin-off into pharmaceuticals. The need to keep the wooden crate makers employed led to an interest in plastics. But there appeared to have been no coherent strategy behind the non-brewing acquisitions in market terms, no real consideration of the expertise needed to manage businesses that were completely outside the board's personal expertise, and no thought of the difficulties in maintaining adequate control over such a large number of different activities with the unsophisticated systems in place at that time.' Each acquisition appeared to have had a sponsor, some director keen enough to recommend the project, which was then voted through by the board without much further ado. The sponsor was then given supervisory responsibility in a general way, often keeping on the existing managers of the newly acquired company. 'The rosiest of rose-tinted spectacles must have been worn to accept the financial projections on which most of these businesses were bought.'

As a result of his site visits and what little financial information he was able to glean directly, Ernest had serious doubts about the prospects for most of these non-brewing businesses. What he had read about them in the analysts' reports and what he knew of the sectors from his own experience tended to reinforce these doubts. And he was becoming aware of fundamental problems facing the core brewing business, which had been starved of essential capital investment for years. Even to maintain product quality there was talk of Ireland alone having to spend £100 million on plant refurbishment. Park Royal claimed they needed a significant sum for modernisation, and there were rumours that their pension scheme had been badly underfunded due to poor investment management. All this made a review of the non-brewing side even more urgent.

In 1981, after some earlier divestment – such as the sale of Crookes Laboratories to Boots – the group's remaining non-beverage interests included Callard & Bowser confectionery, biotechnology, orchids, plastics, car bumpers, Lilo inflatable mattresses, supermarket trolleys, lighting, Tommy Tippee baby toiletries, children's clothes and even snake serum. Services included Lavells newsagents, Drummonds chemists, photographic distribution, advertising and sales promotion. Leisure interests included boating on the Mississippi, Lake Maggiore in Italy and the Loire, cruises down the Shannon, greek flotilla holidays, UK holiday camps, resort development in the Virgin Islands and Topper dinghies. Then there was oyster farming and meat packing in Ireland, property development in the UK and overseas trading in Africa and the Far East. Film production and finance completed a list that was so large and unconnected that it was almost worth an entry in *The Guinness Book of Records*, which was of course yet another offshoot – one of the successful ones.

This list was more diverse than the portfolios of some of the apparently successful conglomerates, but these had management and systems to control and develop their businesses while Guinness had neither.

Ernest: 'I used to look at this amazing collection with some sadness, thinking of what might have been if only the company, having bought the businesses, had known how to build on the potential that must have been there – especially in health products and marketing services, which I personally knew well. But now all we needed to know, urgently and objectively, was what to do next.'

Bain produced their chart of the non-brewing activities with what Ernest described as minimum adequate information on each. Now the board could decide which of three categories they fell into: Some would have to be sold fast because they were losing money and had no future. The performance of a second group might be capable of rapid improvement by cutting costs, with a view to selling later for a far better price than they would fetch at present. And a final group could be candidates for retention, because they were a valuable long-term source of profits. Ernest had to be pragmatic. Time was pressing, and there were no internal resources to do this job thoroughly and quickly. It was his first experience of what was to become a major corporate retrenchment programme.

Almost every Friday evening the results of Bain's investigations were presented by Roux, Rick Grogan and David Hoare, taking anything from three minutes to an hour per company. Ernest dealt with them in batches. Sometimes the state of the business meant that the action needed was obvious. Sometimes more analysis was required. In any case, Ernest would usually take home the Friday packages to review them over the weekend. This process lasted for about eighteen months.

Some businesses, like Callard & Bowser, with its world-famous toffees, were straightforward to deal with. C & B had been losing money for years. There was no way in which the product could compete in the confectionery market of the day without major plant modernisation and heavy advertising. This would make the losses even worse, so it was decided to sell the company as soon as possible. An offer had recently been turned down by the board and there were few other potential buyers, but Ernest knew the managing director of Smith Kendon (who make the tins of Travel Sweets), for whom the C & B range would provide a logical extension. He telephoned to ask if there might be interest. There was, a deal was done, and the losses to Guinness ceased. It was the first important step towards recovery.

The Irish non-brewing businesses were another matter entirely. They consisted of Meadow Meats, a bulk meat packaging unit that tried to sell to supermarkets in the UK; oyster farms; a plastics operation and cruises on the Shannon. They had come together as a result of a deal struck between Guinness Ireland and the Irish government. Guinness would be allowed to raise beer prices by an amount over and above that laid down by the prevailing State price controls in exchange for investing cash in a string of unrelated businesses that might promote employment. This was the 'special penny' arrangement, and put the Irish company under pressure to buy any businesses that were offered to them. Ernest: 'I had enormous difficulty with the Irish board, which included associates of Lord Iveagh, in restricting further dubious acquisitions, even though they certainly would not add to employment if they were unsuccessful – which was likely. I managed to stop them buying a pottery company, but failed to prevent a number of other deals. Eventually I persuaded the Irish company simply to give the oyster farms to the Irish government and end the "special penny" arrangement once and for all.'

In fact the core brewing business was a vital export contributor, and instead of 'special pennies' what Guinness needed were grants to help with the enormous cost of modernising its brewing facilities.

Ernest was scared stiff of the whole leisure division, and especially the planned property development in Tortola, in the British Virgin Islands. It was the dream project of Michael Ogle, a main board director who based himself in a magnificent office complex in Devon, near his farm, and had been largely responsible for the group's diversification into leisure activities. If it had all been finished, Tortola would have embraced a marina, a hotel, villas and a supermarket to be part-owned by Lord Iveagh in a personal capacity. Iveagh later withdrew his investment. Ernest: 'The project had the vaguest of budgets. The last straw came when Ogle bought an excavating company after I had expressly imposed a freeze on the whole development. When we tried to sell many people just laughed. The entire project was considered a joke by professionals in the business. More importantly, the local government had a problem with loss of face. It took ages to deal with this white elephant, during which it had to be managed to contain substantial operating losses. Eventually a deal was done involving the government, and a substantial write-off.'

That, however, was dwarfed by the company's foray into film production and finance. Ernest was introduced to this activity when Ogle casually asked those present at a meeting of directors to meet two Americans who wanted to do a deal connected with film distribution. Ogle wanted Guinness to supply bank guarantees of around £100 million in return for what he claimed would be 'dramatic tax benefits and huge profits'. Apparently Guinness had already had a film production disaster, and was locked into some historic financing arrangements that sounded extremely risky. Moreover, no one but Ogle seemed to know the details. Ernest refused to consider the new proposal and thought that he had stamped on the idea. 'It was well known in the business world that film finance was an area that many had played in and most had lost at, and these were people who knew about the entertainment business. It was simply ludicrous, given the state Guinness was in, to contemplate any such venture.'

It was quite by chance that Ernest switched on the TV in his hotel room on a business trip to New York and heard the renowned US film producer and director Francis Ford Coppola announcing that after being let down by American sources he had found new partners to distribute his new film – including the famous Guinness company in the United Kingdom. Ernest was shocked and immediately picked up the phone and spoke to Peter Guinness. He insisted that no deal was to be done in films until he understood completely what was involved. He was also increasingly concerned about financing arrangements that had been previously entered into to save tax, but which were now being investigated by the Inland Revenue. And there was a lawsuit involving the use of a US Navy destroyer in a film, for which the US government was demanding extra fees.

When he got back to London Ernest immediately commissioned an independent report on Guinness and the film industry from a lawyer versed in the ways of that trade, Michael Flint of the solicitors Denton Hall and Burgin. Flint had worked for Paramount, so he knew what he was looking for, but it still took him nearly a year to unravel the tangle. Ernest: 'His report was so horrific it could have come out of Hammer House of Horrors, but the plan Flint implemented reduced Guinness's commitment and left the group with a far smaller write-off than it originally faced.'

Ogle left very quickly after the problems with his leisure projects had been uncovered. Ernest: 'They could have ruined the company without further ado. Paradoxically, the board considered taking legal action against Ogle and others but decided, in the interests of the company's fragile reputation and that of the family, with some of whom Ogle was personally very close, not to proceed on such a course.' Ogle also negotiated very good departure terms with Peter Guinness.

The Flint report also led to the resignation of Tony Purssell.

The company's sizeable interests in plastics stemmed from a spate of acquisitions which were to have been put under one management and to have resulted in a significant core business. This never happened. All Ernest found was a series of independent companies, some even in precisely the same line of business as others and competing for the same customers, without knowing it. While Ernest was considering what to do about these, invitations arrived for them to tender for substantial contracts from British Leyland and Ford to supply parts for the Metro and the new Cortina. But this involved substantial capital investment up front. Ernest: 'I was persuaded that the Ford investment, at least in part, was necessary to maintain the eventual sale value of the business. This did not prove to be correct, and I tried very hard not to allow myself to be persuaded along these lines again, but it was not always easy.'

Another Guinness plastics subsidiary had a batch of unwanted robots on its hands because a television set manufacturer had complained about the quality of paint the robots were spraying on TV cabinets. So the company lost the paint contract, even though it had already bought the robots.

On a trip to the Far East to see the brewing businesses, Ernest called in on a branch of another Guinness acquisition, MSJ. 'I have never seen so many tea sets in one place,' he says. 'They were piled high, not only in the company's own warehouse and offices but in extra rented space. Allegedly this was going to prove a spectacular profit-maker when the management introduced a series of Tupperware-style parties as a selling-method in the region. My scepticism proved correct: another write-off.'

The group's Topper dinghy was a long-standing family favourite, but it was outdated. New tools had been manufactured to create a new model. But the prototype sank on its first outing: the tools had not been properly checked.

The snake serum was an overhang of a prior diversification exercise involving pharmaceuticals. It was an extraordinary product concept that actually made a profit, but it was hardly the basis of a serious business activity, and was sold off.

Glenco, on the other hand, was a US textile business specialising in baby clothing. It was a classic entrepreneurial rag-trade operation, but was not susceptible to disciplined management from as far away as the UK. Ernest turned to Tom Ward to watch over the business temporarily, as he was on the spot and could have a better feel for the people. Ward was able to establish an American-to-American rapport with the Glenco management, who had sold the company to Guinness, and when it was decided to sell it Ward handled the transaction in co-ordination with Olivier Roux through First Boston, the US bank. It sold for $14 million, well in excess of what had been recommended by First Boston. It was Ernest's first experience of the difference between the theoretical long-term relationship which investment banks in the US claimed to want to develop with Guinness and the reality of simply earning a quick buck on a one-off deal. Guinness would clearly have trouble being taken seriously in the US until they were much bigger. This was a sobering conclusion in view of Ernest's conviction, from his Beecham and Nestlé days, that it was important to have a major US business involvement.

Peter Guinness ran a property portfolio known as Albemarle Developments. He had been with Guinness Mahon, the City merchant bank founded by another branch of the family. In conjunction with John Humphries of the family solicitors, Travers Smith Braithwaite, he developed properties on a small scale and took a profit for either the company or its pension fund. The amounts involved were not significant, and Ernest kept asking why they did not develop the group's own substantial property assets, such as the Park Royal site, in a systematic way. He was to discuss this topic later with others professionally involved in property development, including Gerald Ronson and Jim Gregory, the Chairman of Queens Park Rangers football club, because he felt that Guinness was potentially sitting on considerable sums of money without making the best use of them. He was also to discover that the group's many London office buildings, which were to be drastically reduced, had unfortunately been rented, so denying Guinness any participation in profits from the property boom.

The group's interests in the advertising and marketing services business covered some famous names, including KMP, Pembertons and Imagination, the specialist presentations company. Such a portfolio today would provide the basis for tremendous City excitement, in the light of what has happened in the sector in recent years. But at that time, with only minority interests remaining, and so many other priorities, it made no sense to stay in advertising.

There were times when it was essential to obtain new temporary management for a subsidiary, to put the business into the shape where it could be sold for a realistic price. Experienced consultant managers were hired, usually with satisfactory results. However, it was not until Ernest recruited Shaun Dowling as special projects manager, working with the Bain team, that they were able to rationalise the management of the businesses before they were sold, and get the best prices for them.

Only three of the non-brewing operations were considered worth retaining. *The Guinness Book of Records* was inseparable from the beer business, and indeed had further potential, as demonstrated by

The man who's good for Guinness

This old-established brewing group has taken on a new lease of life since the appointment, last October, of Ernest Saunders as chief executive. John Davis reviews the investment potential

The Ordinary shares of Arthur Guinness have looked much more sprightly since Ernest Saunders took over as chief executive and brought a new sense of purpose and direction to this 223-year-old brewing business. This year the shares have put on 30 per cent, making them one of the front runners in the brewery sector.

Ten years ago Arthur Guinness was one of the UK's top 100 companies by market capitalisation. Today its market capitalisation is some 50 per cent below the figure of £200 million or so that is needed to secure an entry into this elite corporate club. And to add insult to injury Guinness shares, which used to be low yielders, are now among the highest even though the group has a pretty good dividend record.

The main factor in Guinness's undoing was its various attempts at diversification. Considerable management energies and resources have been dissipated during the last decade in attempts to build up important second string businesses. Ceramic tiles, self-catering holidays, film distribution, plastics, materials handling, pharmaceuticals, photographic wholesaling, retailing, plastic injection moulding and confectionery have all been tried.

Although net capital employed has risen considerably over the years, profitability has been disappointing lately. After reaching a peak of £52.9 million in 1978-79, pre-tax profits slumped to £41.8 million in 1980-81, little different from what they were in 1975-76 since when an extra £200 million of net capital has been employed.

But the arrival of Saunders heralded a major policy change. The emphasis is once more on beer and only those non-brewing activities showing a decent return on capital employed are being retained. A steady stream of sales

Price range of Ordinary shares

	high	low
	p	p
1982	91.0	61.0
1981	84.0	50.0
1980	98.0	69.0
1979	108.0	76.5
1978	96.0	73.5
1977	100.5	60.0
1976	75.0	46.5
1975	71.5	28.0
1974	61.0	26.0
1973	92.0	49.0

Ernest Saunders: taking Guinness into the 20th century

has been made by Saunders and more are in the pipeline.

It will be some time yet before the full benefits of the various changes are apparent but group profits have already started to reflect the Saunders touch. For the first half of 1981-82 they showed a modest increase and this has prompted leading brewery share experts, brokers Buckmaster & Moore, to wax enthusiastic about the year's results. They reckon that a 20 per cent rise in pre-tax profits, to around £50 million, is possible and they rate the shares a definite 'buy'.

But it is not only in the area of profitability that an important change has taken place. The group's reporting procedures have been tightened up as part of Saunders's general aim to take 'Guinness into the 20th century'. There are now regular monthly statistics available to the chief executives, allowing them to plan more efficiently.

When Saunders arrived he found no less than 247 different companies operating under the Guinness umbrella. How many of these will still exist after he has completed his cost saving and streamlining exercise only time will tell. But there is no denying that this new broom, who was recruited from Nestlé and who had also done stints with Beecham and GUS, has given the brewing group much to be thankful for.

Comment: A share that has a good yield to back it up, and there is a fair chance that the 1982-83 results will bring a dividend increase, thus further enhancing the yield, now 7.75 per cent. There is also strong net asset backing of 138p compared with a share price of 90p.

Annual events

Half-yearly results: June
Yearly results: December
Report: February
Annual meeting: March

Current year's prospects

For the first half of 1981-82 turnover and pre-tax profits of £454 million and £20 million respectively were reported in June, compared with £375 million and £18.4 million in the first half of 1980-81. Interim dividend was maintained at 1.575p net.

Expansion plans

Entered 1981-82 with £25.6 million earmarked for capital expenditure.

Best known trade mark names

Guinness, Harp Lager, White Child & Beney, Emerald Star Line, J. L. Morrison Son & Jones and Lavells.

Shareholder profile

	% of Ord cap
Institutions	50
Private shareholders	50

Shareholder perk

Shareholders attending the annual meeting can sample the brews.

Ordinary shareholders

31,000

Charity donations

£246,715

	Sales	Exports	Pre-tax profit	Profit margins	Ord div	Net cap employed	Return on cap employed
	£m	£m	£m	%	%	£m	%
1980-81	905.6	71.1	41.8	4.6	28.0	423.1	9.9
1979-80	783.6	59.5	43.3	5.5	28.0	373.4	11.6
1978-79	687.2	59.4	52.9	7.7	28.0	315.0	16.8
1977-78	642.7	57.8	44.9	7.0	23.4	270.5	16.6
1976-77	498.8	48.3	39.4	7.9	21.2	243.3	16.2
1975-76	413.9	36.1	39.3	9.5	19.3	211.0	18.6
1974-75	339.4	24.7	29.1	8.6	17.6	181.5	16.0
1973-74	271.8	16.3	22.6	8.3	16.0	167.3	13.5
1972-73	256.6	6.7	25.7	10.0	15.2	133.7	19.2
1971-72	237.6	7.9	22.3	9.4	14.5	104.5	21.3

Productivity profile

Figures per employee

Employees	Sales	Pre-tax profit	Average wage	Net cap employed
	£	£	£	£
11,585 (UK)	78,170	3,608	5,205	36,521
21,862 (World)	41,423	1,912	N/A	19,353

By the end of 1982 the press was coming round to Ernest's side – and so were the sales figures. The above article appeared in The *Observer*.

the success of the new Guinness World of Records exhibition in the Trocadero complex near London's Piccadilly Circus.

Clares, the supermarket trolleys and shelving business, was capable of producing regular high returns, based on the explosion in the UK retail sector, due to new store openings, refurbishment – and, in the case of trolleys, the propensity of customers to take them home.

Finally, the rump of what had been a grandiose retail operation, known as Guinness Retail Holdings, with luxury offices in Marlow, seemed to provide the only real basis for a second core business beyond brewing – neighbourhood retailing.

Under the energetic management of Nicholas Ward, the business was reduced to the newsagent/tobacconist chain, Lavells, and the chemist chain, Drummonds – then second only to Boots in terms of store numbers. It was capable of producing good profits, and Ernest considered ways of expanding it, as an affordable way into the retailing boom.

The overall result of the analysis of non-beer interests was to sell 149 companies in eighteen months, realising £40 million in cash, reducing borrowings by half to £48 million, and interest charges to £8 million. The turnround was seen as significant by the City at the time, despite the fact that it was necessary to make a reserve of £49 million to cover sales below inflated book values and provisions for topping up the poorly-managed UK pension fund. The process also led to the departure of Stanley Darmon, shortly to be followed by Tony Spicer, who had been in poor health for some time, and Peter Guinness.

During this period, John Theroux had serious worries about the possibility of Ernest being outvoted by the board over the divestment process, particularly as many of the directors had been personally involved in acquiring these businesses. He consulted his colleagues at Boston as to how to handle what he imagined as a problem, even though it did not exist. 'He used to call me at night, to give me the benefit of the Bain partners' wisdom. I felt sure that his real worry was about what would happen to his growing business with us if I were deposed or blocked, since Bain's entire ethos was based on the direct support of the operating boss. If I were deposed, so probably would they be.'

In fact Lord Iveagh's epitaph on the ill-fated diversification programme was that it had been a 'hiccup'.

After the initial stages of the non-beer review process, the implementation was delegated to Roux and the Bain team, together with Dowling and the small in-house legal group that had been put together. Happily, although there were inevitable redundancies at senior level as a result of change of control, there were not the wholesale redundancies that would certainly have resulted if Guinness had decided to hold on to the businesses, and had then been forced to rationalise them later.

Most significantly, the divestment process had given Ernest vital time to start to understand the core brewing business, on which the bulk of Guinness profits depended.

6

FROM GUINNLESS TOUCANS TO GUINNESS GENIUS

The origins of brewing at Guinness go back over 200 years to the brewing in Ireland of a potent black beer originally invented in London and known as 'porter' because it was a favourite tipple of London's thousands of porters in the produce markets of East London and the City in the 1650s. Later the most popular variety became known as 'stout', reflecting the decline of portering as a trade in London, and the fact that it was a heavier beer than ale or bitter. Arthur Guinness began making Guinness porters in Dublin in 1759, with that distinctive taste that allegedly flowed from the waters of the river Liffey. Visitors would come from all over the world to see the St James's Gate brewery, which became the largest in Europe.

The fame of Guinness 'stout' was to spread far beyond Dublin. Its powers as a restorative were claimed in the Napoleonic Wars, and the brew was exported worldwide, its heavy consistency being able to withstand long journeys and storage in distant tropical countries. Guinness stout was always seen as more than simply an alcoholic drink. It became an institution and a piece of folklore. As word spread about the goodness, nourishment and other potent properties of Guinness stout demand grew so great in the larger export markets that the company began to brew it locally. Breweries were established in England, Nigeria, Malaysia, Jamaica and Cameroun. Elsewhere, contract packing was arranged.

In the early days, like many of its contemporaries, Guinness was a completely production-orientated business. It was run by brewers, whose main concern was not unnaturally the quality of the process and the product. Everything else, from price to the level of demand, flowed from that fountainhead. In this century, chemistry graduates, noticeably from Eton and Oxbridge, joined the company, learned the trade and worked their way up the promotion ladder. The brewers' status was emphasised by some extraordinary job titles that persisted until quite recently. Managers handling departments that were strictly outside the manufacturing craft were termed 'Brewer in charge of sales' or 'Brewer in charge of finance'. The head brewer was second in importance only to the head of the brewery. Both were extremely influential, not only inside the company but in the surrounding community.

Until the late 1920s, Guinness stout was hardly promoted, except by newspaper small-ads, beermats and point-of-sale cards in Ireland. But in 1928, just as the company was contemplating building a brewery in England, sales in the UK began to level under the impact of the Great Depression. The company organised a test advertising campaign on posters in Scotland that year. A year later the second Lord Iveagh appointed the S. H. Benson advertising agency to develop a national campaign.

Oswald Greene, one of Benson's best copywriters, visited pubs and asked consumers why they drank Guinness. Many said because it was good for them. Hence the first and still most famous copyline, 'Guinness is good for you'. The first poster with the new slogan appeared in January 1928. The following year, the popular fondness for Guinness and oysters led Benson's self-styled Literary Department to hit on a parody of the Walrus and the Carpenter from Lewis Carroll's *Through the Looking-Glass*, and the whole *genre* of Guinness animal advertising was begun, In 1934 the artist John Gilroy came up with the famous poster of the men carrying the girder to illustrate the other major slogan, 'Guinness for Strength'. A year later Gilroy teamed up with Dorothy L. Sayers, later to become famous as a writer of mystery thrillers, to hatch the Guinness toucan. A brand was born and increasingly became known in the UK as just 'Guinness'.

However, for many years after the Second World War Guinness became a victim of its advertising's very success. As Ernest is fond of pointing out, people talked about the advertising almost as an art form, in isolation from the product being advertised. 'By the time I arrived the Guinness name seemed to involve a number of "products" including Guinness the company, the Guinness family, Guinness advertising, *The Guinness Book of Records* – and only then the beer,' he says.

While other consumer products companies were starting to think about the wider concept of marketing, the opinion round Guinness was that the image created by its famous advertising – together, naturally, with the outstanding quality of the product – would be all that was necessary. This philosophy was fostered by the fact that shortages had led to rationing in some countries, and local firms would even bid for distribution rights. The position of the product in Ireland was protected by a virtual monopoly of drinkers' loyalty.

Back in Britain problems were on the horizon. Guinness, uniquely among British beers though quite commonly for other consumer products, had no control over its retail outlets. After a major rationalisation of the industry in the 1960s, six companies – Allied, Bass, Grand Metropolitan, Courage, Whitbread and Scottish & Newcastle – dominated the trade, and most public houses and many off-licences, hotels and other outlets were owned by the big six. On their own brands they therefore had a manufacturer's, a wholesaler's and a retailer's profit margin, while Guinness had to earn its money purely from manufacturing. The brewers also used their position to demand progressively larger discounts in return for handling Guinness. As these competitor groups became more market-orientated they began to see their pubs both as profit centres in their own right and as extensions of the marketing strategies for their own brands. Guinness sales and promotional efforts in the pubs were thus seen as taking business away from the brewers' own beers, lagers, wines and spirits.

The few Guinness people involved in sales proper had been used merely to receiving orders from customer head offices to meet immediate sales requirements, the price based on a one-way negotiation on annual terms. The 'representatives', as they were called, certainly contacted local breweries and outlets, but their activities were confined to what was known as 'goodwill representation'. The hard sell was regarded as anathema, and in most cases was not even relevant, because of the stranglehold of the big brewers. Ernest: 'Yet, despite these apparent facts of life, the representatives and the hierarchy above them were extraordinarily arrogant. A better measure of their capabilities was described to me by Bob Taylor, who was hired as sales director from outside Guinness. When he first analysed their daily worksheets a significant amount of their time was spent on a category headed "Other" – which turned out to mean playing golf! Taylor said it was clear that we were going to have to change attitudes as well as methods and structures.'

In 1981, when Ernest was recruited, the sales crisis was far more serious than the situation that had hit Guinness in 1926. Sales had been declining continuously for ten years. A new generation of younger consumers wanted lighter drinks like lager, in which Guinness admittedly had a toehold through the Harp lager consortium which had been set up in conjunction with other brewers including Scottish & Newcastle and Courage. But stout was increasingly thought of as an old person's drink in Britain, and overseas it was starting to face tough local competition, particularly in Malaysia. Even in Ireland growth was tailing off. In England, lower public house throughput was giving rise to tales that a pint of Park Royal Guinness did not taste as good as the Dublin version. Ernest: 'This was probably true, since the sheer volume in Ireland, plus the dedication to the product shown by the Irish barman or barmaid, led to a superb drink, whereas the very low volume in the UK, and sales emphasis on the breweries' own beers, meant that quality was at best inconsistent.'

All this made it vital for the company to come up with convincing advertising, that would directly persuade consumers to march into pubs and ask for Guinness, thus obliging publicans to stock and promote it in the teeth of the big brewers' disincentives.

Before Ernest formally joined Guinness he had of course sampled the product in bottled form – and had experienced great difficulty with it. 'It was too bitter and heavy for me, and seemed a specialist taste.' However, from the business point of view the fact was that the brand was centrally important to the group, and had to be given a shot in the arm. In September 1981, still waiting to begin his new job, Ernest had paid a visit to his old friends at the J. Walter Thompson advertising agency in Berkeley Square, who had held the stout brand account since 1969. His plan had been to advise them in confidence of his impending arrival, and to urge them to think about a wide-ranging and objective review of the brand's advertising and marketing. He returned a matter of weeks after taking over, walking round the corner to Berkeley Square from his office in Albemarle Street to repeat his message more firmly. 'Their attitude was that this was something I shouldn't really concern myself with. They told me that their relations with Park Royal were excellent, and the people there thought they were doing a great job ... please don't interfere.'

JWT proposed to slow the decline by reviving the famous toucan in a new campaign. Ernest now reviewed the stituation with the Park Royal management – managing director Michael Hatfield, David Sands-Renton, the marketing director and Jim Reachlous, a bright new marketing manager. That review convinced him that something much more fundamental had to be done. They actually had to turn around sales of the stout by bringing in younger drinkers, as the beneficial impact on profits and morale would be out of all proportion to any campaign costs, and that in turn could have a powerful effect on the share price. But first they had to understand the reasons for the decline. Simple consumer research of the classic quantitative head-counting variety, of which the company had done a little, was not enough.

Predictably, perhaps, Ernest met passive resistance from the Park Royal marketing group when he suggested that they should ask JWT to undertake a radical review. Then, to his dismay, he found that JWT were equally disinclined to look at Guinness anew. He joined his Park Royal colleagues to attend a formal presentation by JWT, the third time he had turned up at the agency's offices in little over a month, only to be told that the decline in sales was really not too bad, and without their advertising input matters would have been a lot worse. Ernest: 'I was really concerned at this attitude, and I let both the agency and the brewery management know that there was no way that we could allow such complacency. As far as the man in the street was concerned, the beer was the company and the plight of one was synonymous with the plight of the other. Then the latest batch of commercials failed their research tests, so JWT had to fall back on old material. One night that November I was sitting in the Albemarle Street flat watching TV, and up came an old toucan ad talking about April Fool's Day! I was livid.'

Ernest had already asked to see the Harp lager advertising at Allen Brady & Marsh, one of whose founders was Mike Brady, a colleague from Beecham days. The firm was riding high, having developed a unique management style under the ebullient showmanship of the chairman, Peter Marsh, and the marketing discipline and planning of David Croisdale-Appleby, the managing director. Their presentation was delivered in an ultra-theatrical style, with their executives in white suits. It made a persuasive case for the proposition that ABM advertising was improving the image of the Harp brand, and, over Marsh's excellent champagne he and Ernest got down to the question of whether ABM might help with the Guinness brand. In sharp contrast to JWT's complacency, Marsh was full of enthusiasm for the prospects of reviving Guinness. Ernest later confidentially asked ABM to produce a proposal for a comprehensive research programme designed to understand how Guinness could be turned round. After a few weeks an enormous document arrived, based on ABM's research, which emphasised the need for a radical reappraisal. It also contained plans for the research, and management support in marketing, necessary to undertake a massive brand relaunch.

'The Guinness situation is desperate,' Marsh told Ernest in confidence. 'This is a very tired, old formula brand. You need younger drinkers. I don't have a reputation for modesty, but even I am not sure we can succeed. Yet can you afford not to try?'

Rumours soon began to circulate in the ever-gossipy advertising trade and its main magazine, *Campaign*, about a possible move of the Guinness account. It was a sensational story in trade terms, for the account had changed hands only once in more than fifty years, when JWT captured it from S. H. Benson. Much of the latest speculation stemmed from the intelligent assumption that any new, marketing-trained managing director at Guinness would have ideas of his own and would inevitably need to review the advertising if he wanted to do something about the stout's declining sales. Furthermore, ABM was a natural challenger for the business, as it was already handling Harp.

By this stage Ernest had concluded that a completely new approach to the Guinness advertising was his only hope. He did not want to hawk the brand around the London agencies, so he told Hatfield that in his judgement the brand should move to ABM. However, before this could be properly organised the rumour machine got out of hand. While Ernest was on a visit to the US the national press in Britain began to take an interest, and for the first time he experienced the powerful impact of media pressure. He quickly phoned the Park Royal management to finalise details. Ideally these needed a round-table discussion to hammer out the detailed arrangements, but by the time he returned to London all that was left was for JWT to be advised that the Guinness account would indeed be moving. The official announcement made the front page of the *Financial Times*. Further, it actually increased the company's share price by 10p – arguably the first time the move of an advertising account had directly improved the advertiser's share price. JWT was upset, and it was unfortunate for them that the media hype surrounding the change was excessive, but they had certainly had plenty of warning. The episode did no harm to Ernest's growing reputation as a determined manager. It also indirectly demonstrated to investors that things at Guinness were going to improve.

There followed a year of industry speculation about what ABM would come up with. While the new agency started work, Ernest decided that if he was going to make the most of a new launch of the brand he had to shake up the way things were handled at the Park Royal brewery. This had been designed by the architect of Battersea Power Station – and looked it. The condition of the building was appalling, and so was morale among its management and workforce. Someone remarked that the offices were more akin to a mental asylum.

In 1982 my parents moved from their temporary accommodation above the Mayfair office to a charming house at Penn, in Buckinghamshire. It was set in a few acres, next to the local church. The house needed substantial restoration which my mother set about with wonderful enthusiasm. It was our first home in England for six years, and Jo, John and I at last had somewhere to come to in our time off from boarding school.

The commute to and from Albemarle Street took Ernest past Park Royal each day, so it was no trouble for him to spend more time on the site reshaping attitudes and galvanising the staff. There was no one else to do it, and it was an area of the business that he could contribute to from his previous experience of handling brands. To make sure things got done, he became chairman of Guinness Park Royal, held weekly meetings to get to grips with the issues, and even contemplated moving the group head office there.

The biggest problem was extensive overmanning. The brewery had been constructed to take at least double its current output. Since the decline in volume sales in 1972 nothing had been done to bring costs down into line with sales. All the competitors of Guinness knew this, but the costs per barrel remained exorbitant, and the company was certainly in the red. As usual, however, the figures were confused and unreliable.

Ernest commissioned Bain to undertake a crash programme to find where and how to tackle the cost problems. Within a few weeks Bain indicated what was needed. An immediate saving of £10 million was necessary for the brewery to make a genuine profit. Ernest: 'I consulted Maurice Freeman, the wise head of personnel. He was an old-timer who nevertheless was exceptionally helpful to me and keen to see the company survive. He had excellent relations with the unions, especially their leader, Larry Grogan, and started to prepare the ground. I met union representatives to explain the urgent necessity for action, and indicated my determination to do something about sales.'

With understandable scepticism, the unions said they had heard

Ernest on his second birthday, October 1937, in traditional Austrian dress

With his parents in 1938 in Vienna

Team sports at school – a St Paul's rowing eight. Ernest is seated, on the right

Cambridge graduation day, 1959: Ernest, aged 23, flanked by his parents outside the Senate House

With his father and brother Peter at the Italian Embassy in 1962. His father is wearing the Commandatore's insignia

My parents' wedding day in 1963 at St John's Church, Hampstead, London

Top: Ernest launching Hunt's mixer range during his early marketing days with Beecham

Above: The magnificent lakeside Nestlé headquarters in Vevey, Switzerland, where Ernest moved to in 1976

Top: With Carole suitably apronned and surrounded by bottles of Guinness, in the flat on top of the Company's offices in October 1981

Above: Watch the Birdie! Carole, myself and Joanna help out Ernest and the famous Guinness toucan during a company promotion in 1982

Left: Ernest with Terry Venables and the QPR team at the start of the sponsorship season in 1984

Below: Ernest in conversation with Prince Charles and Major Ferguson at the Bell's Polo Cup in 1986

Above: My father meeting the Princess Royal at a Save the Children reception at St James' Palace in 1985

Left: In the early 1980s the Guinness revival received royal and presidential support. Ronald Reagan tasted the brew during a visit to Ireland

With Carole and Baroness Phillips after Guinness won the Queen's Award for Export
Achievement in 1985

all that before: how would Ernest succeed where others had failed? Freeman apparently did a fine selling job on Ernest's experience in advertising and marketing, but agreement finally hung on two questions They wanted to know whether Ernest would deal with Irish costs as well, because they had the natural union suspicion that the plan was ultimately to close Park Royal and import all the stout from Dublin. Second, the union representatives were unequivocally contemptuous of the management's lethargy in recent years; they wanted an assurance that Ernest would sort this out, and cut administrative and other costs as well. Ernest: 'I gave them a positive response to both points, and even expressed my determination not just to keep Park Royal open but to get morale up and the place humming again. It was essential, I said, that in the country in which we had our stock market quote we had a vibrant business.'

After a short while the unions reluctantly agreed to the cuts. The details of savings across all sectors of the business were worked out between Bain, Hatfield, Freeman and the unions.

There were to be further meetings and further cuts over the years, but Grogan and his men paved the way for a dramatic improvement in British productivity and morale when sales did start to improve.

Meanwhile, even before the new advertising could be developed and have time to work, the immediate concern was sales. Jim Reachlous, the marketing manager, asked a sales promotion consultancy to come up with promotional campaigns which would have advertising back-up. One was called 'Watch the Birdie', and the other was 'the Great Guinness Challenge'. Such promotions had become commonplace at other consumer goods companies but at Guinness they were regarded as important new steps in trying to do things the 'marketing' way, and to set a pattern for the future. They also showed the breweries who bought Guinness that the company was determined to get sales moving.

Of course, the sales force was untrained to implement this sort of campaign, so they had to be radically reorganised, with major personnel changes. Bob Taylor was recruited from Courage to take on this task, which he did with great energy and determination. 'But it will be a hard slog and take time,' he told Ernest. In the meantime he had to use the existing sales force to implement the programmes as best he could. The results were surprisingly good, and it was in fact those promotions that started to turn the brand round.

Meanwhile, ABM was carrying out field research all over the English Guinness business. They called in Peter Cooper of Cooper

Research and Marketing, an expert in psychological testing who, with his wife Jackie, had carried out research for Beecham. His job was to find out why drinkers, especially younger ones, were not buying Guinness and what form of advertising would get them to change their mind. His findings then provided the research framework against which ABM's campaign ideas were evaluated.

Eventually, after seemingly endless research and pre-testing, ABM came up with a campaign that passed all the agreed criteria. It would, Peter Marsh shrewdly told Ernest, require a bold management decision. It would be very different from anything done before, the board almost certainly would not like it, and it had to focus on draught Guinness alone. But, if they saw it through, he believed it would start to do the job.

The reason for Marsh's caveats soon became apparent, when the 'Guinnless' campaign was unveiled, along with the research explanations, to Ernest and the Park Royal team one day in November 1982. 'I didn't like it,' Ernest admits, 'but my years in marketing have taught me that it was not my personal likes or dislikes that mattered, it was whether I believed that on the evidence of the research the consumer would be persuaded to look at the product in a more positive light. Some of my colleagues had other worries, wondering if other brewers would like the campaign – and what about the Guinness family? I decided that it had enough of the shock value that was necessary if we were to reverse a decade of decline. We had to take our decisions for the good of the brand, and not on the basis of personal likes and dislikes. I had one worry. Would this new approach so appal older, loyal drinkers that they would switch brands? Eventually I decided there was a strong likelihood that the somewhat lonely existing Guinness drinkers – there were so few of them – would welcome the sight of younger people drinking it with them.'

So the board was asked to a spectacular presentation at ABM, and told that in the professional view of the agency and the Park Royal management they should go with the campaign. Ernest: 'It was obvious that most of the other directors did not like the campaign, but – as was beginning to become the pattern – they accepted my professional opinion.' A special series of briefings was organised in London's docklands for the company, the trade financial analysts and the media. Guests were picked up by bus near the Tower of London and taken on a 'mystery tour' through parts of the city most of them had never seen before, creating the impression that they

THE MANAGEMENT PAGE: Marketing

ADVERTISING : BY FEONA McEWAN

The velvet pint pitches for a wider public

IT'S ABOUT the dearest beer in the country; it's unfashionable; its sales are shrinking and it suffers from a surfeit of toucans. A marketeer's migraine or an advertiser's Everest?

From this week, with the launch of its new advertising campaign that has had the ad industry on the edge of its seat for a year, chances are things will be different for the dark velvet pint.

The name of the grain is Guinness, once the tipple of old ladies and pregnant women—medicinal you understand—(Guinness is Good for you), sculptor of bodies (Guinness for Strength); the beer that launched a hundred memorable posters that scooped awards.

So when exactly a year ago today Guinness abruptly dropped J. Walter Thompson after 13 years in favour of Allen Brady Marsh as part of a new management sweep there was the feeling of what next? Now we are to find out. What's promised is a new fresh look at this old favourite—campaigns have been running for more than 50 years—which had become more memorable for ads than product.

The Guinness family of toucans, ostriches, sea lions and other animals are part of adland folklore in what was the most famous poster campaign of a single product in the world. After 40 years with S. H. Benson the account moved in 1969 to JWT where the tradition of familiar good humour and punchy style continued. "Every girl should have a little black drink"; "Who said men seldom make passes at girls with glasses?"

But it is this heritage that comes from being, as one adman put it, a Great British Institution, that was in danger of becoming a tripwire. "The problem," as one JWT man explained it, " is in inheriting a legacy—it's strong, black, good, medicinal—while retaining the magic to sell it to beer drinkers."

Ernest Saunders, Guinness's new managing director and a keen marketing brain, spotted this in mooting the agency move last year. Guinness profits had tumbled from their peak of £53m in 1979 to £42m in 1981 and his brief was to stem the flow. End of year results due this month promise to show that Saunders is certainly good for Guinness.

While aware of the valuable Guinness advertising heritage Saunders believes ads should not just entertain but should sell. "The move to ABM was a dynamic updating of the Guinness image," he said this week. "I felt the advertising had lost a little of its relevance to the target market."

The man he chose to spearhead the new direction of Guinness was ebullient Peter Marsh, arguably the most talked about man in the ad industry. His flair for self-publicity is matched only by his zeal on behalf of his clients. Since becoming chairman of ABM in 1974, he has steered the agency in a vertical direction, overdrive all the way. It now lies sixth in the UK's top 10 agencies (Campaign)—the only all-British agency there.

Long silence

"The Guinness heritage is a terrible trap," Marsh admitted this week. "What the hell had toucans got to do with it? We're talking about people drinking beer in pubs. Advertising is about telling people how to use a product with ease and comfort.

"What we had to do was bring it back to today. Plug it into attitudes common to beer drinkers, make ordering a pint a desirable thing to do, take Guinness back to session drinking."

From the outset Saunders and Marsh agreed to "get it right." This has meant one year's research of the most painstaking, no-stone-unturned sort. "The most researched campaign we've ever done," concedes Marsh.

The long silence during 1982 led tongues to wag about problems between clients and agency. "All the talk that we were about to fire ABM was rubbish," says Saunders.

"It's a great credit to the hard work of the agency that the campaign is bang on our strategic target, enjoyable and," he adds emphatically, "going to sell."

ABM's research pinpointed the target market: male draught drinkers (79 per cent of all beer drunk last year was draught) in the C2DE social groups (which make up 71 per cent of all consumers) in the 20- to 34-year-old range (these constitute half all beer drinkers). The aim, too, was to lower the age profile long term and it was decided that volume gains were likely to be made by persuading the occasional Guinness drinkers to drink more.

"Our brief," says account executive Peter Bear "was to normalise the choice of Guinness and popularise the experience of drinking it."

So what about the campaign? This viewer was impressed, amused and even moved to try the dark velvet. The word to conjure with is "Guinnless," which refers to people who have been too long without a Guinness. All the ads feature Friends of the Guinnless helping the Guinnless overcome

Enjoy a quiet Guinness at home.

Top: the beginning of the Guinnless wonders, a campaign derived from one of half a century ago (right). Peter Marsh aims to take Guinness back to "session" drinking—an image far removed from the toucan's message.

their Guinnlessness.

This idea lies at the heart of the £7m campaign which breaks on TV tomorrow night. The ads (three commercials so far) take the form of a spoof: in one an amiable fast-talking young man approaches a pair of punks in a pub and asks them how long they've been Guinnless. "A couple of weeks," says one. Persuaded to try a pint, one punk responds with the killing line: "This past fortnight's been a cultural vacuum for me."

From this central idea will flow the Friends of the Guinnless concept which is sure to be fully exploited in the months ahead. Posters, car stickers ("I'm Guinnless, I'm driving"), girlie calendars for the trade, beer mats, lapel stickers (saying "I'm Guinnless, buy me one") will make sure we are all in on the joke.

Which reminds me, I'm feeling rather Guinnless myself right now. . . .

The above article appeared in the *Financial Times*.

were about to be let in on a great secret. Once there, they were subjected to a massive dose of Peter Marsh's showmanship, complete with flashing lights, dry ice and special effects. Sadly the oysters, specially flown from the company's farm in Ireland, did not survive the journey well: quite a few guests suffered the consequences.

Up went the now-famous teaser poster, 'Guinnless isn't good for you'. Marsh hyped it, the press sneered at it, acres of print were devoted to discussing it – and the company's phone lines were swamped with people claiming that the spelling was wrong. It had been noticed. The campaign unfolded. The Friends of the Guinnless society was launched. A vicar in Wandsworth erected a sign outside his church which said 'Godless isn't Good for You'. Within a few months nearly nine out of every ten adults in the country had registered awareness of the campaign, and sales of draught Guinness stopped falling. The first objective had been achieved – and the cynics proved wrong. Young people were taking a new look at Guinness.

It was, however, going to take far longer for newspapers to stop writing old-style stories about Guinness being given to horses and centenarian ladies. Indeed, Ernest had a montage made of the free Guinness publicity he did *not* want, and sent it to the Park Royal marketeers as a reminder. They took the point, but some habits die hard. People like the familiar Guinness associations, such as the word

'Seven million quid of advertising campaign ruined at a stroke.' This *Punch* cartoon was one of several that showed that the new Guinness advertising had been noticed.

of mouth publicity that doctors recommend Guinness for pregnant mothers. The company had to focus on its new strategies, but meanwhile a little of the old mystique probably didn't do any harm.

In any case the Guinnless theme had always been seen as short-term. It was already time to plan a positive, sustainable campaign that could be the basis of long-term recovery. Gary Luddington, the recently-appointed marketing director, produced a comprehensive and sophisticated advertising brief spelling out exactly what was required. Unfortunately, ABM was having difficulties in coming up with a solution to the brief, so Guinness decided to undertake another advertising review. When the media got to know of this, and despite Gary's careful pre-selection of a small number of agencies, over eighty applied to show their work. The choice came down to two: ABM and Ogilvy & Mather, parent company of S.H. Benson, the original Guinness advertising agency, several of whose overseas subsidiaries still handled the business.

Ogilvy & Mather won the account with a stylish revival of the visual link between the words Guinness and Genius, which had been exploited from time to time since the early days. The latest version was to be 'Guinness: Pure Genius'. Again, 'pure genius' became a catch-phrase overnight, but it did not cause the controversy of Guinnlessness. Ernest: 'That was fine, because we wanted this one to have more acceptance, to give it a longer life.'

The next move was to tackle the condition of draught Guinness at the bar, and in particular cooling equipment that would get the product closer to the temperature younger drinkers liked, especially in summer. This involved much technical aggravation and sales force legwork, but gradually the presentation improved and sales grew. With the support of the new advertising Guinness, instead of being regarded as thick, black and stodgy, was now seen as cool and refreshing. The other brewers, owners of so many tied public houses, realised that they had to start backing Guinness again.

Putting draught Guinness back on the road had an enormous impact on morale at Park Royal. The next step was to give bottled Guinness a lift. 'I felt that it had always been a mistake to ignore the fact that draught and bottled or canned Guinness were essentially different products, appealing to different customers. So we revitalised packaged Guinness with a new name – Guinness Extra – a new label and a foil wrap around the neck. The liquid inside was just a little less bitter. It was a success: a new brand had been created.'

The marketing team started winning professional awards for its sales promotion campaigns. This was a nice bonus, but what was important was that the campaigns were working and sales were improving. The company had teams operating mobile bars and the brand was given prestige by selling black velvet – Guinness and champagne – in special glasses at upmarket sporting and social occasions. The most remarkable external tribute to the marketing team was from *Marketing Week*, the marketing trade magazine. It put Guinness high on its marketing performance list, and top in some cases, for alcoholic beverage companies. This was only a few years from the time when, other than being amused by Guinness advertising, no marketing professional would have considered Guinness as having any standing in this field.

By 1986 Guinness Park Royal had a completely new management team. Ernest recruited Peter Libscomb from Beecham as managing director, completing the transformation into a fully marketing-orientated operation and the model, Ernest hoped, for other operations in the beer group.

Two years previously Ernest had capitalised on the revived mood at Park Royal by signing a deal to sponsor Queens Park Rangers, the west London soccer club which had just been promoted to the first division of the Football League under the dynamic managership of Terry Venables. Loftus Road was already a favourite resort for many Park Royal employees on Saturday afternoons, and the sponsorship fitted in with Guinness's new youthful image. Apart from the publicity value, the club's Guinness Lounge enabled Ernest and the Park Royal management to meet trade customers and other important guests in relaxed and agreeable surroundings. Ernest would preside over an afternoon or evening reception complete with lunch or dinner and a complimentary bar from which sportily-clad promotional girls

'Times have changed since we used to slap 'em in the face with a wet sponge!' The sponsorship of QPR was to last the best part of three seasons.

would serve the group's products while everyone had a first-class view of the game. Afterwards, players from both teams would come up to the Lounge for the presentation of the Man of the Match award. Thanks to the sponsorship agreement, the Loftus Road stadium was probably the only place in Britain where Guinness was sold at a price determined by Guinness, and the condition of the product in all the bars was under Guinness supervision. It was priced at only a marginal premium to lager, and sales were phenomenal.

Unfortunately, Terry Venables was lured to Barcelona at the end of the first year, and despite the lack of problems at Loftus Road itself the image of soccer rapidly deteriorated due to hooliganism, and severe restrictions were imposed on club entertainment. After 3 years the sponsorship was not renewed. Even so, it had served its purpose: along with the other marketing initiatives, it had helped to put Guinness back on the map.

It was now Lipscomb's task to take a more robust line with the other large brewers. Backed by the evidence of product success, he had to bring an end to the years of excessive discounts and the traditional view of the company as nice clubbable people who entertained well at race meetings. Edward Guinness had done an excellent public relations job within the industry, becoming chairman of the Brewers' Society, but much more would be required for Guinness to develop properly in the UK again. New products were now being nurtured – a non-alcoholic lager, for one – and needed distribution. A different era was about to begin. The arrival on the brewing scene of the Australian entrepreneurs, John Elliott and Alan.Bond, together with a review of the tied-house trade by the Monopolies and Mergers Commission, indicated that the momentum for change was gathering pace. Guinness could only gain. (In March 1989 the MMC published their report advocating significant changes to the tied-house system. On the day the report came out, all brewers' shares were down, with the exception of Guinness, who were up 12 p.)

To the vast majority of beer drinkers, and notably visitors to Ireland, Guinness stout was Irish, and one of Ireland's best-loved products. It was part of the Irish drinking culture, and equivalent to good wine in France. To tourists a pub visit was not a pub visit without a pint of the local brew, still sometimes referred to as a 'pint of plain' by the locals, carefully pulled and then left to stand for just the right number of minutes to make the famous Guinness head. It was an unforgettable sight – a row of Guinness pints on the bar, ready to be drunk – and a dream for visiting UK executives to aspire to.

The mecca of Guinness Brewing was the famous brewery at St James's Gate, for years the largest brewery in Europe, and virtually a self-contained town within Dublin, like the Vatican City within Rome. It had everything from railway yards to printing works, and two large tankers that carried the bulk brew across the Irish Sea for bottling in Liverpool for the export trade. Its huge production unit served the Irish domestic market and much of the rest of the world.

The Irish management not only regarded their country as being the true home of Guinness stout, but also Dublin as being the real headquarters of the group. The 1886 London stock market quote and shareholder base was seen as a mere historical technicality. It was a source of deep-seated resentment that potential Irish shareholders had been ignored at the time of the introduction of the equity in London.

There was a Guinness board in Ireland, chaired by Lord Iveagh, with a number of his nominees as outside directors. Iveagh had his company office in Dublin's St James's Gate and spent a great deal of time there, largely to look after his extensive livestock and farming interests, the investments of the Iveagh Trustees and other matters unrelated to the business. Through being based in Ireland he had for a time also enjoyed a favourable personal tax position. His presence there was useful for maintaining contact with the Irish government. Ernest: 'It also gave the Irish top management an excuse to prevaricate over executive decisions that had been agreed, or required agreement, with the London head office, and to push for heavy investment which in fact needed careful overview on a group-wide basis.'

The Irish sense of independence went further. They held their own press conferences at the time of the announcement of the group's results in London, making their own comments and carefully removing Ernest's photographs from the literature, even though he was group managing director, and replacing them with those of the Irish managing director. Ernest: 'The Irish management also provided sectors of the Irish press with background material which attacked me personally for all the unpleasant changes that were having to be introduced – whereas the credit for any success went to the locals! Ireland was the birthplace of my "Deadly Ernest" nickname. According to Irish journalists I talked to, it was supposed to represent grudging respect for a determination to grapple with problems my predecessors had chosen to ignore.'

So the Dublin management had over the years manoeuvred itself into a position where it was extremely difficult for the group head office to control the Irish market. Yet the group's immediate profits depended on the need for profit growth from Ireland, and this would require significant changes in Irish policy, practices and attitudes.

Guinness stout dominated the Irish beer market to an extent seen nowhere else in the world. Over half the market still consisted of stout, and ninety-five per cent of stout sales were accounted for by Guinness (the rest came from Murphy's and Beamish, produced in Cork). There had been a slow decline in volume from the all-time high, but heavy advertising, consistent quality, powerful distribution and one other factor kept Guinness in this enviable position. The other factor was price. Unlike the rest of the world, in Ireland Guinness was cheaper than other brews.

Ernest: 'The core problem lay in dramatically reducing the cost base of stout production, with sales now static at best, in a country where inflation was a real problem, both in terms of cost build-up and consumption. And other problems lay in the need to develop the lager brands.'

At the heart of the cost problem lay overmanning in all sectors of the business, historic restrictive practices, direct involvement in activities that should have been bought in, and the terrible state of the plant. Massive investment was needed simply to avoid breakdown and maintain quality, let alone improve efficiency.

Prior to Ernest's arrival a plan had been floated to invest around £100 million in return for union agreement to manning reduction by natural wastage, extremely heavy up-front payments for early retirement and modifications to restrictive practices and 'contracting out'. But the proposed timescale was lengthy and, given the level of inflation at the time, the scheme would not have provided the necessary immediate profit improvement. More would have to be done.

Once again, Ernest asked Bain to look at the basic economics, pinpoint cost savings that had been overlooked and produce a realistic prognosis for the next ten years. Bain had enormous difficulty, and initially much passive resistance, in getting at the numbers. Ernest: 'It is no exaggeration to state that the Irish technique of charming troublesome visitors meant the replacement of several Bain team members who had had their determination charmed out of them.'

Negotiations between the Irish end of Guinness and the Dublin government were as difficult as those within the company. Ernest insisted on the Irish government contributing a grant, which eventually they did, but the Irish cost problem was to remain a factor of major significance throughout his period of office.

Although progress was made – especially when top management changes wrought a more enlightened attitude locally – a fundamental shift happened only when the burly, dependable Vic Steel came in from Beecham to take over as managing director of Guinness Brewing Worldwide, the new management unit for brewing, and Alfons Walser, after having served for many years as a member of the Irish management, became technical director worldwide. It also helped when Brian Slowey, the Irish managing director, was brought into worldwide brewing affairs, so that he could see for himself how vital the Irish business was to the group. Ernest's early months in Ireland had shown him the need for a management unit that would link all Guinness's worldwide brewing activities, and so develop a team spirit enabling individuals to learn from each other and eliminate the 'not invented here' attitude. This was the genesis of Guinness Brewing Worldwide.

The advertising of Guinness in Ireland at that time involved a high degree of 'not invented here'. However, research did show that, given the unique position and history of Guinness in Ireland, the UK approach was not particularly appropriate – certainly not the Guinnless campaign. Indeed, the most important aspect of Irish marketing was its emphasis on the condition of the product at the bar. And that was at risk from the appalling state of St James's Gate. There was an air of decay: beer vats were literally held together with string after hasty repairs. Pigeons roosted in the rafters, their droppings falling into the vats, and it was not surprising that the workers were most unhappy in their work.

The Irish sales force needed a new approach also, especially since even in Ireland supermarkets were developing in the big cities and required specialised attention. Furthermore, when Heineken bought Murphy's in 1984 Guinness suddenly had real competition – and competition was something the firm was not used to handling.

The Irish technicians developed a form of packaged draught Guinness known as 'Bottled Draught', which was sold with a special syringe to make the 'head'. Although it was not economic in its original packaging all research indicated that it would be a winner once the technical problem had been overcome, and Ernest made a canned version a priority development project for the group worldwide. This product is now available in the market-place. Indeed, the

Irish had research and development resources that were soon to be adopted for even wider group purposes.

The Irish connection had one other dimension: the IRA's terror campaigns. Each time there was an outbreak of terrorist activity in the UK the image of Guinness as a Dublin-based company suffered around the world. Ernest reviewed this problem with the Irish ambassador in London and met the then Irish Prime Minister, Dr Garret Fitzgerald, who was very concerned for Irish exports. Bomb threats at any of the company's offices were always taken seriously and the buildings evacuated.

Ernest: 'I was particularly concerned for the safety of my children who were away at school, and we took professional advice on security.' On the day Freddy Heineken was kidnapped in Amsterdam Ernest was due to meet him. Indeed, he was prevented from catching the plane for Amsterdam only by a mysterious telephone message to the gatehouse at Park Royal just as he was about to drive off. 'When I subsequently met Freddy he impressed on me the need for stringent security precautions in my office.'

Beyond Ireland and the UK, Guinness business overseas was global: there was a bottle of Guinness to be found on the better bars of every country in the world – even if it got there by unorthodox means, such as smuggling! But volume sales were to be found in only a few countries, notably hot countries in the developing world such as Nigeria, Malaysia, Cameroun and Jamaica. Here bottled Guinness was brewed locally and volume sales had been developed over the years after pioneering by old-style exporting from St James's Gate.

In most cases the product was – and still is – the Foreign Extra Stout version, which is closer to the original strong porter. Local consumers believe it to be much more than just a dark beer. It is seen as a brewed tonic drink with magical properties. When Ernest was in the developing countries for Beecham he was taught that the basic advertising concepts were health, sex and success, and Guinness was thought to contain the potential for all three. The explicit sexual advertising still allowed in some developing countries gave full rein to themes with lines like 'Keep on top with Guinness', 'Keep it up with Guinness' and 'Guinness for both of you'. Certain ladies within the Guinness nobility objected to one poster showing a beautiful girl with the slogan 'I'll have a Guinness today'!

The largest Guinness overseas market was Nigeria, where there were a number of breweries. Over the years the market had been developed in conjunction with Unilever, and there was now a residual minority holding by Guinness, with sizeable local financial participation. But supply was vastly exceeded by demand, and distributors paid for the privilege of distributing Guinness.

The political situation in Nigeria was particularly unstable. At one stage draconian import restrictions were imposed on raw materials. This was the biggest crisis Guinness had faced in the country, since the bulk of the ingredients had to be imported. But while most competitor breweries were closed, or on drastic short-time, Tom Ward somehow managed to make arrangements from the US for licences that kept Guinness plants rolling, and a vital source of Guinness profits intact.

In all the other major overseas markets Guinness was starting to feel the pressure from lager, and beer competition in general. This caused many problems, since analysis showed that profits had previously been maintained largely by price increases rather than by appropriate marketing and advertising. The tougher conditions exposed the company's basic lack of a proper marketing operation for the group as a whole, and time would be needed in which to recruit marketing personnel of sufficiently high calibre. In the meantime, to make adequate profits, and to fund necessary increases in marketing spending, cost reductions had to be implemented and efficiency enhanced everywhere.

In Malaysia, a major form of promotion was to hire mini-skirted girls to persuade people to drink the required brand of beer. Guinness had originated this technique – but it was immediately followed by all other brewers in the territory. Ernest: 'In most bars I visited on a trip to Malaysia, there were more promotion girls than drinkers!' When he introduced market research to the local management there, the consumer base was found to be very narrow – a few drinkers drank a great deal. 'I asked whether in these circumstances it was worth advertising in mass media. Why not telephone them?'

In Cameroun, on the other hand, the brewery was literally in danger of disappearing altogether, since a massive crack had appeared in the ground, and the brewery was beginning to tilt into it. Ernest sanctioned major refurbishment, and the plant kept going.

In Kenya the Guinness distributor had found Guinness was good for killing snails, and the public relations he used to spread the word about this to the locals was so persuasive that it eventually found its way back to Europe! In Italy, Ernest found little Guinness on supermarket shelves, but plenty of three-year-old bottles and cans in laundrettes and bakeries, because on one occasion a sales team had made their targets by just selling to anyone. No one knows what sales pitch they had used.

Dublin-produced Guinness had been in the US for a long time, peddled by a sales force consisting largely of middle-aged expatriate Irishmen. The base for this operation was a building in downtown Manhattan, next to a cemetery which the boardroom directly over-looked. There had been an attempt to brew Guinness at a small brewery acquired on Long Island, New York, but this proved futile: customers who wanted Guinness in the US wanted the real thing, and that meant product imported from Ireland – for which they were prepared to pay the requisite premium. The brewery soon closed.

The US sales operation had been consistently uneconomic, so it had been decided to obtain additional revenue by buying a dis-tribution business to sell and distribute other beers in parts of New York. Although sales of one import, Bass, were promising, this operation as a whole made substantial losses.

Ernest: 'On my first visit to New York for Guinness, I decided that we needed a total re-orientation of the business. We should position ourselves as importers of speciality beers, appealing to the increasing US interest in beers that had a distinctive taste and image.'

So he pulled out of the New York distribution business, moved the offices from 'death row' to Stamford, Connecticut, hired new management, and put together the beginnings of a viable portfolio.

Ernest: 'Sales developed extremely well from the inception of the "importer of speciality beers" concept. It appealed directly to the affluent American, who above all wanted something exclusive when out with friends or entertaining. This was a concept that could well be replicated in other large development markets, such as Japan and continental Europe. It was a small niche to start from, but a valid one.'

The Guinness Import Company, as the Stamford business became known, was headed by an American, Bob Kinsey, and Ward was both his legal counsellor and on the board to give local support, since there were many legal problems involved in the changes of distributor necessary if a thriving network was to be rebuilt.

The new business was able to take advantage of the fact that the annual St Patrick's Day parade down Manhattan's Fifth Avenue provided it with a sales boost. Many millions of Americans had Irish origins, or knew the product from trips to the West Indies, and over and over again it was demonstrated that sampling was the key to success.

Ernest: 'On one occasion we occupied the President's Box at the Kennedy Center in Washington. We brought our own sixpacks of Guinness – and left them behind for the President! The company has many mementoes of President and Mrs Reagan photographed with Guinness, thanks probably to the fact that Tip O'Neill, Speaker of the US House of Representatives until 1986, was an Irishman – and proud of it.'

Another useful event was the 1982 opening of the Walt Disney Epcot centre next to Disney World in Florida. Epcot, the Experimental Prototype Community of Tomorrow, was supposed to depict life in the future. Bass and Guinness sponsored a joint venture – a pub for the English village, where pints are served with excellent pub food. Ernest and Carole attended the ceremonial opening where brass bands played a selection from *My Fair Lady*.

The occasion gave Ernest his first experience of appearing on network radio and television in the States. He was asked about a range of subjects, and eventually he casually told the interviewer that Guinness was excellent for making Christmas cake. The radio station was immediately bombarded by eager listeners wanting the recipe. My mother was listening to the programme in their hotel room, and could not believe her ears when Ernest, who had never cooked more than a boiled egg, started dictating the recipe. He began: 'Pour in six bottles of Guinness . . .'

I am always tickled by the pictures of Ernest standing outside the Epcot pub with a glass of Guinness in his hand or to his lips. He dislikes all beer, and Guinness in particular, but he could never admit it. As chief executive, trying to convince other people to drink it, he had to be seen to drink it himself. Over his five years with Guinness there must have been over a hundred receptions where he had to be photographed drinking the stuff.

Jo and I went to university in 1984. Jo went to Exeter to read philosophy, while I went to my father's old college, Emmanuel, Cambridge, to read law. John at this time was at boarding school near Southampton. Jo and I would often travel to London to attend publicity functions, and it was always fun to watch what Ernest would do with his drink. He had three favourite solutions. One was to order a half-pint in a pint glass and slosh it around so it looked as if he had drunk half already. This was particularly effective, because the same glass would do for the entire evening, and he would not have to drink any of it. If someone put a full pint in his hand he had a second ruse, 'the switch', but for this he needed me. I would be standing at one side of the room with an almost empty glass, and he would casually walk over and switch glasses while we were chatting. For real emergencies he brought a third ploy into action, involving the nearest flowerbed or indoor plant. Unfortunately this was once captured on film by an alert photographer! However, Ernest did enjoy champagne, and after he had discovered the delights of Black Velvet it was served at every function.

Guinness had seen the growth of lager coming since the 1970s, and had thought of it in production terms simply as a way of compensating for the decline in stout sales. But they underestimated both its

SUMMER BEGINS THIS WEEK AND

Summer Thirst starts in Ernest

I'm Ernest— Guinness cures my thirst and renews my strength

FIVE MILLION THIRSTS ARE CURED EVERY DAY BY GUINNESS

G.E. 3361. C

Research into the Company's archives revealed this appropriate ad – first used in 1960.

attractions as a lighter drink and the commercial complexities of marketing and distribution. The Harp lager brand was developed in Ireland by a German brewer, Dr Herman Munder, and while the inherent strength of Guinness restricted lager to a modest share of the total beer market there for many years it remained the leading Irish lager brand.

In the UK, Guinness got into the lager business with Harp through a consortium including two other large brewers, Scottish & Newcastle and Courage. This proved initially to be a satisfactory entry-point into the market, but led in the long term to severely restricted growth and almost to its demise. When the brewing industry, including members of the Harp consortium, saw how the potential for lager threatened their traditional sales of bitter it was every man for himself. They all developed their own brands, or licensed established European and Australian brands. And as the brewers controlled pub distribution they were able to shape the deals to suit themselves and promote their own brands with lavish advertising budgets.

Harp inevitably suffered from lack of promotion. The original consortium had broken up after tortuous negotiations among the partners before Ernest arrived, leaving only two regional brewers – Greene King and Wolverhampton & Dudley – to partner Guinness, with Courage using the brand in the take-home trade as a loss-leader, which did not do its brand image any good at all. Harp's market share plummeted. Another valiant reconstruction was conceived in 1985 when Scottish & Newcastle came into the picture again because its own lager development had not been successful.

Ernest: 'When I got round to studying the new Harp arrangements I was alarmed by the terms exacted by Wolverhampton & Dudley, on whose board sat Edward Guinness – his brother-in-law was chairman of W & D. The deal was very hard on Guinness, but if Guinness had fallen out with W & D, who stocked Harp in their pubs, the whole enterprise would have collapsed. That would have been seen as a disaster for Guinness in lager because its overall position was already so weak. We could resist threats to import rival stouts from Ireland, but Harp, although a "me-too" brand with little going for it, was our only foot in the lager market door.'

In Ireland, by contrast, Harp was the first brand in the market and it held a virtual monopoly for many years on the back of the distribution dominance of Guinness stout. But even here Harp was to come under attack. With the high beer consumption per head in

Ireland, and the invincibility of Guinness in stout, competitors were not going to leave all the lager market to Harp.

Ernest: 'In my view the Irish management had adopted a "King Canute" policy with regard to lager. They believed that the unique status of the Guinness brand would actually restrict lager development. I kept telling them that this was wrong, and that they needed to think positively about improving the product and the image of the Harp brand, which seemed to me to be vulnerable to its international competitors. I also suggested taking on other international lager brands on a franchise basis.'

But while Ernest could try to keep a daily eye on Park Royal he could not effectively control the Irish operation simply by telephone and fax machine. Harp's share of the Irish lager market started to shrink rapidly when Heineken bought Murphy's brewery in Cork, and others launched cut-price brands which fragmented the market. Then the Harp brewery in Ireland was hit by a strike.

The local management decided to stand firm, and the strike lasted several months. That gave Heineken and the others a chance to get their products into pubs that had previously been exclusively Harp stockists, and become established in drinkers' minds. Once in, they stayed. The competition had established a beachhead and proceeded to advance.

As Heineken progressed, and Carlsberg pressed, others made distribution arrangements in Ireland, and a battlefield was laid out. But the market was too small for that, so the battle shifted towards outlets which had not traditionally been strongholds for stout. That meant a further sales force re-organisation. Far too late, the intransigent Guinness Irish management started to undertake consumer research. It told a predictable story. Harp was in big trouble, both in its image and as a product. As well as support for Harp, new brands were required. A first attempt was made with the licensing of a top-quality German beer, Furstenberg, and the initial results were encouraging, but by then Guinness had lost its lager dominance and would probably not regain it without major moves to acquire or license other brands. Negotiations to distribute Carlsberg were initiated in the light of this strategy.

Beyond the UK and Ireland, Harp had a successful franchise in Nigeria, again due to overall demand for lager vastly exceeding total supply from all manufacturers; but whenever Guinness faced competition in the lager business it failed, due to an initial lack of marketing competence – and the time it subsequently took to hire marketing people and get the right strategies in place.

In Cameroun the brand made advances, but was then wiped out by local competition. In Malaysia two separate attempts were made to launch a lager. Both failed. It was clearly necessary to rethink the company's participation in this growing but highly competitive sector. Ernest: 'We could try to buy or license a well-known competitor's brand, but, better still, wasn't the Guinness name still magic in the world of beer? Surely we could position ourselves as marketers of speciality beers on the back of Guinness's worldwide reputation, and perhaps share distribution costs with other brewers'.

The first concept to emerge from this new approach exploited the Guinness name on a luxury lager product called 'Guinness Gold', to be priced at a premium to Heineken and Carlsberg. But in parallel, the Irish R & D Group had developed a technical breakthrough in lager – good-tasting, non-alcoholic Kaliber. If Guinness had missed the boat, worldwide, with Harp, then maybe the trend towards alcohol moderation would give the company an international potential through Kaliber.

After a low-key launch in Ireland it was decided to make a significant effort in the US and then the UK. The marketing task was to overcome the psychological resistance to something that looked right both on the shelf and in the glass, tasted right, and fitted in with current lifestyles – but wasn't really beer. Could people be seen to drink a non-alcoholic beer? At first the omens were not good. The mighty Budweiser spent millions on a product in the US called LA. It failed. Ernest: 'We took the view that mega detergent-type launches would not work – and we could not afford them in any case. What was required was the right background image, to back sampling. Getting the drinker to taste the product, and realise it tasted good, was the most important factor.'

Consumer research was conducted in abundance – and in the UK the launch of Kaliber was successful, using the formula of sampling and image endorsement by two comedians who were hugely popular with young people, Billy Connolly and Lenny Henry. In the US the product also showed considerable promise, but the local management were perhaps wanting to run a little too fast with what they believed was a winner.

Ernest: 'However, the consumerist pressure on alcohol moderation in the US showed every sign of providing Kaliber with the ideal environment to catch on, and it did. I had no doubt that Kaliber would become a second major Guinness brand.'

Finally, the most important long-term factor in the tough struggle to convert Guinness from a failing one-product company into a successful participant in the world beer market of the 1990s lay in forming the management unit known as Guinness Brewing Worldwide. In this way all the strengths of the individual operating companies, wherever they might be, could be made to work for the good of the whole. 'Not invented here' could be eliminated, and strategic marketing direction could be made to work.

Ernest: 'In 1985 I was able to lure Vic Steel away from Beecham to become managing director, with a seat on the main board and fully responsible for beer activities. Vic was a fine international consumer products manager, and from the moment he arrived his detailed attention gave Guinness Brewing Worldwide exactly the impetus it needed.'

Ernest's personal interest and his contacts in marketing enabled him to persuade a number of first-rate people to join the brewing group, and they recruited others. By 1985 Guinness became known as a top-class marketing company and headhunters actually began poaching from them – a telling sign.

Strategically there remained one fundamental issue: was Guinness to be in the beer business or the much larger drinks business? In Ireland Guinness, in association with Allied-Lyons, was involved in the whole range of drinks, from soft to spirits. The group needed more international brands, and would need to consider distribution arrangements to exploit them, whether they were developed by Guinness or acquired. The 'beer versus drinks' question would have to be settled.

7

LIFE WITH THE GUINNESSES

For three years, from 1981 to 1984, Guinness reported improved profits and earnings at each successive half-year. The share price reacted accordingly. When Ernest joined in 1981 the shares were trading at 49p and the company was valued at £90 million. At the beginning of 1984 the share price was around 120p and the market capitalisation had risen to £200 million. Although Guinness was still outside the stock market's 100 biggest companies, helped by warmer press coverage it was attracting the interest of City stockbrokers' analysts and the investing public. The new Guinness advertising campaigns kept awareness of the company at a high level. The City was still sceptical of the company's ability to sustain this performance in the long-term, but morale in the company had improved and the board was gratified, especially the family members who had large shareholdings. Their wealth had been substantially increased.

Although it was accepted that a great improvement in the status of the company had taken place in a very short time, scepticism remained because it was clear to analysts that the profit improvement at this stage was largely due to the divestment programme, cutting out loss-makers, reducing costs and keeping a firm grip on the on-going businesses. This was all good housekeeping, but the volume sales of Guinness stout were still basically static. The new marketing approach had yet to bear fruit, and there was a need to invest in marketing and improved productivity.

So from where was the future growth to come? There were two basic necessities. First, Guinness needed to accelerate the upgrading of their internal management to cope with their expanded organisation – and at the same time cut their need for expensive consultants like Bain! Second, they would have to look at possible takeovers, despite the failures the company had had down that path in the past.

These would present a different type of challenge to credibility in the City, but they could not keep profits rising at the expected rate in any other way.

Meanwhile they had to keep the business running despite major deficiencies in management and systems. This entailed not only hard work and long hours, but an acceptance of the realities of the situation, and a considerable degree of flexibility and delegation. It was impossible to stick rigidly to programmes and timetables. Meetings were forever being changed, postponed or cancelled.

The cornerstone of the day-to-day management was the weekly control meeting Ernest held every Monday morning at head office, with key members of the head office departments present. They reviewed the previous week's sales for the whole group against the current budget and the previous year's out-turn. Once a month there was a review of the sales, costs and profits of the previous month. Ernest: 'As I hadn't been trained in, or been inclined to get into, financial analysis I applied a crude rule-of-thumb control using an old-fashioned ruler on the simple charts: whether sales were going up or down, the slope of the ruler on the costs line had to be in proportion to the sales line, so that profits would be secure whatever happened. It was a terribly simple formula, but it worked. It also cut out the previous complacency under which profits were simply allowed to decline if sales failed to meet budget.'

Any deviations in performance were taken up by the controllers with the operating companies concerned, bringing in Ernest only when needed. 'In the early days the controllers used to enjoy playing a waiting game with the monthly figures, to see if I had spotted the critical variations. But I got fed up with this and eventually, as I acquired complete faith in the controllers' abilities, I reversed the process, leaving them to advise me of problems and propose corrective action, which at this stage usually involved cost-cutting.'

Phil Rhodes was group controller, while Olivier Roux, the head of finance, had overall charge of the financial side. He had many other financial responsibilities that required attention if Guinness was going to be able to operate as an up-to-date international business. Roux was of course helped by Bain and by Price Waterhouse, the group's new auditors. Rhodes and the other controllers 'followed profits like hunters stalking tigers', according to Ernest. As a marketing man, he was therefore able to focus on sales and marketing problems. 'I had learned over the years that if the brands were on target the rest would somehow follow.'

The weekly control meetings gradually developed a permanent agenda that went beyond performance monitoring to range over the entire business. Again, it worked by exception. Beyond a brief verbal status report by each department, matters were brought to Ernest's attention only when major decisions were required, when there was trouble, when something new or unexpected occurred or when his views were needed. So basic yet successful was this system that similar control meetings were adopted by the operating companies.

Ernest had to try to ration his time carefully throughout the week. In addition to sales and marketing matters, he focused mostly on senior personnel recruitment, external relations and the Park Royal company, visiting other major operating companies when he could. Although he was inevitably concerned with strategic decisions on financial, legal and administrative issues, he delegated the detail to the experts, from whom he received one-page weekly update reports. These became the back-up to control meetings he couldn't attend. The operating managers were supposed to produce similar reports, but it was notoriously difficult to get them to comply. 'Roux was the worst offender. He just didn't think it was necessary for him.'

Normally the control meetings merely had 'action minutes', indicating who had to have done what by the next week's meeting. When more formal decisions were required, a number of the more senior managers convened as a management or executive committee to produce conventional minutes for the board.

The problems that bore in on Ernest in the early years forced him into an eighteen-hour day, seven days a week. Health and family life were suffering, and he realised he had to get help. He was using the Bain consultants far more extensively than he would have liked, and he hired two young ex-Boston Consulting Group men, Ian Cheshire and Stephen Hill, as personal assistants. Ernest: 'But the major problem was that it seemed to take an agonisingly long time to recruit managers of the right quality for many key positions, and I had to balance the need to replace almost every senior manager with the practicalities of keeping the business going. The result was an unsatisfactory and enormously frustrating compromise.'

It was not hard to see why ambitious experienced managers were reluctant to work for Guinness at this stage. The company had an appalling reputation, particularly in marketing and sales. Its salary, conditions and benefits had fallen badly behind market rates. The salary scales were quickly updated, but the company's poor image on the management career ladder was a tougher problem. All the leading consumer brands companies were recruiting in the early 1980s, and it required enormous persistence to compete against them. Candidates had to be persuaded to have faith in Guinness's future, and as they wanted to hear that message from the boss, Ernest had to get involved in nearly every case. The major executive search companies waxed rich on the company's predicament. The new personnel director, Colin George, had an enormous recruitment task, and he worked methodically through it. His weekly update on progress made depressing reading, yet Ernest felt they were right to reject candidates who did not fit their demanding criteria.

Indeed, whenever under this extreme time pressure Guinness appointed someone they inwardly knew was not quite right, they always lived to regret the mistake. Such people never walked out voluntarily. There was a classic example in the head office finance department. After Tony Spicer, the finance director, had decided to retire because of ill-health, Ernest called in a leading executive search company with a reputation for finding senior financial people. It was an important and urgent appointment.

'After a number of weeks, Peter Guinness and I were persuaded to offer the job to the finance director of a public company, whose name inspired glowing references. Somehow I wasn't personally over-impressed, but allowed myself to be persuaded, because of the urgency. The appointment was to be straight to the main board. The search company insisted on this, whereas Lord Iveagh would have preferred to have a newcomer "prove himself" first. It didn't work out. One reason was the man's personality. The other was the depth of knowledge and authority that Roux had established within the company in his original role as controller. I asked the new man to leave, after representations from other directors, especially those from Ireland. Having talked it over with Iveagh and George, we decided to ask Roux to take the job himself.'

Ernest thought that he would be flattered by being offered the opportunity at his age. He was not at that time aware of how much Roux was earning from Bain. Roux declined with some ambivalence, but whilst remaining on full-time secondment from Bain he took on the functions and became known as head of finance.

It was a role that Roux took to as if he had been born to it. 'He mesmerised the board with his highly articulate and well-prepared presentations. He always got his financial budgets, capital projects, acquisition proposals and budgets approved, so that he could get on and implement them with the least fuss.' In July 1984 Bain was asked to agree to his appointment to the board as a non-executive director. Ernest: 'This was a pragmatic arrangement, to suit Roux's personal career perceptions, give him status, and to fit in with Guinness's need for continuity, both internally and externally at the time.

Ernest next tried to fill the finance directorship with a permanent candidate by appointing someone without the title and trappings, but with the understanding that he could become finance director before long. Roux was committed to training him. But this appointment did not work either. Ernest was unwilling to trust anyone immediately with the same degree of almost totally delegated authority that he had gradually bestowed on Roux. 'Since my days at Nestlé I had learned to respect the Swiss philosophy that recruits had to earn their superiors' trust. Once earned the individual would have my complete trust and confidence unless or until he let me down. Equally, it always struck me that Roux was deep down even more ambivalent than he admitted about handing over the responsibilities, the authority and the prestige that went with the finance directorship. He certainly did not make it easy for this candidate to succeed.' With each hiccup Roux's position became stronger and Ernest became more reluctant to replace one of the few experts he could delegate to. He took the title of director of financial strategy and development at the time of the Bell bid, to remove any external doubt as to who was Guinness's finance chief.'

The search for a permanent finance director continued. Howard Hughes, the senior partner of Price Waterhouse, was constantly on the lookout, although the hunt slowed during the bursts of takeover activity.

The other principal recruitment problem lay in the area of marketing and sales. The group needed at least fifty senior managers. Finding them took forever, and in the process the heads of a number of executive search firms became extremely wealthy.

The company had for many years been a pillar of the Brewers' Society, partly out of self-interest because of its lack of tied public houses. But beyond that, its relations with the outside world were patchy. Ernest: 'I felt ill at ease in this situation. I had no establishment roots, and indeed no worthwhile connections at the right levels in Whitehall, the City or Fleet Street, and the rest of the board seemed unable to be of much help either.' At first the most urgent task was to improve the company's relations with the investment community.

Brokers had in the past complained that they found the company's response to their enquiries completely unsatisfactory. 'I was told of one visit by an analyst who asked how the group budgeted for so many subsidiaries. He was told, "We don't budget. We just count the costs at the end of the year."'

Ernest felt that he needed to learn how to communicate the company's progress better, so he took advice from public relations consultants and brokers' analysts who followed the brewing sector. He developed a formula that was to become successful: a twice-yearly presentation to analysts, followed by press enquiries handled on an individual basis. Ernest would chair the analysts' meeting, introduce it, and answer non-financial questions, leaving Roux to present the financial results.

Ernest: 'Roux did so with such confidence that he completely overwhelmed his audience from the outset with his grasp of the numbers and his own presentational style. Bain trained its executives superbly in the art of presentation, and Roux was utterly plausible, even on the most flimsy facts.' Roux developed an on-going relationship with the analysts, whose broking firms would hold lunches for Guinness executives to present their latest results to representatives of the institutional investors, such as pension funds, unit trusts and insurance companies. 'I remember those occasions well, because we had to get across London from Mayfair at midday, arriving hot and bothered only to be pitched straight into a lunch that others ate while Roux and I talked. It was one way of losing weight.' But they were not meeting the company's major non-family shareholders directly, and regularly enough, a failing that hit them when they needed support for big acquisitions.

Roux argued for a change of company stockbroker, ultimately recommending the appointment of Wood Mackensie to replace James Capel. Woodmac, as it was known in the City, is a Scottish broker with an extensive London office. It is now part of National Westminster Bank, but it was then independent and had a strong reputation as a research house. Its analytical approach appealed to Roux's own methodical style. But Ernest felt Guinness would ultimately need additional clout when it came to making big acquisitions, so he told Woodmac that he reserved the right to bring in Cazenove on such occasions. Additionally Guinness had no formal arrangement with a merchant bank before the takeovers began. They had merely consulted Rothschilds on a one-off basis during the sales of subsidiaries.

Ernest also started to develop relationships with newspaper City editors. The decision to replace J. Walter Thompson as advertising agents and bring in Allen Brady & Marsh had made the press sit up. Who was this tough new managing director, they wanted to know! On the advice of public relations consultants, Ernest made himself available to City editors and senior financial journalists, but initially he found it an ordeal. Ernest: 'The media's appetite for information about Guinness' future plans was insatiable. I didn't know the ground rules, and I didn't have the experience to judge the ethics of the situation. Journalists wanted exclusive news, but I had a duty to the Stock Exchange and my shareholders. As I studied financial pages to see how other companies handled the problem, I found myself in a quandary. Our PR advisers were pressing for more openness, while my gut-feel urged caution.' Nevertheless, on the whole the company was starting to get a good press on the back of the improving results. The fact that the media coverage was largely about Ernest was due to the fact that people, not numbers, make news. For years the media had wanted a human face to put alongside the toucan. Now they had one. However, his contact was mainly with the financial and marketing press. Ernest still hardly knew most of the national and regional newspaper editors.

Equally, the company's connections at top levels with City regulators, the Bank of England and government departments were non-existent. Contacts with top industrialists were also thin, outside the Brewers' Society. After one of Ernest's visits to Boston to review Bain's work with Bill Bain, John Theroux suggested that their London adviser, Sir Jack Lyons, who apparently knew everybody, could help. Theroux arranged an introduction. Ernest: 'Sir Jack certainly knew his way around. He was often photographed with the Queen or the Prime Minister, and was a major benefactor to such organisations as the Royal Opera House, Covent Garden. He said he would help. I tried hard to develop connections at the right level, where I felt it was important. I made some progress over the years, but time was always a problem with the difficulties of the business to worry about. It was a major disadvantage not to have personally had these contacts, and disappointing that the other directors couldn't help. But then the family-oriented board was itself in need of evolutionary change to meet the new status and objectives of the company.'

*   *   *

By 1983 Ernest was virtually the only non-family director left in the company, as the survival exercise described earlier exposed the severe limitations of most of the other directors. But while his official position in the company strengthened, he was left in doubt about his personal status in the eyes of the family. At the first Guinness wedding he and Carole were invited to, at Lord Moyne's magnificent Hampshire home, Ernest was introduced as 'the new brewery manager' and they were seated at a table with the company secretary and the Moyne estate manager. They were gradually promoted to more important seats but, apart from the Moynes, the Guinness family largely excluded them from all but the most formal social functions.

The Guinness family, or 'Guinnessty factor', as it was known out of their hearing, was inextricably linked with the company in the public mind as a sort of eccentric dynasty which added spice and occasional scandal to the company's image. Their activities were covered in everything from the William Hickey column in the *Daily Express* to the more salacious revelations in the *Sunday Sport*. Despite the fact that Sabrina Guinness was at one time vying with the then Lady Diana Spencer for Prince Charles's affections, the family publicity was rarely positive, since over the years the family had been involved in more than its fair share of divorces, mistresses, drugs, kidnapping and even AIDS. Tragedy intervened regularly enough to inspire talk of a curse on the family.

To the company, the misfortune of having a member of the family – Paul Channon – in the Government indirectly led, Ernest believed, to some of the difficulties experienced in later years.

Ernest and Lord Iveagh had many talks about the ideal composition and role of the board. Ernest had also discussed the issue with Howard Hughes, senior partner of the company's auditors, Price Waterhouse. Iveagh had been gestating a plan for equal numbers of family members, non-family non-executives and non-family executives on the board, including a significant Irish representation. Ernest, on the other hand, was primarily concerned to recruit competent executive directors to take responsibility for major sections of the business. Ernest: 'As far as non-executives were concerned, I felt that the company needed additional experience from outside the family and from outside Ireland: an American, a European, expertise perhaps from the law, banking and probably from politics.' Iveagh did not disagree, but was nervous about appointing people he did not know. A seat on the board was still considered by the family as a very special honour, and particular care had to be taken after the finance director episode.

It was in the event pragmatism that led to the appointment in 1984 of Tom Ward, the American lawyer who had impressed the board with his work in the US and help over Nigeria. With Iveagh's agreement, Dr Arthur Furer, a banker as well as a director of many international companies and chairman of Nestlé, was approached by Ernest after the Irish-born chairman of Unilever had found it impossible to join. Furer and Iveagh met, and they got on well together. Roux's appointment brought another European on the board. Peter Keehan, already a director of Guinness Ireland, replaced Ken Whittaker as the Irish representative.

That left the board short of executive directors, a gap that could be filled only when the right people had been hired. In the meantime, there had already been a significant number of changes, and with the major policy developments, Iveagh felt that unity of purpose was more important than anything else. Ernest agreed. If it was regarded as important for the board to get into a particular subject in depth, the executive within the company would be asked to attend the board meeting and explain. The management and the board worked well together.

Ernest and Iveagh developed a good and largely informal working relationship. Iveagh spent most of his time on his diverse private interests – farming and horses in Ireland, the family estates, property in Canada and family investment trusts. But the two would discuss everything of importance before it came to the board, and Ernest would always patiently take him through the entire agenda ahead of board meetings, explaining the items that required special attention. The two spoke regularly on the telephone, and Iveagh later paid Ernest the compliment that my father had never failed to keep him informed, so that he had never been embarrassed by his ignorance as had been the case in the past. In the early days Ernest briefed Simon Lennox-Boyd (later Lord Boyd) in a similar manner, but eventually time pressure made this usually impossible. There were also growing personal difficulties between the two top Guinness family representatives, and Ernest did not want to be caught in the middle. 'I noticed that on the extremely rare occasions when anything near criticism of the executive was voiced at a board meeting, the intention appeared to be as much to embarrass Iveagh as to get at us. There was apparent resentment that the chairman was so well-informed.'

The directors at this stage, being predominantly family or family-linked, were content to be part of a group that was participating in a well-publicised and significant turnaround. Most either said nothing, or waited to make an intervention of some sort for inclusion in the minutes and then rushed off. They were very well-informed on how the company was doing – Ernest was even asked on one occasion to reduce the amount of detail in the performance report for each meeting. In most cases, they lacked the relevant experience of the commercial world to be able to make an objective contribution, so their inclination was to support whatever changes were put before them, and Ernest cannot remember a single proposition being turned down. But, of course, they had few grounds to do so. Although the company had narrowly escaped disaster, by 1984 it was heading in the right direction. Those board members with big shareholdings were already considerably richer.

Ernest: 'The chairman on one occasion mentioned with delight that his recent dividend cheque had enabled him to purchase a number of new bulls for his farm! Lord Iveagh made it as easy as possible in an informal way, to get approval for plans with minimal procedural fuss. He would often pre-handle board members himself on anything that might prove difficult. The board was playing its role in the recovery in a pragmatic and supportive way. They were flexible and unbureaucratic, and aware of he enormous pressure on me to get things done and produce results. In one note to me, Lord Iveagh was kind enough to end by saying that the family considered me as an adopted Guinness, so maybe the family representation on the board was even larger than it appeared!'

Small shareholders, whom the board saw only at Annual General Meetings, also gradually became appreciative of what was happening to improve the position of their company.

The Guinness AGMs at Park Royal were typical of those held by the older consumer products companies. The institutional investors stayed away, leaving the field clear for private shareholders to have a day out, heckle or applaud the board, taste their company's products and go home with a bagful of gifts – a few bottles of stout, a selection of Guinness-emblazoned tankards, aprons, oven gloves, tea towels and a copy of the *Book of Records*. Each year about six hundred people, mostly aged over 60, would be picked up by coach from Hanger Lane underground station and ferried to the Toucan Inn at the Park Royal brewery. The meetings had a party atmosphere as everyone looked forward to the free drinks in the lounge afterwards.

There was nearly always the obligatory awkward customer to bowl a few verbal bouncers at the chairman, but that was part of the fun.

In Guinness's case the annual moment of drama usually came from a serious-minded Irishman who would rise to his feet and announce: 'O'Hegarty – ordinary stockholder.' A ripple of anticipation would spread through the room. For years his questions had been very critical of the board, and made them squirm. When I myself attended I would naturally watch to see what the board would do to head off the O'Hegarty challenge. On one occasion my father defused him by calling for him to speak before he could choose his own moment. The rest of the stockholders loved it even when, after a few years, his complaints turned into equally wordy plaudits.

However, in 1984 the meeting nearly collapsed in confusion. Iveagh, a painfully shy man, hated the AGMs and for one reason or another, due to tax domicile or a claimed illness, had not routinely attended stockholders' meetings. He had not attended my father's first two AGMs. But Ernest was very keen that Iveagh should be publicly seen to be fulfilling his role as chairman, and by 1984 the results were sufficiently positive for him to be able to persuade Iveagh to appear. But a BBC journalist called John Roberts, who was also a shareholder, asked a tricky technical question, and it completely threw the chairman. Iveagh dropped his papers, the company secretary could not find the answers, and the board would have lost an important resolution if the chairman's eyesight had been good enough for him to count the subsequent show of hands accurately.

Luckily, the financial reporters from the London dailies did not usually bother to turn up at the Guinness meeting because it was so far out of town, so the incident went unreported. But afterwards senior representatives from the company's stockbroker and auditor came up to Ernest and said that something had to be done about the board's lack of professionalism – including the chairman. Howard Hughes and Ernest subsequently discussed the idea of Iveagh becoming president of the company, and either Ernest or Lord Boyd becoming chairman. Hughes floated the plan at a meeting with Iveagh, who was not keen. His principal reason was that he did not want to be pilloried in *Phoenix*, the Irish equivalent of the London satirical magazine *Private Eye*. But all this was put to one side as takeover activity gathered momentum later that year, although Boyd continued to handle shareholders' meetings involving votes on technical matters.

*   *   *

The need to keep the company's profits moving forward had led Ernest to think hard about an acquisition programme. Although borrowings had shrunk as a result of the divestment process, massive sums were already committed to modernising the Irish brewing operation, so cash-flow was still going to be negative for the foreseeable future. Nevertheless, Roux's soundings in the City suggested that Guinness now had the credibility to make acquisition moves to demonstrate that the company was past the pure recovery phase and ready to move forward. As the group's stock market capitalisation had climbed from its low of £90 million to £200 million, the stockbrokers' view was that Ernest could consider a takeover worth up to £100 million, which could be partly financed by using new shares. Ernest: 'In fact, the view in the City was that the right acquisitions would be seen positively. But of course a wrong move would have done immense damage to Guinness's still-fragile credibility.'

At first, they considered buying another brewery company as a quick way to expand the group's limited beer brands portfolio. But this option was ruled out in the UK by Guinness's dependence on the other brewers for public-house sales. They would not like to find Guinness competing with them in their pubs, and might refuse to stock Guinness in their other retail premises. Bain was asked to survey available breweries and brands in Europe, the US and Australia. Ernest then made a few tentative enquiries, but there was nothing Guinness could afford. So the search for a takeover was widened to the group's other arm – retailing.

In the early 1980s Britain was in the midst of a high-street boom. Men like Sir Terence Conran, Rodney Fitch and Michael Peters were redesigning the look for familiar names like Boots and W. H. Smith, and the stock market was hungry for new retailing ideas. Successful companies were using their muscle to buy up their rivals. French Connection went public in 1983, Conran was taking over Richard shops and Heals, the new management at Woolworths was beginning to show its paces, and Dixons was eying Currys. Sir Ralph Halpern had revived Burton Group and had let it be known that he was prepared to wave his chequebook.

Ernest knew that he could not compete in the highest reaches of the high street, but Guinness already had a profitable 'neighbourhood' business based on the Lavells newsagents chain and Drummonds the chemists, and just as he was considering his options, W. H. Smith launched a hostile bid for Martins the Newsagents, a much larger business than Lavells. The Guinness head office team in Albemarle

Street urged Ernest to make a counter-offer. He called in Bain to analyse the situation and Roux called in Morgan Grenfell, the merchant bank, to advise on the shape of an offer. While he was in the US on business Ernest received a call from Albemarle Street suggesting he telephone John Martin, Martins' chairman, to see if he might be interested in a friendly deal. He did, but while Martin said he would consider it, he intended to remain independent.

Two weeks later, however, Martin asked to meet Ernest at Albemarle Street. He said that if Schroders, his merchant bank, and Morgan Grenfell could agree a price he would be prepared to do a deal. Ernest: 'It was a real eye-opener to see how the two big merchant banks encouraged their clients to come to terms. In effect Roux, Tony Richmond-Watson at Morgan and his opposite number at Schroders reached agreement very quickly. Maybe this wasn't surprising, as we had been encouraged to go for what was called a "knockout" bid. This was a new word to me in this context, but I soon leaned what it meant: you pay what you have to to get the other side's acceptance. You don't know if the price is too high until you have bought the company and seen its earning potential for yourself. Initially it's a matter of faith and guesswork.'

Roux and Morgan Grenfell persuaded Ernest that they should bid £47 million. His only personal involvement after his initial meeting with John Martin was the deal completion meeting at Morgan's offices late one evening in June 1984. 'Tempers were hot on both sides. Lord Iveagh hired a private jet from Ireland and got lost on the way from the airport. In fact, he never turned up at Morgan's at all.'

When the agreed bid was announced to the stock market, Guinness shares fell sharply. The rationale of the deal had not been explained clearly enough, thus rekindling fears in the City that Guinness was about to embark on another bout of wild diversification. But the shares recovered when the logic behind the takeover became apparent.

Once the group controllers and Bain executives had got inside Martins they recommended integrating it with Lavells under the leadership of Nicholas Ward and John Bristow, who had rationalised Lavells and would do the same at Martins. Ward subsequently asked that Guinness should buy the Lewis Meeson tobacconists chain from Barker & Dobson and the R. S. McColl Scottish newsagents business from the Dallas-based Southland Corporation.

That gave Guinness a chain of more than 1,100 neighbourhood

shops. These enabled the company to reap the full benefits of bulk buying, and become a leader in the confectionery, tobacconist and newsagent sector. To that was added Neighbourhood Stores, a small company which held the UK franchise for 7-Eleven, the convenience store concept that had been developed in America to sell everything from papers and hot snacks to beer, 24 hours a day. Ernest: 'I couldn't help hoping that this might give me the opportunity to control some of my own outlets for Guinness and launch new brands.'

Ernest also cast his eyes abroad for speciality retailing expansion. Guinness picked up the Hediard business in France. He felt that, in addition to its retail outlets, the Hediard brand could be exploited worldwide to carry luxury food and drinks with a French cachet. In the US Guinness acquired Richter Bros., which already had a reputation for selling high-quality imported food and drink products and so would be an ideal vehicle for Hediard and future luxury brands in the US. A toehold outside beer had been established in Europe and the States.

Additionally, Ernest had been convinced since his days at Beecham and Nestlé that there was tremendous potential in marketing the concept of positive health through nutrition and exercise. Kaliber had been designed to make the most of the trend towards health-consciousness, sales of lighter food were rising, and this was the era of aerobics, breakfast television's Green Goddess and the Jane Fonda Workout. But while half the American population was regularly using vitamins and other dietary supplements, only a twentieth did so in Britain. Ernest: 'I could see the possibility of putting together at low cost a group of businesses that would over time grow into a really worthwhile division, and we already had the Drummonds chemists chain as a starting-point.'

In November 1984 he bought Champneys, the 'Rolls-Royce' of health spas, from Grovewood Securities, part of BAT Industries. Then Daphne Swan and her partners sold Guinness the Cranks health-food chain, and Sir Jack Lyons introduced the Nature's Best mail-order vitamin business. Meanwhile Guinness bought Dietary Specialities, which marketed a natural vitamin supplement called Seatone. So for around £5 million the Group had assembled the nucleus of a very promising healthcare business.

In all, Guinness had invested some £100 million, with which it had created a significant retail business and the nucleus of a health business, as well as acquiring class brand names with potential. These were put together to form a development division, and the search began for a main board director able to manage it.

Meanwhile the office in Albemarle Street had become impossibly cramped and inconvenient. Ernest: 'I had a visit from Alan Bond, the Australian entrepreneur. He told me that my office was a disgrace, and if the Group were to be taken seriously we would have to move to more suitable premises. His was the final impetus that led to the move to Portman Square late in 1984, and also the source of the layout of my office suite there. At Bond's suggestion it was made big enough, and had enough telephone lines, for several parallel meetings and conversations to take place – just like a large hotel suite.'

8

THE BID FOR BELL'S

By the end of 1984 Guinness had spent around £100 million on acquisitions, and its equity was valued at £470 million on the stock market. It had a growing retail business, a foothold in the positive health business and a collection of excellent brand names with real possibilities internationally as well as in the UK. But the group was no larger than some of the regional brewers, and it was still regarded as essentially a brewery company by the City. It was tiny by comparison with the likes of Bass or Allied-Lyons. The bull market was raging, everyone was doing deals, and it seemed to be necessary to be seen to keep moving just to stand still, or even to remain independent.

Early in 1985 Ernest was invited to dinner at the luxurious Connaught Hotel, discreetly tucked away between London's Berkeley and Grosvenor Squares. His hosts were Christopher Reeves, Morgan Grenfell's chief executive, and Anthony Forbes, joint senior partner of Cazenove, among the most prestigious stockbroking firms in London, and one that was keen to develop an association with Guinness. 'I was curious. Here I was, chief executive of a brewery company still struggling to get out of the second division, having no personal City connections, being entertained at a top restaurant by two pillars of the City establishment. I couldn't imagine what they had in mind.'

As the meal progressed, they unfolded their plan. Guinness would have to make a major acquisition if it was to promote itself from the second division. And they would help. Guinness should get to work on something big now, even if it meant a contested takeover bid. The company was well regarded. Ernest had the credibility. There was no time to be lost, because of the danger that a predator might have a go at Guinness itself, if the company did not make a move.

This was heady stuff. Ernest went to the office the following day and told Roux and Lord Iveagh. 'We were all tremendously flattered by the attentions of such powerful City figures. If they were correct, surely we should take steps to add to our drinks base, where a major bid would be accepted as a logical move. A UK contested bid in beer was still felt to be impossible, given the group's restrictive relationship with the brewers – but spirits might be another matter. The bid should not be worth more than about £400 million, as that was considered the largest justifiable expansion. The target should preferably be a British company, since we needed to improve our UK earnings – too much profit was currently coming from Ireland and third-world countries. We needed above all another well-known brand with export potential, to fit in with our plans for making Guinness an international brands group.'

Bain, Morgan Grenfell and the Guinness head-office team set to work and researched several possible targets – and Bain and Morgan Grenfell came up with the same suggestion at more or less the same time: Arthur Bell and Son. It was a drinks company dominated by one product, whisky, with a quality brand that had done extremely well, but now appeared to be stagnating. As well as a glass and transport business to bottle and deliver the product, Bell owned the luxurious Gleneagles Hotel Group with three hotels in Scotland and one in London, and a small American wine business. It was the right size, but there was a serious problem: it was Scottish and Ernest was aware of fierce resistance to English takeovers from the so-called Scottish mafia. He called on Charles Fraser, an Edinburgh lawyer and chairman of Morgan Grenfell, Scotland, to advise. And the word was that Raymond Miquel, the chairman of Bell, was not part of the charmed circle north of the border. He had a reputation for being a loner, and took no part in the strongly nationalistic organisations devoted to promoting and defending Scottish commercial interests. His aggressive takeover battle for the Gleneagles group had upset local opinion, and the tartan fund managers were concerned at his future strategy. A marathon-running fitness fanatic, he was known to be keen on getting into the sports industry. His son-in-law was the golf professional at Gleneagles, and he was supposed to be looking at Wilson Sporting Goods, the US golf and tennis equipment firm which was then owned by Pepsi Cola.

He had built the Bell's brand by single-minded leadership of a meticulously drilled military-style sales force which concentrated almost exclusively on pubs and clubs, focusing their attention on the position of the product in the row of spirits optics behind the bar. The salesmen had to put in long hours, always wore green or tartan jackets and were expected to share their leader's devotion to physical exercise – including running in marathons. Raymond Miquel had no compunction about using the many licensed trade charities to muster support against his rivals, many of whom were owned by brewers, and his salesmen would give up their evenings to fly the Bell's flag at social events organised by branches of the Licensed Victuallers' Association, contributing to collection boxes and allegedly making sure that the less glamorous girls always had a dancing partner. They were specifically not allowed to fraternise with 'the enemy' – other whisky company salesmen.

Ernest: 'The centrepiece of their so-called marketing, which was not much more than sales or sales promotion, was a film starring Raymond in every sequence. It was shown to the many trade visitors who came to the Perth head office, and to the financial institutions, who were treated to sales talk rather than financial projections.' Nevertheless, the business had flourished until quite recently, helped by a fashion among whisky drinkers for the less 'obvious' brands from 'independent' distilleries, which in the consumer's mind had an aura of exclusivity when compared with the older, mass-produced image of Haig, Johnnie Walker and other Distillers company brands. According to Guinness's research, Bell's had enjoyed this exclusive status in the past, but it was now being eroded by Famous Grouse, from Highland Distilleries, which had taken over brand leadership in Scotland, thus removing a valuable Bell's promotional claim.

Ernest had made discreet inquiries the year before about the possibility of a friendly deal with Bell. The Saunders family solicitor was Henry King of Denton Hall and Burgin, who was on the Bell board. Ernest casually asked him to think about the idea, and Henry eventually raised the thought with Miquel. The reply was clear: Miquel would never contemplate such an idea, and particularly not in a case where he was unlikely to emerge as boss.

So the almost certain prospect facing Ernest was a hostile bid, of which he had no experience and towards which he felt much trepidation. 'We were going to have to bid in Scotland, with all the difficulties that involved, and against an opponent who, although not apparently a member of the Scottish Establishment, had a formidable reputation as a fighter. We would face a tough battle and I frankly wondered whether we should take this on. Plainly, we would need a first-rate team of advisers.'

Morgan Grenfell continued to push for action. They told Ernest that Guinness needed scale and needed it now, or the group might itself be vulnerable to predators. They also had information regarding Miquel's acquisition searches, which they felt would not impress the City. Indeed, Miquel told Ernest after the battle that he himself had been looking at Guinness as a possible takeover target. So, in great secrecy, Bain prepared an in-depth analysis of Bell and came up with a price that Ernest could justify to Guinness shareholders and the board. 'There was another factor I had to take account of. The Moyne side of the Guinness family had for generations been fanatically against any involvement in the spirits industry. But I had kept Lord Iveagh in the picture as usual, and he told me that when the time came he would handle the matter himself.'

The analysis indicated that Bell would indeed make a good acquisition, and at a board meeting on June 6 Roux outlined the broad strategy of the need for a major step. The board was prepared for a contested bid, but for security reasons only a very limited number of directors was aware of the identity of the target. Mid-June was selected as the time to launch the bid.

On June 10 the operation suddenly had to change gear from highly secretive, systematic and detailed planning, with the involvement of people only on a strictly need-to-know basis, to preparations for immediate action. The Bell share price had started taking off, which inspired a trickle of press stories about a possible bid and Guinness as a possible suitor. The trickle became a flood. When Roux and Ernest were in Scotland on June 13 for a routine institutional visit, they woke to read a major article about their plans in the *Glasgow Herald*. The Bell share price started to run away, and Guinness no longer had time to buy a stake as a platform for the takeover campaign. They would have to bid immediately at a higher price than intended, or abort.

Ernest called a board meeting the evening he and Roux returned from Scotland, to gain formal approval for a bid, and to agree terms. The meeting was marked by an emotional outburst from Lord Moyne's son, Finn Guinness, who usually said nothing and merely took copious notes at board meetings so that he could report back to his father. Jonathan Guinness asked Iveagh to speak to Moyne, which he apparently did. The board agreed to go ahead, and the announcement was scheduled for the following morning, June 14: Guinness was bidding £330 million for Bell.

That night, after the board meeting, Ernest contacted Brian

Basham of Broad Street Associates, the company's public relations adviser, at a restaurant, and he came round to discuss the proposed announcement with Ernest and Chris Davidson, Guinness's in-house public affairs director. They had already decided they would need a Scottish-based PR man, so Davidson brought in Colin Liddell of Charles Barker Scotland. Sir Gordon Reece, who had recently become a consultant to Guinness after his spell as publicity adviser to Mrs Thatcher, liaised with Basham and with Andrew Gifford of the parliamentary lobbyists, GJW. Saatchi & Saatchi was hired to prepare a corporate advertising campaign.

On the night of the board meeting the PR team drew up a plan of action. They would hand-deliver a note to Miquel in Perth first thing in the morning. Ernest would then telephone Miquel, and after that Guinness would announce the bid to the Stock Exchange. It was agreed on Liddell's strong recommendation that Ernest should hold a press conference in Scotland. Basham and Roux would handle the London press initially, while Ernest went to Scotland to chair the press conference at the Sheraton Hotel in Edinburgh. The plans were not finalised until 3 a.m., when Ernest climbed into bed at the Churchill Hotel in Portman Square for a few hours' sleep.

On the financial and legal side, Roux worked with the Morgan Grenfell team and Freshfields the solicitors to produce the documentation. The Morgan team was headed by Antony Richmond-Watson. Wood Mackenzie's Scottish connection would of course be very useful on the stockbroking side but, as they had been warned when they were originally appointed, additional stock market muscle would be needed. Cazenove & Co was asked to come in alongside Woodmac. Ernest broke the news to John Chiene, senior partner of Woodmac, who was none too pleased, but the two firms worked out a means of operating together. Ernest also believed that Morgan Grenfell's contribution should be balanced by having a Scottish merchant bank on board. 'Charles Fraser, Morgan's man in Scotland, was understandably reluctant, but I had heard good things about Angus Grossart of Noble Grossart and made a note to see if he would help.' Roux of course was able to turn to Bain's UK adviser, Sir Jack Lyons, with all his political and financial contacts, including his close associate the broker Anthony Parnes.

In the morning Ernest called the Bell's office at about eight o'clock. He was put through to the company secretary, who said that he had received Ernest's letter, but Bell had no comment to make since Mr Miquel was in America. 'I couldn't believe my luck. Miquel was apparently woken in Chicago at about three in the morning local time, and promptly compiled an aggressive rejection statement. He said that the bid was ridiculous and an insult to Scotland. He was besieged by the press on the phone, and was apparently very prickly about the whole thing – but he refused to return to the UK until the end of his scheduled trip, so I had a whole week to claim the initiative.'

After announcing the bid to the Stock Exchange, Ernest flew to Edinburgh for the press conference, with Davidson, Liddell and Alan Stewart, Davidson's deputy, all of whom are Scots. The entire Scottish media turned up, including representatives from newspapers, TV and radio stations in every corner of the country. 'The questions were hostile, but not as bad as I had anticipated. I emphasised the key objectives of restoring Bell's leadership in Scotland, turning round the declining UK brand share trend, and building Bell's into an international brand – which would boost exports. The questions were very parochial, and related almost exclusively to the fact that a company registered in England was bidding for a Scottish company, and that was inherently bad for Scotland. I decided I would have to spend more time with the Scottish media, as I did not know them at all.' As the bid developed, Ernest often used to go up to Scotland at weekends to update the local journalists, as well as making himself available on the phone from London during the week. 'I think with hindsight that I probably overdid it, because they got used to a high degree of personal input and so became resentful when it was not possible to devote that sort of time to them later, during the Distillers bid.'

In the early days the principal people involved in the bid used to meet every morning in the Portman Square boardroom for coffee at 8.30. There were Richmond-Watson, Roux, the brokers, and Alan Peck of Freshfields on financial and legal matters; Davidson, Stewart, Basham, Reece, Liddell, and Andrew Gifford for PR and lobbying; and Jennifer Laing for advertising advice. Basham was always late, and Reece always arrived with a large cigar in hand. After a review of the press, the meeting usually fragmented, with Roux attending to the financial, City and legal tactics while Ernest concentrated on the PR and advertising aspects. After the first few days the meetings were less well-attended. People would turn up when they could. The brokers in particular felt that their time was better spent at their desks in the City. 'This was the genesis of the so-called "war cabinet" which the media, fed by Basham, incorrectly attributed the

Distillers's bid. In effect it was a logical extension of the normal Monday head office control meeting, and a useful co-ordinating mechanism.'

Reece made it clear early on that Ernest should have one immediate personal objective – to avoid having the bid referred to the Monopolies and Mergers Commission on 'Scottish interest' grounds. There was the direct precedent of the bid by Hiram Walker for Highland Distilleries, which had been blocked by the MMC. To escape the same fate, Ernest would have to work virtually full-time on addressing the Scottish issue and its attendant politics. As Liddell and Gifford concurred with this advice, Ernest accepted it and from then on spent a great deal of time out of the office and on the Glasgow and Edinburgh shuttles. It was no coincidence that the draught Guinness fonts at Heathrow miraculously obtained prime positions at the Terminal One bar during the bid.

On his next visit to Scotland, Ernest arranged to meet Angus Grossart, who said that he would have to think about the proposal that Noble Grossart should join the Guinness team on the bid. Ernest got the impression that Grossart was going to consult James Gulliver, chairman of the Argyll Group, whom the press had indicated was a close friend and client of his. He duly came back to Ernest and said that he had indeed spoken to Gulliver, who had raised no objection! We now know why: Gulliver would have been more than happy for Guinness to become embroiled in the bid for Bell while he himself was, in fact, preparing for an assault of another whisky company. Indeed Gulliver positively encouraged Ernest to go ahead, and wrote a formal note saying that he was not interested in Bell.

But Grossart did have a price for his participation: Noble Grossart to be billed as prominently as Morgan Grenfell in the offer document, which would of course be seen by virtually every influential figure in the British financial community. This was a hard pill for Morgan's people to swallow, but eventually they did and Noble Grossart joined the team. Their man was Peter Stevenson, one of whose most valuable contributions was to write an aggressive model defence document of the sort an on-the-ball Bell might use against them. However, he had used Guinness information for this, and Ernest was subsequently very concerned when Noble Grossart acted for Gulliver in the Distillers bid that Gulliver might have had access to this confidential information, some of which exposed potential Guinness weaknesses.

Raymond Miquel returned from the US on June 16, and immediately irritated the Scottish media by giving his first press conference in London, at his usual venue of the Hilton Hotel in Park Lane. He was apparently tired and irritated, and seemed most uncomfortable answering questions related to financial and political issues. He followed this tactical blunder with a second conference at the Caledonian Hotel in Edinburgh, where he repeated the message, threw out the TV camera crews, and delivered a blistering personal attack on Ernest. He said that no price was acceptable for Bell, and that there was no purpose at all in contemplating a meeting with Guinness, which Ernest had suggested might be useful. He concluded by stressing how he would never work under the Guinness regime. (What he was referring to, as he explained to Ernest after it was all over, was the different way the Park Royal sales force was run, compared with Bell's. At least, that was what he said!) Ernest invited the press to come to the Sheraton afterwards in case there were any questions that he could answer. They all came.

Meanwhile Bill Walker, MP for Tayside North and a close associate of Miquel, was making noises of his own on Bell's behalf. He was feeding the press with constant attacks on Guinness, and demanding the intervention of Parliament to block the bid. This may have gone down well with the Scottish newspapers, but it cut no ice at all in London.

Bell's first counter-attack of its own was an attempt to unseat Morgan Grenfell as Guinness's advisers. Bell was advised by Lord Spens, at this stage employed by the merchant bank Henry Ansbacher – but the association had begun when he was at Morgan, who had floated Bell on the stock market and had also worked on the Gleneagles acquisition.

Encouraged by Spens, Miquel and Walker made a huge fuss, threatening to take legal action against Morgan, and settling for an assault through the City Takeover Panel. A meeting of the full Panel was convened to hear Bell's plea that Morgan should be prevented from acting for Guinness. Morgan was represented at the hearing by Christopher Reeves, the chief executive, and Graham Walsh, head of corporate finance and a former director-general of the Panel. This was a sign of how seriously they took the challenge. Ernest had never seen the Panel in action, so he asked to sit in on the hearing. Initially his request was refused, but he was eventually allowed in to hear the final speeches and the verdict. He was treated to the sight of Lord Spens in full spate. His performance was in direct contrast with Walsh's laid-back approach, which won the day. Bell promptly hired Warburg to act alongside Ansbacher. Ernest: 'I must say, in retrospect, Morgan should have told me more about the history of their relationship with Bell.'

A schedule was prepared for Ernest by those who knew the Scottish political scene and the emotional impact of the so-called 'Scottish ring fence'. It involved visits to the Scottish Office, both in Edinburgh and Whitehall, where he talked to the economic adviser, Dr Gavin McCrone. Ernest met the Secretary of State for Scotland, who was then George Younger, and his deputy Sir William Fraser. Ernest: 'It was what proved to be a typical Whitehall meeting. I was ushered in to see the Secretary of State and his senior aides. They listened politely, thanked me for coming, and said nothing. But the expression on their faces gave no grounds for confidence.' As a brewer, Guinness came under the aegis of the Ministry of Agriculture, Fisheries and Foods, and they too were lobbied and proved supportive. The relevant DTI Minister, Alex Fletcher, was polite, but clearly inclined to support Bell.

Ernest also went to the Scottish Development Association in Glasgow, whose managing director, Dr George Mathewson, seemed more concerned to relate details of his achievements at the SDA, and delicately hinted that he would soon be available to the private sector again. Ernest visited many other Scottish political institutions. He introduced himself to the chairman of the Scotch Whisky Association, John McPhail, who was also chairman of Highland Distilleries, producer of Famous Grouse. McPhail was a former Bell director who had fallen out with Miquel and claimed to be at least neutral towards Guinness.

In addition Ernest and Roux went to see the major Scottish institutional investors, such as Scottish Widows, Scottish Amicable and Ivory and Sime, and toured the Scottish banks. There Ernest met Sir Thomas Risk, Governor of the Bank of Scotland, for the first time. He was polite but disinclined to be supportive. When they were meeting the Scottish financial institutions, Guinness had the assistance of Wood Mackenzie's Edinburgh operation as well as Cazenove and Noble Grossart.

Ernest: 'My reception at these Scottish visits was polite but hardly warm. I rapidly learned to understand the general concern in Scotland about takeovers "from the south", as they called them. And there were specific issues in relation to Bell, concerning supply arrangements with small independent distilleries who had historically supplied part of the Bell's blend, and about the future of its hotels. I put these concerns into context with encouraging proposals regarding Guinness's plans to really do something professional about Bell's export business, which was stagnating.'

Specifically and on the recommendation of its advisers, Guinness gave assurances in its offer document that there would be no redundancies as a result of the takeover. Guinness wanted the Bell's blend unchanged, so there was no problem as far as the small distillery suppliers were concerned. Bell would continue to be managed from Perth, and the plan was that the Gleneagles Hotel would be developed, possibly as part of a luxury health and leisure group in conjunction with Champneys. The document was non-committal about the Piccadilly Hotel in London, a recent Bell acquisition which had not yet been completely refurbished and was allegedly running well over budget.

Ernest: 'In relation to the Gleneagles hotel group, about which we were to be much misquoted, I talked to Sir Hugh Wontner, chairman of the Savoy Hotel Group, and Michael Richardson, his merchant banker and co-director, about a possible link with the Savoy, believing that Gleneagles, the Savoy and perhaps the Hong Kong-based Mandarin Hotels could form a superb luxury group. Every conceivable company was in any case putting in offers for the Bell hotels as soon as we announced our takeover bid. Some were getting involved in the bid itself as a means of forcing our hand, or trying to, but only the Piccadilly had an immediate question mark over it.'

In London, Bill Young from Bain and Freshfields' Nicholas Spearing were putting together a comprehensive dossier on the Bell bid for Guinness to submit to the Office of Fair Trading. Ernest felt that there could not be a competition problem with the bid, because Guinness did not have any whisky interests, so any difficulty would probably centre on the Scottish factor. He met Sir Gordon Borrie, director-general of the OFT, who like other officials listened and said nothing.

Silence was not something the Scottish MPs Ernest saw at the House of Commons shortly after they had been lobbied by Miquel could be accused of. Ernest: 'Bill Walker and Nicholas Fairbairn, the MP for Perth and Kinross, were most insulting and went way beyond mere aggression. The whole meeting, which lasted an hour, was extremely unpleasant. Walker and Fairbairn simply didn't want to listen to us. I had had no previous experience of this sort of event, and it was obviously more hostile than usual as one or two of the other MPs, including Sir Hector Munro, took me and Chris Davidson for a drink afterwards because they felt that the meeting had been unnecessarily antagonistic.'

Walker and Fairbairn continued throughout the bid campaign to make extremely hostile comments. Walker tried to get the matter raised in the House on a number of occasions, referring to the takeover with phrases like 'skulduggery in smoke-filled rooms'. Eventually, despite objections from the Scots and, more surprisingly, some English brewers who seemed to want to ensure that Guinness was kept in its place, on July 23 the OFT recommended to the Department of Trade and Industry that the bid should not be referred to the Monopolies and Mergers Commission. Guinness had surmounted the formal political hurdle, but even so the entrenched antagonism from Scotland never died.

Despite Miquel's public refusal to contemplate such an event, on June 25 Ernest had one brief meeting with Miquel and Henry King, the solicitor. Tom Ward had maintained contact with King and they set up a meeting at the Sheraton Park Tower, where Miquel normally stayed when he was in London. Inevitably, it came to nothing. Most of the time was spent on deciding what would not be said in a press statement to be issued afterwards. 'But the meeting left me convinced that Miquel would fight to the bitter end.'

Tony Richmond-Watson of Morgan Grenfell calmly orchestrated the bid strategy and tactics like a military operation. Ernest: 'He had a timetable organised around documents and dates. There were dates for sending out the offer document, closing dates for increased bids, final closing dates and all sort of procedures related to the workings of the City Takeover Code. I never really understood it all, and was happy to delegate this side of things to Roux, working with Richmond-Watson, Noble Grossart and Freshfields while I concentrated on developing the fundamental sales message to shareholders, which research told me should focus on the proposition that Bell had lost its way.' This demonstrated that Bell, after years of growth, had been consistently losing UK market share and Scottish brand leadership to Famous Grouse. Its valuable claim about being Scotland's 'No. 1' was, Ernest emphasised, an important asset that Bell had lost. They had also made little progress overseas and attempts at diversification had been haphazard. The rebuilding of the Piccadilly Hotel, which had been bought as a means of bouncing people arriving from Heathrow up to Gleneagles, was way over budget and suffered from a complex arrangement with the Kuwait Investment Office over the lease. 'As for the rest, we felt that lorries, glassmaking and Wellington Wines in the US were irrelevant to the core business. Bell would do better under Guinness.'

Morgan's tactical manoeuvrings, using all their traditional skills, undeniably had a material effect on the course of the bid. Not experienced in these matters, Bell had been forced to bring in a new merchant bank late in the day, and Miquel spent considerable time travelling between London and Perth by rail, which put him out of action at key periods.

Guinness had started the bid without any Bell shares, but a block became available from the Kuwait Investment Office, who had apparently been instructed by their government to sell their interests in alcoholic drinks. On the advice of Noble Grossart, Guinness bought their shares. Ladbroke Group bought a three per cent stake in Bell, saying that they wanted 'trading arrangements'. They eventually sold to Guinness. There were continuous tactical flurries involving the Takeover Panel, most of which Morgan won. 'One got the impression that there was a sort of business game going on between the City people and the regulators, in which the client was an amateur in a club of professional players. Roux was clearly exhilarated by what he was learning from his day-to-day involvement with the City. He told me on several of our trips how he enjoyed the City, and how his career thoughts were moving in that direction, rather than in consultancy or business management.'

Although many of Bell's shareholders were south of the border, the biggest single investor in the company was General Accident, the insurance company whose head office was across the road from Bell's in Perth. Angus Grossart decided that a special effort should be made to court General Accident. He arranged for Ernest to meet Sir Norman Macfarlane, a director of the insurers, before Sir Norman's planned day at the Wimbledon tennis championships. Ernest: 'Sir Norman was pleasant, he listened and asked questions, including some about supply arrangements for whisky bottle caps.' Sir Norman owned a company that made such caps, but he was not then a supplier to Bell.

For the other institutional shareholders, Roux prepared a flip-chart presentation of Guinness's case, and he and Ernest took this round on a roadshow through London and Scotland mapped out by Cazenove and Wood Mackenzie. The Guinness case was supplemented by a Saatchi & Saatchi advertising campaign on the theme

'Bell's has lost its way: Guinness is Good for You'. It was a highly visible campaign, using full pages in the national press, and it was the first time that a consumer products advertising agency had taken part in a corporate takeover battle. They were able to use the old, but now banned slogan, 'Guinness is Good for You', because it referred to Guinness the company rather than the stout.

Ernest: 'In retrospect we probably overdid the amount we spent on advertising, but at the time we felt that we had more of a job to do to convince Bell's shareholders than in fact proved to be the case.'

As the dates on Richmond-Watson's chart passed, one question remained. Did Guinness need to raise its bid? Without exception, the media seemed to think so. Feedback from institutions was mixed. Ernest met a number of fund managers on a wet Sunday in July at the Windsor Great Park polo ground. His impression was that Guinness was expected to make some additional gesture. Morgan, Cazenove and Wood Mackenzie were giving Roux similar advice. Richmond-Watson formally recommended to the Guinness board that the offer for Bell be increased. On August 7 the bid was raised from £330 million to £370 million and declared to be the final offer, so that it could not be improved any further under the Takeover Code. At that point every broker's circular and, in due course, every newspaper City editor in London supported Guinness. Ernest: 'It was as if we had paid our dues to the financial community, who all wanted a little bit more. Maybe it was naïvety on my part to agree. Maybe we could have won without the increase.'

Miquel rejected the new offer, but Peter Tyrie, the former head of Gleneagles Group before Bell bought it, decided to dissociate himself from this reaction, and instead recommended shareholders to accept the Guinness bid. Through the introduction of Noble Grossart, Ernest had met Tyrie, since he wanted to know about Guinness's interest in the hotel and leisure business. Ernest: 'I told him in confidence about my thoughts regarding the possibility of developing a health and leisure group which might embrace the Savoy, but it was Peter Stevenson of Noble Grossart who encouraged Tyrie to dissociate himself from the rest of the board and recommend Bell's shareholders to accept the bid.'

On the last weekend of the bid, when it was clear that it was going Guinness's way, Bell stirred up a 'white knight' scare, suggesting that the Rothmans International tobacco group was considering a friendly counterbid. Ernest found this incredible, but took the trouble to find out if it was true. As Rothmans is ultimately South

African-controlled, he contacted the South African ambassador in London, who was a friend of Sir Jack Lyons, but could get no confirmation from Johannesburg. Eventually Sir Robert Crichton-Brown, Rothmans' UK chairman, was contacted in Australia by the media and denied that his company was involved. A formal repudiation was issued on the Monday, in which it was clear that Rothmans had told Bell as long ago as the previous Thursday that it had 'no plan or intention' to make a bid. Ernest subsequently found out that the two firms had indeed talked, but on what basis and on whose initiative he could not discover.

The story was inflated by the Scottish press, but the end result was merely to make Bell look desperate. The emergence of Rothmans produced the unexpected bonus of blowing the Liberal Party leader, David Steel, into the Guinness camp, since he was adamant that a South African organisation should not be permitted to run Bell at a time of general disinvestment in South Africa. He pointed out that Miquel could no longer claim to be in the business of keeping Bell independent when he was seen to be supping with other potential masters. Miquel did indeed insist, even after Rothmans withdrawal, that he was talking to 'one or two' other interested parties. But Morgan Grenfell punctured that claim by inquiring whether Bell had passed any material information to any other companies. When Bell had to admit that it had not, the game was up. On the last day of the bid, at the last hour before the offer closed, General Accident told Miquel that it was assenting to the offer. At that point Guinness was assured of winning more than the fifty per cent of Bell's shares necessary for control. The battle was over.

Just before the bid ended, Brian Basham of Broad Street Associates irritated the Guinness board by allowing himself to be quoted in *The Sunday Times* as claiming that he virtually controlled the entire Guinness campaign, everyone else including the Guinness management being little more than his puppets. He gave the impression that all major bids, not just this one, involved manipulation by public relations people, whose skills largely determined the outcome. Some institutional shareholders, Ernest was later told, actually changed their minds and decided to stay with Bell as a result of this – but not enough to make any difference. Ernest: 'It was also in this article that Basham referred to the so-called "war cabinet", which was entirely his definition of Guinness's meetings, and which he then described as the alleged decision-making cabal during the Distillers bid. He was not even acting for Guinness in that campaign.'

Guinness had won its first contested takeover against a tough and vociferous opponent, but one not supported in the City or even to any significant extent in Scotland.

'We felt that we had won a tough, tiring and aggressively unpleasant battle, but Guinness had done its planning and was well prepared. Bell never really got organised. It was a comparatively easy victory in the end, but it did not seem so at the time.'

As soon as it was all over Ernest briefed a meeting of Guinness managers at Park Royal. 'They were bubbling over with enthusiasm. It was hard to believe that morale had sunk so low just a few years before.' He also consulted Henry King as to the best way to handle the defeated Miquel. King advised waiting a few days. Ernest: 'In the interim I formulated the view that since Miquel had allegedly devised the Bell sales system personally, and had exerted such a strong personal control over everything to do with the sales force, maybe I had better think the hitherto unthinkable and persuade him to stay on, at least on a temporary basis, to ensure a smooth transition.'

When King told Ernest that Miquel had calmed down, they arranged to meet. Miquel agreed to stay for a while, and Shaun Dowling from Guinness would come into Bell as vice-chairman. Ernest also put Bill Young of Bain on to the board since he had done so much of the detailed analysis on Bell, and in some ways knew the company better than they did themselves.

For the next few weeks Ernest and the rest of the Guinness team sampled the Miquel management style at first hand. 'Whether we were in Perth, Gleneagles, London or New York, we were subjected to a non-stop monologue of sales-orientated lecturing, with the odd diversion on how the cloth on billiard tables should be maintained.'

Dowling instituted at Bell the weekly control meetings which had been so effective at Guinness. They became his means of getting into the operation systematically. Eventually Dowling came to Ernest with the request that Miquel should no longer stay since split loyalties were getting in the way of performance. Ernest: 'Raymond was paid off with an excellent deal, including life membership of Gleneagles and his precious Aston-Martin car with personalised number plates. But, although he went happily at the time, I realised later that his bitterness obviously lingered, as did the resentment of others, including the two MPs, Walker and Fairbairn.'

Dowling was an excellent asset-stripper by nature, and concentrated on short-term profit improvements. His focus was primarily on the non-whisky side of Bell, which included the hotels, but also on cost savings on the whisky side. It was decided to sell the Piccadilly at the best price, because its costs were wildly overrunning and there was no sensible way in which the bedrooms could be brought up to the necessary five-star standard. Fortunately, Guinness was receiving offers for the hotels all the time. One marketing idea that Ernest put into action at the Piccadilly was to install a Champneys London club, which the Champneys people had always wanted but had never been able to afford.

The Gleneagles Hotel in Scotland also needed money spent on it, and Ernest was happy to agree to that. The Mark Phillips Equestrian Centre was developed to encourage custom. The Caledonian Hotel in Edinburgh was also upgraded.

Before long Peter Tyrie, the former Bell's rebel, was tempted by an offer to join the Mandarin Hotels Group. Ernest: 'His departure caused the first reassessment of our future in the hotel business – other than the Gleneagles Hotel itself – which the Distillers bid was to solidify.'

Sir Peter Parker, chairman of glassmakers Rockware Group, put in a bid for Bell's glass business, but while negotiations rumbled on the two sides could not agree on price. Guinness had to invest in a new furnace if it was to maintain the operation, but in the end the glass business too was affected by the Distillers bid.

Wellington Wine was in a far worse state. 'It was a total mess,' says Ernest. 'There were major personnel and management problems, and it made sense only as part of Bell's distribution arrangements.' It was eventually merged with Distillers' US operations.

On Bell's export side, the first priority was to stop the US losses stemming from the costly programmes that had been Miquel's personal creation. 'The advertising and sales operations there were entirely inappropriate,' says Ernest. 'National advertising and the odd billboard on the way to Kennedy Airport to support a few outlets in Florida did not make sense, especially as the stockists down there would destock as soon as Miquel's back was turned. This operation was discontinued.'

The most important strategic marketing venture in which, for once, Ernest was unable to get adequately involved due to pressure of work, was a new advertising campaign for the Bell's brand. 'It needed a new image: we needed to understand how to reposition Bell's, because by then in car terms it was being seen as an old Ford Cortina, while Famous Grouse was the BMW!'

Ernest was asked to participate in the final selection of an advertising agency. They choose Wight Collins Rutherford Scott, who had an excellent reputation through campaigns like 'Less bovver than a hovver' for Qualcast lawnmowers. They were also the agency for BMW cars, so they had a feel for the fashionable consumer goods market. Unfortunately Ernest never saw much of WCRS, which was out of character with his normal way of operating. Coincidentally or not, Guinness was one of the few clients who failed to get a memorable campaign out of that agency. In the end Ernest transferred the account to Frank Lowe of Lowe Howard-Spink, because he felt that at least he knew how Lowe operated. Lowe's Campaign worked.

Bell had agreed to sponsor the Ryder Cup golf tournament in the autumn of 1985 as a result of Miquel's personal sporting tastes. The hospitality tent for Bell at this event was enormous, but Ernest was shocked to see both how few guests were there and who those guests were. Bell had apparently not made any attempt to use this major sporting event to attract many of the potential large customers who were not stocking Bell's. 'Everyone, especially the bar staff, was enjoying the festivities, but it was a wasted exercise from a business point of view.'

The idea of associating whisky with sport worked well. Guinness subsequently arranged for Bell's to sponsor a polo match at Windsor, which was a great success. They had also inherited a soccer award known as 'Bell's Manager of the Month', in which a Football League club manager would be presented with a huge bottle of Bell's for the month's outstanding achievement. Ernest is a great soccer fan, and was a director of Queens Park Rangers through Guinness's earlier sponsorship of the west London club. To my mother's irritation he went to every home match, and started to watch out for the Bell's Manager of the Month presentation. He also ensured that Bell's was available at QPR, but was annoyed to discover that it was not available in the directors' bar at many grounds – even though the home club's board would happily watch their man receive the Manager of the Month award. As the applause died away at such occasions, many a chairman would find Ernest at his side expressing disappointment that his 'favourite' whisky was not to hand.

One of the earliest new promotional ideas was for a bell-shaped porcelain decanter to be produced bearing portraits of Prince Andrew and Sarah Ferguson, in honour of their engagement. This was particularly popular with homeward-bound tourists when they stopped off in Heathrow's duty-free shops.

Perth remained Bell's headquarters. It took six months for Ernest to recruit from Seagrams an excellent marketing-orientated managing director, Rob Hermans. Work then began on a comprehensive consumer research programme to supplement the work that had been done on Bell's before the bid. Particularly urgent was the market situation in Scotland, where Bell's was losing ground fast. 'As with Guinness in my early days, we needed a promotional programme to tide us over while we developed a new advertising campaign and a fresh marketing approach.'

Hermans got to work on this and the new advertising. He also built a marketing department, which Bell had never had. On the strength of his progress, Ernest ultimately decided to merge the whole Distillers UK sales and marketing operations with Bell, and let Bell run the lot – from Scotland.

As a result of the takeover, the financial press was very much in favour of Guinness's achievements. Ernest had many requests for interviews and articles, and the share price went to an all-time high, taking Guinness to a market capitalisation of nearly £1 billion. His personal standing was also high. Guinness shareholders, including of course the Guinness family, were six times better off than when he had joined the company. He was proud of what had been achieved in only four years. He was also exhausted. We all badly needed a holiday. He was worried about the aspects of the business that had inevitably taken second place during the Bell bid, but we forced him to take a two-week break at the end of August 1985.

9

THE DECISION TO BID FOR DISTILLERS

While Ernest was on holiday he learned from the *Sunday Telegraph* that James Gulliver, Chairman of the Argyll Group, intended to launch a highly leveraged bid for Distillers.

'My reaction to the *Sunday Telegraph* article was nothing very much initially, but over the next few weeks after I got back to the office we had to start thinking about the possible significance to Guinness and Bell if anybody, not necessarily Argyll, took over the biggest player in the international whisky business. I was not at all concerned, as has been suggested, about the Bell's brand in the UK market, because our research had shown quite clearly that in terms of which drinkers might switch from Bell's it was in direct competition only with Famous Grouse and Teachers. None of the Distillers brands seemed likely to have an impact on Bell's.'

However, Ernest gradually became concerned about the effect of a change of ownership at Distillers on the stability of the global marketplace. Raymond Miquel had rightly insisted that the price in the UK could and should be maintained at a high level. If anyone started slashing the price, consumers might feel that the drink was no longer fashionable. There was reckoned to be a cycle in the UK whisky industry. A less well-known private brand like Famous Grouse or Bell's would start to become fashionable. Sales would rise to the point where it would become a mass-market brand, and that would leave a gap for a new brand to become the cognoscenti's favourite. Distillers, with long-established brands like Johnnie Walker, Haig and White Horse, was not in this game at all. But whisky was a declining market internationally, and there was a large surplus of unsold stocks – a whisky lake. Distillers was widely regarded as a poorly managed company. If Argyll did not make a bid, Suntory or Seagram or somebody would, so the risk of market instability would not go away.

But time was against Guinness: it needed breathing space in which to reorientate Bell, and meanwhile, on September 2 1985, James Gulliver had been forced by the mounting speculation into making a statement that Argyll would not bid for Distillers 'at the present time'. The Takeover Panel had got them to agree that that meant at least three months.

Ernest: 'We discussed the situation internally at Guinness, in relation to what we needed to do to speed up our plans for Bell. At the back of my mind there was always the thought that, whoever got Distillers, there might be an opportunity for us to pick up some additional brands – particularly if somebody did a leveraged buyout and needed to sell something off. There was a lot of joking from stockbrokers, suggesting that we had gone for the wrong company in buying Bell, but that was nonsense. Our biggest acquisition before Bell had been Martin the Newsagent for £47 million, and even that had knocked our share price because the City didn't think we could cope with it. Bell was pretty big, and there was no way that we could have gone for anything bigger. I had in fact asked Morgan Grenfell about Distillers when we were discussing Bell the year before, and Christopher Reeves had laughed, saying that the City would never wear it.'

At this stage in the rumours about Distillers, Ernest told his top team to keep their ears to the ground while he remained open-minded and drew up a list of brands that he might like to buy if the chance arose: Booth's or Gordon's gin, Pimm's, one or two of the brandies.

In October Olivier Roux visited Hoare Govett, who were admirers of Guinness as well as being Distillers' stockbrokers. The brokers were left with the impression that Guinness would be willing to help Distillers to fend off Argyll. Word got back to Gulliver, who knew my father well enough to get on to him direct. They knew one another through their mutual interest in football: my father was a director of Queens Park Rangers, while Gulliver was on the board of Manchester United. Ernest invited him to lunch at the Guinness office.

'Gulliver came rushing round to lunch. He said to me, "Are you still interested in brands?" I said, yes, of course I was still interested in brands. Was he saying that if Argyll took over Distillers there might be some brands floating around? He was non-committal. He asked me about Roux having allegedly said to Hoare Govett that we'd like to stop Argyll. I said that if he said that, he said it without my authority, but we were certainly interested in knowing what was going on. Gulliver had come to lunch on a fishing expedition.'

Ernest's prevailing view at this stage was that Distillers was simply too big for Guinness, and anyway my father was personally exhausted by the Bell acquisition.

Ernest: 'I had not enjoyed all the aggro with Miquel during that bid, even though it had been a good victory. I was spending a lot of time in Scotland, looking at Gleneagles and McColls, the retail chain. I gave a talk to the Scottish Institute of Directors, at which Malcolm Rifkind, the Secretary of State for Scotland, was the after-dinner speaker. We had a pleasant chat.'

In November Ernest went to what proved to be a pivotal event: a meeting at Gleneagles of the Scottish Council for Development and Industry, a regular gathering of that country's great and good. He was conscious of the need to meet people in Scotland now that Guinness owned Bell and was therefore part of the region's community.

Ernest: 'Charles Fraser, the lawyer chairman of Morgan Grenfell Scotland, introduced me around. Most of the chat was about Distillers and how awful they were, and how somebody should take them over because anyone would be better than what they had. Everybody assumed Argyll would bid, but not everyone was in favour.'

Gulliver had for some years owned a spirits firm called Amalgamated Distilled Products, which had been brought into Argyll. But its whiskies had been lampooned in the satirical magazine *Private Eye*, as 'Mickey Mouse' brands. They had names like 'Glen Scotia' and 'Scotia Royal' that seemed to have been dreamed up to give them an instant history. This sort of transparent marketing was anathema to the Scottish establishment, which prided itself on its genuine centuries-old traditions. And it had not gone unnoticed that, although he was a Scot by birth, Gulliver had left the homeland at the age of 31 to make his fortune. He had joined the Scottish Council for Development and Industry and the Scottish Economic Council to keep in with the local sources of power and influence, but there were still question marks about him in the minds of the more conservative cliques. And furthermore Argyll, primarily a retail group and not a thoroughgoing drinks company, had its head office in Hayes, Middlesex.

In the light of these reservations, Charles Fraser had been thinking about forming a consortium to bid for Distillers, on the lines of the Paternoster bid for Woolworths in 1982. He raised the subject with Ernest at that Gleneagles gathering. As managing director he was thinking of Gordon Waddell, a former Scottish international rugby player who had married Mary Oppenheimer, a daughter of the South African mining tycoon, Harry Oppenheimer. Ernest: 'Fraser said to me that maybe there could be an investor role for Guinness as a member of this consortium. I thought, maybe I can get hold of some brands.'

Shortly afterwards Ernest met Reeves and Graham Walsh, the head of corporate finance, at Morgan Grenfell. It was an ad hoc chat about strategy. Talk fell to the question of Guinness's size in what had become a mega-bid era. American and Japanese banks were rushing around trying to persuade people to do deals, which would generate huge fees and interest payments to them, on the back of what was then a roaring bull market on the Stock Exchange. The Morgan men pointed out that, even after the Bell takeover, Guinness was still no bigger than a largish regional brewery group in the drinks field. It was still miles behind combines like Bass or Allied-Lyons, in which the Australian entrepreneur John Elliott's Elders IXL had taken a stake, so it was by no means safe. And the real giants, like Seagrams and Anhauser Busch, were making noises about global expansion.

Ernest: 'I had an uncomfortable feeling that we were probably still too small, and for two reasons. First, we could be vulnerable to a takeover. Second, the drinks business would surely be dominated by world giants, where you either had to be up there with the biggest or resign yourself to becoming a regional or specialist operator. There was therefore a dilemma about what we should do. Were we going to be one of the giants, or were we going to take a role as a specialist?'

Reeves and Walsh took a very bullish view. They were, after all, the number one merchant bank for mergers and acquisitions at that time, and they had suffered one or two setbacks recently. They needed a big victory to restore their reputation – and of course another large bid by Guinness would generate a huge income for them. There were also rumours beginning to circulate about Morgan Grenfell going public in its own right, which it did in 1986. So they were pushing Ernest quite hard, telling him that he could not rest on his laurels, and it would be good for Guinness shareholders if the company was among the top twenty British companies, and to achieve that Ernest would have to make one more big move.

'At that, I just sighed. I went home and told Carole, and thought, "What am I letting myself in for?" The idea of going through another Bell campaign was just awful. I talked about it to a number of people in the company, including non-executive directors like Arthur Furer. If we had to make an acquisition in order to get scale, I asked, why not go further into retailing? It was a booming area. Or what about the health business? Champneys and Nature's Best were just a toe in the water, and we had added the Cranks restaurant chain that month. I began to think, fancifully but aloud to Morgan Grenfell, what about Beecham? I would love to go for that, and they were having management problems at that time. But I suspect that Morgan were looking at it with another client. Retailing, then? I thought of Boots, which has a strong health aspect, but they too were a Morgan client. I thought of linking Champneys and Gleneagles to make a super luxury hotel group, with a Champneys in each one.'

At another level there was also talk of a joint venture with Underwoods, another Morgan client, who were interested in some of Guinness's Drummonds and Martins outlets. That was when Ernest first met Roger Seelig, who was a director of Underwoods and one of Morgan's star corporate finance people. Another idea of Seelig's was to develop *The Guinness Book of Records* business in conjunction with Paul Hamlyn's Octopus Books, where he was also involved.

Ernest: 'I was impressed with Roger Seelig. He struck me as a dynamic, forceful individual. I knew his reputation, Reeves had described him as the most entrepreneurial man in the bank and I could see him working out ideas as we were talking: he seemed to be able to think of several things at once.'

Walsh subsequently reported that Morgan had had an internal review made of the Boots/Beecham/hotels ideas. They reckoned that Beecham was just too big, and lots of other big players would get involved as well as the government, and they did not think that Guinness could cope with that, to which Ernest replied that maybe the answer was for him to offer himself to the headhunters as the next chairman of Beecham. That did not go down too well, but Walsh was not keen on the Boots plan, although he offered to make an introduction. And the other ideas would not be big enough to have an impact on Guinness's strategy.

Then Walsh said: 'You must bear in mind that no company can feel safe today, with merchant banks running slide-rules over every company in Britain. The thing to do is to put yourself on the map in the drinks business. There are only going to be five or six companies in the business in a few years. You should go for Distillers, it's in play, we'll back you all the way and we've shown with Bell that we know how to win bids. Guinness has the credibility, and it needs to use it.' From Scotland, Fraser was pushing too, becoming more and more positive and reporting growing discontent with the idea of Gulliver winning Distillers.

Ernest: 'I thought about it for a couple of days. I was busy doing other things. It was a huge dilemma. I thought about Morgan's motivations for not considering the other possibilities I had suggested. Only later did I discover that Gulliver had been to Morgan in the early days, maybe two years before, to get them to take him on in his original thoughts about Distillers, and they turned him down. I remembered they had been Bell's bank at one time as well. I talked to Roux and Iveagh and Ward. We agreed that from the point of view of stock market credibility and the world drinks market and a wonderful brands portfolio passing us by, maybe it did make sense once and for all to make it to the top of the world drinks league. Iveagh was extraordinary. He was completely positive and said he would support any move I wanted to make. He said the family could have been the British Rockefellers or Rothschilds, with the Guinness Mahon Bank as well, but they had lost their way. So anything that could put the Guinness family back in the big time he was in favour of. Even though the Moyne branch of the family had disclosed during the Bell bid that they had reservations about the spirits industry.'

Nevertheless, it seemed worth getting Bain to upgrade the considerable amount of background information they already had on the spirits market, to get some idea of values and see if a bid for Distillers might make financial sense. Bill Young of Bain was sent off to work on that exercise. But my father still had doubts.

Ernest: 'Personally, I was not at all convinced that we could do it. I wanted to keep our options open on the small deals I had mentioned to Morgan. We still had not got the top management we needed. Vic Steel had only just joined the company from Beecham: at last I had got a main board director for beer. But I hadn't got a director for the development group. And we still had the long-term problem of finding a successor to Roux. I was frantically busy with Bell, and catching up with the rest of the business. I had an ongoing personal conflict between my own feelings about not wanting to get into another big bid so soon, and the fact that on a professional level I felt I owed it to the shareholders of Guinness to put their company into the big league. Was I putting the company at risk by not doing it? What other British company would become available, where we could use shares to make this jump?'

My father might not have wanted to get into a Distillers battle for personal reasons, but the professional in him, bred to a sense of duty by my grandfather, was starting to take over. Bill Young produced an up-to-date analysis. Ernest was putting himself in the position to be able to take a proper decision somewhere down the line. He told Morgan that there was no way he would take on Distillers on a contested basis. 'I said that I would certainly prefer the brands to the business. But if and when there was a call for a white knight, only then would I contemplate a full bid.'

Ernest renewed contact with John Connell, the Stowe and Oxford-educated chairman of Distillers. They had met after Guinness won Bell, as part of Ernest's round of meetings with senior people in the whisky industry. Then they had talked amicably about the whisky lake, and Connell had revealed that he had been at school with Edward Guinness. This time the mood was very different: Connell was a man at bay.

Ernest: ' I went to see him at the end of November, just about the time when they appointed Sir Nigel Broackes to their board. He had this wonderful office overlooking St James's Square. He said very little, but there was a large Scotch in his hand. He struck me as a man already bowed by the pressure he was under. He said, "That horrible little grocer wants that chair," – pointing to his own "and this office. He won't sell this office: he wants to sit here." Connell wanted advice on PR. I didn't say anything about what I had at the back of my mind. I wanted to see how he was reacting. I recommended Tim Bell in London and Colin Liddell in Scotland, two advisers I had used. I also recommended he find a more aggress-ive financial PR company than Streets, because I understood that Brian Basham of Broad Street was in the wings behind Gulliver. Basham had acted for me in the Bell bid. We agreed to keep in touch.'

Guinness completed the purchase of the Cranks health-food res-taurant business, and Ernest had a meeting with Paul Hamlyn about a tie-up with *The Guinness Book of Records*. Nothing was decided about Distillers. At this time, my father would abruptly walk out of meetings and go for a stroll round the garden in Portman Square, turning the options over in his mind.

On December 2, Argyll bid £1.87 billion for Distillers. Suddenly, the pace changed. The bankers went to action stations. Decisions had to be made.

Ernest: 'It was like a tidal wave. I felt we were being dragged along faster and faster. I was getting reports from Bain and Roux that the numbers looked reasonable: we could make a bid that added up. With all the excitement in the place, I talked to Steel, Iveagh, Furer and Ward. The more we talked, the more people caught the mood. My colleagues were moving from "we don't want to tackle this" to "maybe we should" to "isn't it tempting?" The momentum was gathering.'

Anthony Richmond-Watson had been the Morgan man acting for Guinness during the Bell bid, but towards the end of 1985 he became involved with yet another Morgan client, United Biscuits, in its three-way struggle with Hanson and Imperial Group. Ernest: 'I said that if I'm going to be expected to tackle something giant, I want the best man you have on my side.' Reeves asked for time to think about the matter. Eventually he phoned to say he had decided that Seelig should be the man. Reeves added: 'He is a very powerful personality and will want to do things his way.'

My father found himself engulfed by the general enthusiasm for this vast project, an enthusiasm which was being fuelled by Morgan and Bain, who were both highly motivated to get into the battle: both would be getting handsome fees. A major review of the situation was fixed to be held at Bain's office on December 23. Apart from Ernest, there was Fraser, Ward, Roux, Seelig, Salz, Mayhew and the Bainies.

The clock was ticking. If Argyll's bid was cleared by the Office of Fair Trading, Guinness would have a mountainous task to catch up. They faced an aggressive competitor, James Gulliver, with excellent advisers and very well prepared. And he had been planning his bid for possibly two years. Although Guinness knew about the Scotch whisky industry, there had not been enough time to analyse Distillers comprehensively. If Ernest and his team were going to enter the race, speed was vital. They risked a reverse of the Bell situation, where they had been much better prepared than their opponents.

'At that review meeting we spent a lot of time discussing the advantages of the white knight strategy, under which we would wait for Distillers to call us into the fight as their saviour. There was general enthusiasm for the idea. Roux said he would need to do more work on the numbers over Christmas. Salz was asked to prepare an OFT submission. Fraser said why bother about the white knight strategy, why not just go for it. I said no, we must wait until Distillers are prepared to give up the thought of remaining independent, and then we might move in.'

Ernest went to Switzerland as usual to be with the family at Christmas, but he did not have much of a holiday. At Les Diablerets he can think more clearly than anywhere else. He mulled over the implications of what was happening. He was now strongly tempted by the idea of turning Guinness into a world brands company in one leap, after which he could relax. And my father is unashamedly patriotic: he was attracted by the thought of being able to play a significant role in improving British whisky exports.

'Skiing gives me a boost, but I was tired. I was taking on a tough, ruthless opponent. He had hired Brian Basham, an equally ruthless public relations adviser, Saatchi & Saatchi, the number one advertising agency, and Noble Grossart, the aggressive Scottish merchant bank. All three had been on the inside of our planning for the Bell bid, and we were forced to keep Basham on for the time being, because if we severed links with him it would have been as good as admitting that we were thinking of entering the contest. And the scale of the whole thing was frightening.'

Tom Ward came over with his family. With their wives, the two of them met Arthur Furer for dinner at the Montreux Palace. As is still the custom in Switzerland, after dinner the wives were ushered away into a corner while the men talked. The size of the Distillers bid did not seem particularly spectacular to Furer, for Nestlé was itself huge. He was enthusiastic.

Ernest: 'Furer talked about what he saw as the necessity of getting Guinness shares quoted on the world's stock markets if we were to be a world-scale company. I could see the glint in Furer's eye. Bank Leu, where he was a director, could be put on the map by becoming the Swiss lead bank in an international stock market listing programme, which did later happen.' So, like many others involved in the battle, Furer's enthusiasm had other motives.' Ward was also very positive about the idea, but basically reckoned that the risk of a Guinness bid being referred to the Monopolies and Mergers Commission, or losing the bid itself, was such that the Guinness board would never buy it, and the shareholders would be up in arms. He felt we would have to come up with some way of protecting our downside on the bid costs.

On New Year's Eve, our family had dinner at a local restaurant with our friends, Walter and Uly Pacht and their children. Ward and my father turned up for the coffee. 'Ward had come to the conclusion that we definitely had to hedge the costs. He said we would have to find some way of making Distillers underwrite our bid costs. I said that that had never been done before. Ward said that didn't matter.'

On December 30, during that dead week between Christmas and New Year, Distillers had published its formal defence to the Argyll bid. It contained few surprises, saying 'Argyll is unsuited for the stewardship of the Scotch whisky industry because the majority of its business is as a UK discount supermarket operator. Where Argyll is in the Scotch whisky industry it also trades predominantly on low prices.'

But on the Saturday after the New Year, January 4, *The Times* sent up a flare with a story speculating that Guinness was about to make a counterbid. Ernest: 'Sir Nigel Broackes, who had just joined the board of Distillers, was very keen on the white knight idea and he was a great pal of Kenneth Fleet, *The Times* finance and industry editor. But in my view this was a Basham tryout to see what reaction it produced.'

There are no deliveries of British newspapers to Les Diablerets at weekends, so the earliest the article would reach us in Switzerland was on the following Tuesday. In the meantime Melvyn Marckus had been trying to phone my father on the Saturday, but he decided not to talk to the press. Bay Green, the Kleinworts man acting for Distillers, phoned and read part of *The Times* article.

Ernest: 'I said we couldn't possibly talk about it on the telephone. We agreed to meet in London when I got back. I returned the following day and reached the office on the Monday, January 6. The Guinness annual results were due to be presented on the 14th, and I had a big review meeting with Vic Steel all day. He had joined the company in October, so he had been with us long enough for me to want to know what his thoughts were on the beer business.'

Ernest met Green for breakfast on the 8th, at the New Piccadilly Hotel, where Ernest was staying. Green brought Mark Birch with him. Green said that he thought the OFT would clear the Argyll bid. Distillers were talking about white knights: was Guinness interested? My father was very carefully non-committal, and suggested that Green have a chat with Seelig. The two bankers knew one another well, because they were both working on the bid by Sir Terence Conran's group, for British Home Stores. Ernest suggested waiting until Argyll was formally cleared by the OFT, and then they could meet again. 'I didn't say yes and I didn't say no,' he remembers, 'but the subject was now on the table.'

He promptly told Roux about the meeting, and phoned Iveagh. He then put Steel on alert, in case he might be needed. At lunch that day he had to cope with a fishing expedition by Kenneth Fleet over a previously-arranged lunch which was also attended by Chris Davidson, the public relations director at Guinness. Ernest: 'We got into discussions about what chief executives do if they are asked questions by journalists which they cannot answer. Kenneth said, "For example, if I were to ask you about a certain subject of topical interest, you wouldn't feel able to answer, would you? And I wouldn't expect you to." "You're dead right," I told him.'

The next day the OFT cleared the Argyll bid. Ernest: 'I made a tentative arrangement for a meeting with Connell on the Monday. On Saturday Ward and I went to Scotland to talk to Charles Fraser. Ward was very enthusiastic, working with Salz on his bid costs scheme. Fraser said getting through the OFT would be tough, but not impossible.

Ward indicated that the company had gone confidentially to the OFT for unofficial guidance, and that Ernest had asked Dennis Ford, the OFT case-officer, to tell him if a merger of Guinness and Distillers was bound to be referred to the MMC on current competition criteria, because if the whole idea was in his opinion completely futile, Guinness would go no further. Ernest: 'Far from taking a negative view, Ford was positively enthusiastic, and urged us to make a formal submission as soon as possible.'

When Ernest got back to London he had a drink with Seelig on the Sunday evening. They shared a bottle of champagne in the euphoria of the eve of battle. 'Seelig was very excited and pushy. Morgan Grenfell had lost a number of bids lately, and he was sure that we could do this, we had to do it, now was the time, we would never forgive ourselves if we didn't, and so on.'

Ernest and Ward met Connell the next day at Green's flat in Chelsea. 'It was a funny meeting,' he recalls. 'It was all very general. We discussed the idea of getting together to compete with Argyll. The idea was that I would run the company. It was our management that was going to develop this business, and so we had to run the show. Connell wanted to be chairman. I had no objection, but guessed Lord Iveagh would have. If I had wanted to be chairman as badly as everyone has subsequently alleged, the time to have said so would have been then rather than afterwards. There was discussion about how we might structure an offer. I asked whether we could follow the Storehouse concept, whereby it seemed we did not actually have to make a bid, but instead the investors in the two companies would swap their shares for shares in a new holding company. I naïvely thought that we could avoid making a bid this way and it seemed a cheap way of going about it. That was how we got the idea of having a holding board for the two companies.'

Names of possible directors for the new holding board were jotted down. Apart from my father, Guinness would have Iveagh, Boyd, Roux, Ward, Furer and Steel. Distillers would put up John and David Connell, Broackes, Spengler and one or two other non-executives. Sir Thomas Risk was mentioned as a possible candidate by Connell, as he was Distillers' banker in Scotland.

It was then left to the merchant banks to work on a structure and hammer out possible terms, with Ward and Roux representing Guinness in the discussions. Meanwhile Ernest had to handle the Guinness annual results, for which the timing could not have been better. Profits before tax were up by twenty-two per cent to a record £86.1 million, and the dividend payout was increased for the fourth year in a row. At the conference for city analysts and the press, there were plenty of questions regarding the rumours, for every paper had picked up on *The Times* story. But Ernest maintained a strict 'no comment'.

That evening he was due to go with my mother to a gala evening at Covent Garden. Their guests were Philip Wilkinson – then chief executive of National Westminster Bank, which was Guinness's main bank – and his wife. The Wilkinsons were neighbours of ours at Penn.

Ernest: 'It was an all-star evening, although Pavarotti cried off with a cold. I don't know anything about opera, and it was a peculiar work with very long intervals. The bars were full of top people. Midland Bank were the main sponsors. Everyone was talking about the Distillers situation. I met a lot of people who were saying hello to Wilkinson. They were trying to find out if I was going to have a go at Distillers, and they were encouraging me as if I were a gladiator about to enter the ring. Wilkinson being a very discreet man, I said no more to him at the end of the evening than "I may have to see you shortly." I noticed Broackes and Fleet sitting together.'

By this stage my parents were beginning to stay at the New Piccadilly Hotel all the time. Ernest was sleeping extremely badly, resorting to the sleeping pills he had used during the Bell bid. We knew that Carole would need to have a serious operation soon. Everyone was talking about the bid non-stop, they hadn't had a proper Christmas holiday, and my father had not been back to Penn since he had returned to England. For Carole, a bid for Distillers was an awful thought, as she knew very well what it would mean to our domestic life for weeks on end. So my father was personally very troubled, and still far from convinced that he should go ahead with the bid.

On January 15 he chaired a major review of the Guinness retail business at Martin Group's headquarters. He concentrated on finding out their plans for strategic development, to get a feel for whether to push ahead on this front, to see if it would make better sense to link up with Underwoods or make a bid for Boots. In the evening he had another meeting with Paul Hamlyn about *The Guinness Book of Records*.

Meanwhile Iveagh had put the Guinness board on standby, so that head office would know where everyone was. That effectively told them that a big bid was imminent, and they could guess what was in the air. After that it was difficult to maintain tight security.

The next day, Ernest was invited by Lord Richardson, former Governor of the Bank of England, to a top-level dinner at Brooks's Club for the chairman of an American bank. There for the first time my father met David Walker, then a director of the Bank of England, and others of that level.

Ernest: 'I had been loth to go with so much on my plate, but I didn't know any people of this standing in the City, so it was an opportunity I felt I couldn't pass up. Richardson, who happened to be on the board of GEC, talked a little bit about the Distillers bid, and indicated obliquely that Lord Weinstock, GEC's managing director, was uneasy about Gulliver, but thought that Distillers were hopeless. I got the feeling that GEC was going to sell its holding in Distillers, and the next day they did just that. Walker talked to me about "Great Britain *Ltd*" operating on the global stage, as opposed to "Little England", which was a great theme of his.'

Meanwhile, the tempo was hotting up. Seelig had reported back on the idea of a Storehouse-type merger, saying it wouldn't work because Distillers shareholders had to be able to compare two competing offers, and they would not be able to do that with this sort of scheme. There had to be two straightforward rival bids. Guinness would have to be the bidder, as Distillers had no credibility. That brought to the fore Ward's plan to get Distillers to pay for Guinness's bid costs. Ward, Roux and Seelig all worked hard at trying to persuade Kleinwort that this was a good idea, and how Guinness could not be expected to come in as a white knight without some protection of this sort.

On January 16 Distillers had a board meeting at which they agreed in principle to the idea of getting together with Guinness. For the next three days there were constant discussions, particularly about whether or not Distillers was going to agree to foot the bill.

Fraser had come down from Scotland and was pressing Scottish issues very strongly, almost obsessively. He wanted to see the combined group become a Scottish company with a Scottish head office. Ernest: 'I didn't object – most people thought Guinness was an Irish company anyway. But I had increasingly come to the view that whereas London was essential for the financial people who had to deal with the City, if we were going to be a worldwide business then I myself would be spending a lot of time in New York, Europe and Japan, so where I had my official head office made no difference to me. And since I had hardly been at home since I had been at Guinness, the idea of having a second home in Edinburgh was not a problem.'

Gulliver was to make a monstrous suggestion to the press the following May, after the battle was over, that we were turning our back on Scotland and househunting in Oxfordshire. He had met my mother at a reception for Dame Kiri Te Kanawa, the opera singer, and said something to the effect of "how's the househunting in Scotland?" Carole told him that she had other preoccupations at that moment, but what about him? To which Gulliver replied that HE was looking for a house in Oxfordshire. Then he told the papers that we were! The reality was that Ernest intended to get the company to buy a flat in Scotland, and split his week between Edinburgh and London – as many Scottish businessmen do. The Edinburgh and Glasgow shuttles are busiest on Monday afternoons and Thursday evenings.

What was rapidly emerging as the real obstacle to a deal was the idea of letting John Connell become chairman of the new group. Fraser was adamant that Connell would not be acceptable in

Scotland. Gulliver and the press had savaged him over his handling of the defence against Argyll's bid. Iveagh could not see why he could not be the chairman, as Guinness were doing the taking over, and he and Ernest had had a successful partnership. But Fraser and the banks were determined that the new chairman should be a Scot. The obvious candidate was Risk, whom Connell had mentioned as a possible non-executive director. And, unbeknown to Ernest, his Scottish bank adviser, British Linen Bank, was a joint venture of Morgan Grenfell and Risk's Bank of Scotland. So Risk was already involved.

All this was being debated at high speed, for Argyll had been cleared, and was racing away with the initiative. Ernest: 'Compared with the big decisions, questions like the name of the company, where I lived or who the chairman was, were liveable with. I got in touch with Risk as he was on his way to Edinburgh Airport to catch the shuttle to London, and asked him to come and see me with Seelig.'

At the Portman Square office Ernest told Risk what he had in mind. He pointed out that neither board had been told of the proposal that Risk could be a possible chairman. Guinness and Distillers had not yet agreed a deal, but there was a feeling that the new group should have a Scottish non-executive chairman – even though both John Connell and Iveagh thought that they should be chairman. 'I spelt out exactly the basis of the proposed arrangement, which was as it appeared in our offer document on March 3, that the company would be managed by Guinness under my leadership. And I described the success of Guinness, in which we had done a great deal in a short space of time. I said: "People may say the Guinness board is not very bright, but they have been totally supportive and there have been no boardroom politics. Management and board have agreed completely on philosophy. The executive decisions have been sound, and look at the results." I addded that what we now wanted was a Scottish Lord Iveagh. He asked about Scotland, and I told him what was in mind there – how we would make a big effort to participate in the Scottish community. But what we were talking about was building a great Scottish brands company worldwide. The future lay overseas, and it was from the success of the brands in world markets that the benefits would flow.'

Risk raised the question of the group's banking requirements, as Bank of Scotland had got part of Distillers' banking business. What

Scotland. Gulliver and the press had savaged him over his handling the banking business if he took the job as chairman, and indeed he wanted more of that business. Ernest parried, pointing out that Guinness had a good relationship with NatWest in the UK, but banking arrangements were a question of competition and he could never see the group having just one bank. Risk said that he would have to talk to his board about becoming chairman, and he should have a better idea by Monday. But Ernest insisted that he had to know by the weekend, because he had to sell the idea to Connell and Iveagh. They parted.

Ernest told Iveagh of the plan, and he accepted the idea of this combined structure and someone else being chairman, with himself, Connell and Ernest as deputy chairmen. He also agreed that inevitably a number of the Guinness family would have to come off the new holding company board: over the years he and Ernest had discussed the fact that it was no longer a family company anyway. But Iveagh was concerned that the growing Scottish dimension should not wipe out the Irish element, because the Irish government would not like that. Iveagh, Ernest and Roux provisionally planned to launch the bid on Monday, January 20.

On January 18, Fleet wrote in *The Times* that the management of Distillers now believed a merger with Guinness would be the best option for its shareholders. He claimed, accurately, that initial soundings at the OFT had been promising. Fleet added: 'Both Guinness and Distillers see the maintenance of the Scotch whisky industry as being of primary importance ... (the merger) fits in well with Guinness's international ambitions.'

Ernest was travelling in his car that day and, after what he claims were many attempts, Gulliver finally got a message to him that he wanted to talk. Ernest called him back from his car, and Gulliver asked about the Fleet article. Ernest: 'I told him that Guinness was not interested in making a contested bid for Distillers. Everybody knew they were looking for a white knight. then the phone went dead. I didn't cut him off: I think Gulliver must have gone running off to talk to his advisers. Everyone was frantically running about in different directions. We had too much to do with too little time and too little co-ordination.'

The key people on the Guinness side at this stage were Ward, Roux and Seelig. My father regarded Ward as the negotiator *par excellence*. Roux was putting together the financial and legal documentation with Freshfields and working on the financial aspects of the deal with Morgan, Cazenove as well as his Bain advisers. After the Fleet article they decided Guinness had the weekend to get the bid off the ground, or pull out. They knew that the City Takeover Panel would demand the sort of statement that Argyll had had to make in September, saying whether or not they would bid. But nothing was coming out of Distillers' elegant headquarters in St James's Square. Ernest: 'Later in the day I phoned Lord Rockley of Kleinwort Benson at his home and said we had to have a decision because we had to do something on the Monday.'

That night he went to see John Connell at his home at Burhill Golf Club near Walton-on-Thames, Surrey. My father arrived at about 9 p.m. He had a whisky, while Connell had a goodwill Guinness. He had not read the newspapers. They were lying there unopened, so he had not seen the *Times* article.

Ernest: 'He was clearly very uneasy and very uncertain. I had to convince myself that he was for this deal, and could sell it to his board. I said I had to tell him something he would not like, that it was the unanimous view of the advisers that he had been massacred by the press, he had no credibility and we needed someone else as chairman of the new group. I had been advised to go for a Scot, and Risk had agreed in principle by phone that evening. I said I had not formally offered Risk the job, but he would do it if asked. Connell was very upset. I said I'm sorry, but that is the way people feel. It was a miserable moment.'

Ernest asked Connell how soon Distillers might consider the matter, and Connell said that the Distillers board was due to meet the next afternoon, Sunday. My father argued that that would be too late, so Connell agreed that if he could get in touch with the other directors he would get it brought forward to the morning. Meanwhile, Kleinwort and Morgan would meet to iron out any problems.

On Sunday morning, Ward, Seelig, Reeves and Ernest went with Rockley to Distillers House to see Connell. As Seelig and my father got out of their respective cars in St James's Square, of all people they saw Jacob Rothschild. He said: 'I know where you're going!' He and Sheridan Dufferin, one of the Guinness family directors, were trustees of the National Gallery, and Dufferin had told him they were on standby. So much for secrecy.

The Guinness delegation had a brief discussion with Connell, and were then politely told to leave. Reeves and Seelig went off, while Ward and Ernest went to the Bain bunker in Connaught Street to prepare for the Guinness board presentation which would follow if Distillers agreed to the deal.

The main sticking points were the chairmanship and the bid costs. Ernest made it plain that he was flexible on everything except those two points. He felt Ward was right: there was a great risk of being referred to the Monopolies and Mergers Commission, or losing the bid, and so the costs had to be covered.

Discussions in the Bain bunker were protracted. Roux was in one room working on his figures. Ward was on the phone to Kleinwort, trying to negotiate the costs agreement. By 9 p.m. Ernest decided that they had to call in his directors, who duly installed themselves in the bar at the Portman Square office while events unfolded a mile away in St James's Square. They had to wait until 11 p.m. before word came through that Distillers had agreed to Guinness's demands, and the Guinness board meeting could be formally opened. They were being asked to give the go-ahead for a takeover bid worth £2.2 billion. Roux, Ward and my father took the rest of the board through the plans, including Distillers paying Guinness's costs and the fact that some of those in the room would not be invited onto the holding board, which did not go down too well.

Ernest: 'I am sure that they would not have agreed without the costs agreement.' In the event Roux emerged with a bid budget which Ward had reckoned could go as high as £80–100 million, largely underwritten. 'A number asked if we were really going to be able to cope with such a large takeover. I said I had agonised over this and we just had to do it, in the interests of shareholders.'

After obtaining the necessary unanimous approval from the Distillers board, the meeting broke up at about 1 a.m. The Guinness acquisition team worked through the night to complete the paperwork. Ernest worked with the public relations people on his press conference presentation: he was going to announce the bid in Scotland first, then have a second press conference in London. The Distillers board meeting was still meandering on, and John Connell wanted to see the proposed Guinness press release so that he could make his own announcement.

That morning, for it was by now already Monday, January 20, Ernest flew to Edinburgh with David Connell, John's brother, and Bill Young from Bain & Co. They travelled in a private plane with a party of Scottish journalists who had flown in from a visit to Distillers' US operations. In Edinburgh my father made contact with Risk and Fraser, and they went to the press conference venue, which was Guinness's Caledonian Hotel.

Ernest: 'The atmosphere in Scotland was dramatically different from when we were last there, during the Bell bid. The Scottish press, whom I had got to know the previous year, were terribly hostile. It was as if they were all reading from the same script, one penned by Argyll. It said: "Distillers is awful. By association, Guinness is now awful. Surely this new bid must be referred to the Monopolies Commission." It was clear the Argyll message was "Refer, Refer, Refer". It was as if we were being accused of intervening in someone else's private tennis party. Argyll was fighting Distillers – why were we getting involved? We'd had our match with Bell: this was someone else's game. And Argyll was run by Scots, even if from Hayes in Middlesex.' Most of the questions were about the likelihood of the deal being referred by the Office of Fair Trading, and Scottish issues. The press there did not want to know about what my father regarded as the key aspect of the bid: that this had the potential to make a great Scottish-based international brands company to compete with the biggest people in the business, that would do great things for exports.

Ernest: 'It made no impression on them. We had a repeat show for the London press at the International Press Centre off Fleet Street. By chance Argyll had a meeting next door, and they were naturally watching us. I felt uneasy about Brian Basham, our former public relations adviser, who had now resigned, standing outside the door of our meeting, but going into Argyll's.'

The London press evinced no interest in Scottish questions, but were also negative. They noted the following day that Distillers' agreement to the bid effectively destroyed their argument that it already had a sound management that was turning the company round. The *Financial Times* pointed out that Guinness could get higher earnings per share with Distillers by selling its British Petroleum stake and rationalising the company. 'Argyll could also do this, of course,' it added unhelpfully. Most papers argued that Guinness might be overreaching itself with such a large bid so soon after taking over Bell, and speculated whether the OFT would accept the international benefits from the merger or instead focus on the combined group's thirty-eight-per-cent share of the UK whisky market.

Guinness's immediate problem was how to convince the big institutional investors that it had made a genuine bid. They would not be inclined to take it seriously until Sir Gordon Borrie, director-general of the OFT, had given his verdict. If the deal went to the Monopolies Commission, it would be on ice for up to six months. As Argyll had already been cleared, they would have the field to themselves and could make their bid unopposed, which would be unfair on Guinness and unfair on Distillers shareholders, who were entitled to a choice.

10

VICTORY

The duel with Argyll rapidly generated its own momentum, rushing with gathering speed to the climax in April. Ernest always felt a sense of scrambling to catch up with the well-drilled and highly professional team that had been amassed by Argyll. Although Guinness had a strong group of advisers, because of the rush there was a lack of cohesion and even some dissension in their ranks: for example, John Chiene, the Scot who headed Wood Mackenzie, the stockbrokers, resented playing second fiddle to Cazenove & Co. And this group included 'stars' in their own right who did not find teamwork easy.

'In football terms it was like Liverpool versus Everton or Arsenal versus Spurs. Argyll had bought some of our players from the Bell bid, but we still had a powerful team. The problem was that there was so much to do that it was simply not possible to keep track of everything. We had to decide priorities quickly. It was a question of pragmatic delegation of responsibilities.'

Guinness's manager for the City aspects of the bid was Roux, with Ward to oversee the legal side and handle Distillers. Ernest could bring in Vic Steel too, but his prime responsibility was to keep making profits. For that reason, my father largely kept the other line operators out of the bid. 'I saw my role basically as the marketing of the bid, explaining to all and sundry why it was that Guinness rather than Argyll would do the best job with Distillers. This was what I could do best, and no one person can do everything.'

In the earliest days there were a few attempts at morning gettogethers, as had taken place during the bid for Bell. But the Bell deal had been far more straightforward: Guinness and its team had done all their planning in advance, and they had an opponent who in the end did not put up much of a fight. Guinness had had the luxury of spending an hour or so each day, routinely discussing strategy and progress. But there was no time to strategise over Distillers. Basham's claim that Guinness had a 'war cabinet' was completely erroneous. In any case, the brokers preferred to see Roux at the end of the day. So the morning meeting soon boiled down to an analysis of the newspapers with Chris Davidson, Tim Bell and others, with endless cups of coffee for whoever else wanted to come. It was a very fragmented 'war effort', lacking co-ordination.

Ernest: 'On the second day after the press conference, Roger Seelig and Gordon Reece made it perfectly clear that as far as I was concerned there was only one priority: given Argyll's political clout, employing Sir Alex Fletcher, ex-DTI Minister, and with Cranley Onslow, chairman of the Tories' backbench 1922 Committee, on their board, I would have to do everything to avoid our bid being referred – exactly the same plan as we had carried out in the Bell bid. If strategic decisions were required, I would be contacted. But although I had to remain involved with the PR side, I would have to concentrate on the OFT problem.'

The other problem was Guinness's 'partner', Distillers. The rules of the City Takeover Code prevented Guinness from getting all the information on Distillers that they wanted, because both sides had to receive equal treatment and Distillers did not want Argyll to get their hands on all this material. But the situation was more difficult than that.

Ernest: 'They were playing a pretty dangerous game, for in their hearts a lot of them were probably hoping that in some way both bids would fail and we would all go away, so they didn't want to give us any information anyway: I nicknamed Distillers 'the tranquillised rhino'. They worked at a snail's pace, it was terrible. It was a situation we should perhaps have foreseen, but none of us had experience of being a white knight in a contested bid.'

Ward's role proved critical. People involved in the bid used to criticise him for picking up Ernest's phone in the office, but he held things together with Bill Spengler and David Connell, the two alert directors of Distillers. Without that relationship, particularly the American tie-up between Ward and Spengler, the Guinness bid would have floundered.

Ernest: 'The workload was just terrific. From the first day I realised that my car boot and the conference table in my office and my bedroom at home and in the hotel would not hold all the paperwork I was supposed to look at. The piles of unread papers and unanswered phone calls grew daily. I tried to keep a general grip of what was going on, but there was so much that in reality the task was hopeless. My office, and the boardroom, and the secretaries' office in between, were full of different groups of people, phoning, holding splinter meetings. Ward remarked on the chaos.

But it was impossible to escape the logic of Reece's advice: all the effort would be in vain unless Guinness could stop its bid going before the Monopolies and Mergers Commission. That meant Ernest spending considerable time in Scotland as well as lobbying in London.

As the bid got under way in late January, Risk, Fraser and Gifford were urging my father to do the entire round of Scotland without delay. In any case, the City still did not consider Guinness had made a bid worth considering seriously, because of the Monopolies danger.

Meanwhile, the other side was making the running. On January 27, a week after Guinness launched its bid, Argyll complained to the Takeover Panel over the agreement by Distillers to pay Guinness's costs. The Panel rejected the complaint, so ten days later Argyll raised the stakes by making a formal allegation that the costs agreement broke the Companies Act. On same day, it increased its bid for Distillers to £2.3 billion.

In Scotland, Ernest went round the same people he had lobbied during the Bell bid, stressing the advantages to Scotland if Guinness won. He argued that in terms of competition policy, it was irrelevant that the Distillers' whiskies were produced in Scotland. What mattered was that the market was worldwide, and in a worldwide context Guinness and Distillers would only have a small share. 'I met hostility and indifference. In fact they were so hostile you wouldn't have thought we had ever met before. I was very concerned that the OFT would clearly get nothing but negatives from Scotland.'

Ernest also made a brief courtesy visit to Guinness's Scottish investors. The only encouragement came from General Accident, one of the biggest investors in Guinness since its holding in Bell had been converted. They shared Ernest's vision of the world drinks market, and they did not particularly like Argyll. 'But most other influential people up there were blindly concentrating on Scottish administrative details. We were down to discussing the number of secretaries we were going to bring from the south, and precisely when. The concept of a great international drinks business did not excite them.'

To overcome this indifference, while Tim Bell worked on the

public relations strategy in London, Frank Lowe produced brilliant advertisements, showing for example how the whisky industry could suffer the fate of the motorcycle industry if it remained parochial, and how British companies needed to compete on a world scale.

Ernest went to see David Walker at the Bank of England, who was encouraging. To support the formal submission to the OFT, Bill Young and he then had several meetings with Dennis Ford, who had been making promising noises before Guinness announced its bid. 'Ford had a great sense of his own importance. He kept saying he had just been on the phone to Gulliver, even though the Argyll bid had been cleared.' Ernest also saw the director-general, Sir Gordon Borrie. One key argument was that it would be unfair to refer the Guinness bid after Argyll had been let through. 'If you refer us,' he told Borrie, 'the investigation is going to take six months, and you would basically be giving Argyll a walkover and in the process denying Distillers shareholders freedom of choice.'

Guinness had Sir Peter Carey for consultation. He was a director of Morgan Grenfell, and had been Permanent Secretary at the DTI. Sir Jack Lyons was also very helpful, writing to Mrs Thatcher and seeing other political contacts, among them the Cabinet Secretary.

The media push for referral to the Monopolies and Mergers Commission was considerable. The financial journalists, many of whom had backed the Guinness bid for Bell, just did not want to hear my father's case for avoiding referral this time. Ian Watson of the *Sunday Telegraph* told him: 'We have chosen our man for this bid.' Some told him not even to bother sending them the Guinness press releases or documents relating to the bid. That was why Guinness ran press and TV adverts designed to appeal directly to the civil servants and politicians who would make the vital decisions: the press was by then effectively a closed door.

Ernest: 'We answered all the OFT's questions, and we were getting favourable indications that they were sympathetic to the international approach. But I was at Gleneagles when we heard on the TV news that Paul Channon had been appointed Secretary of State at the DTI in succession to Leon Brittan in the wake of the Westland affair. Channon was related to the Guinness family and would want to demonstrate his impartiality by stabbing us in the front as well as in the back. On top of that, in my opinion Borrie was extremely sensitive to public opinion, and every newspaper was saying that we should be referred.'

On the morning of February 13 Roux gave the board a com-

Some of the advertising undertaken by Guinness at the time of the Distillers bid.

prehensive update on the bid at the meeting of the full Guinness board. Some directors argued that it was essential to regard the offer as a business deal which would be pursued only for as long as it was to the advantage of Guinness shareholders, and should not turn into a 'win at all costs' campaign. Ernest accepted that as the basis on which to proceed. However, in the late afternoon they heard from Ford that they had been referred.

'I was furious. They had handed the bid to Argyll on a plate. I am told Ford recommended to the mergers panel that we should not be referred, but the mergers panel had been split. The first thing I did was to get Gordon Reece to draft a letter which was hand-delivered to the Prime Minister, with a demand to see a Minister at the DTI. I felt at a tremendous disadvantage in not being able to see the relevant Cabinet Minister – Channon. We got a call from the duty officer at the DTI, suggesting that we should contact Borrie.'

He was unavailable, but Ford was contacted, and he offered to come and explain, and did. But Ernest still insisted on seeing the decision-makers in Whitehall. The next morning the junior ministers, Michael Howard and Geoffrey Pattie, were not there, or made excuses not to see my father.

However, an appointment was made by Downing Street for Ernest to see Hans Liesner, deputy secretary and chief economic adviser to the DTI, and a senior civil servant in the DTI's competition department. 'He must have been uncomfortable, because he surrounded himself with about twelve civil servants. We talked for an hour or so, and I tried to find out if they had sent the formal order for the Monopolies Commission to begin their investigation. They said that they had. I had cooled down by this time, so I asked them just to explain the process to me. They said, you are now out of the DTI's hands. You are in the hands of the Monopolies Commission, which is like a court. So if you want to know what you can do, you should see the chairman of the Commission, Sir Godfray Le Quesne, but it probably won't do any good.

'I went back to the office late that afternoon and saw my desk. After six weeks of non-stop work on the bid, it was piled high. The other thing I found completely demoralising was the way our advisers, who were collecting fat fees, just said 'cheerio, better luck next time', and cleared off. I had never felt so depressed in my life. People kept coming in for a sort of farewell drink. The only thing I could think of was, "Thank God for the costs agreement".'

Ernest went home, had a few whiskies and woke on the Saturday morning to read the newspaper reports of the referral. He made a few phone calls, including one to Charles Fraser in Scotland. As a director of United Biscuits, he was involved in the other major bid at the time, by Imperial Group, which had also been referred. UB were discussing trying to get out of the referral by reversing the situation: UB would bid for Imperial. My father asked Fraser if he had any ideas for Guinness. Fraser replied by asking if Ernest had talked to any really good counsel specialising in competition policy. He recommended Jeremy Lever and John Swift, who were going to a dinner at All Souls College, Oxford, that night. Fraser arranged for them to meet a Guinness team at the office on Sunday evening.

A car was sent to Oxford with some papers on the bid for them to read before the meeting.

'We discussed the germ of an idea to come up with some sort of reconstruction of the bid for Distillers. I had spoken to Sir Hector Laing, chairman of United Biscuits. They guessed that they had been referred because Imperial owned Golden Wonder crisps, which would give UB a large share of the UK snacks market if it was combined with UB's leading brand, KP. The point is that the OFT never say why they are making a referral. We guessed that in our case it was the combined Guinness-Distillers share of the UK whisky market, which would amount to thirty-eight per cent. The idea of our agreeing to sell off some whisky brands in order to escape a monopolies investigation had apparently come up in discussions between Ward and Seelig, because Seelig probably knew what was happening at UB, another Morgan client. We discussed this idea with Lever and Swift.'

Ernest made an appointment to see Le Quesne on Monday, February 17, accompanied by Young, Ward and Swift. It was soon apparent that Swift and Le Quesne knew one another and had an excellent relationship, so Ernest let Swift make the running. Over a series of meetings lasting three days, Swift persuaded Le Quesne that if Guinness agreed in advance to sell off enough whisky brands to bring their and Distillers combined UK market share down to twenty-five per cent, that would be sufficient for Le Quesne to recommend to the DTI that they should let the first bid lapse. They could then make a fresh bid incorporating the promise to divest. But Ernest and the others were made to understand that the second bid would still have to go through all the OFT hoops again, with no guarantee that it would be cleared.

While Ward, Swift and Young were working on a detailed proposal to put to Le Quesne, Ernest went back to talk to Borrie, Rifkind and Geoffrey Pattie about the national importance of taking the broader global view of market share in this situation. Was Britain going to allow the Japanese to take over the world's markets?

At about five o'clock on the evening of February 19 Bill Young picked up his portable telephone outside the DTI and reported to Ernest that Le Quesne would recommend to the DTI that the first bid should lapse. The office in Portman Square was full of people anxiously waiting to hear the decision. Roux and his financial people, with the brokers, had been working out new bid terms on a contingency basis. Two hours later the official word came through from the DTI.

Shortly afterwards the entire Morgan Grenfell first team arrived: Reeves, Carey, Walsh and Seelig along with Forbes and Mayhew from Cazenove. They had come to celebrate the second bid.

Ernest: 'It was an extraordinary gathering. The Morgan people in particular were very excited at the fact that we had come up with a means of getting back into the race, as their UB bid had been referred. Ward was ebullient – he had done a lot to make it happen. Roux was, as usual, inscrutable.

'But I had had enough. I had kept my doubts to myself before, but this time I expressed them to the group. After this, there would be no going back, and I was already whacked. I saw ahead the nightmare of more OFT lobbying to get this new bid through, with the possiblity that the press and the Scots lobby might get us referred again. Even though we would have the costs covered, I questioned the capability of our very small group of people to continue to operate twenty-four hours a day without sleep. I said I didn't want to go ahead. I can't explain why I didn't come out with my misgivings earlier: I just didn't.

'There was a furious argument. Ward said it was my duty to the shareholders to go on. Having gone this far, he said I couldn't jump off now. I said it was all very well for him, darting to and fro from the States, but I had to live with this all the time. Later I said to Ward that if I was going to go ahead I wanted him with me. But the real blast came from the Morgan group, led by Reeves. The bank could no doubt see the millions of pounds in fees disappearing. He said it would ruin my reputation. Nobody in the City would ever listen to me again. We would never have the credibility to make another major bid. My reputation was at stake, so was the company's, so was Morgan's.

'We argued for I don't know how long, then I told them I had made up my mind and was going into my office to call Lord Iveagh. I went alone to my office and phoned him. I told him we had got permission to make another bid, but I didn't want to go ahead. I had heard what the board had said on February 13, and like them I was not in favour of winning at any cost. We could make a credible withdrawal now without loss of face. I expected Iveagh to say, 'If that's what you want, it's up to you,' but he didn't. He was extremely disappointed. The board had not meant that at all. Would I please think about it? I then called Lord Boyd, another Guinness family director, who I thought would be pretty pleased at pulling out. Not a bit of it: if anything, he was even stronger than Iveagh, talking about duty and would I think about it again?

'So I found myself in an extraordinary situation. The chairman and deputy chairman of the company did not agree with me. I rang Iveagh again and had another talk. He tried very hard to persuade me. He asked what the others were saying. I told him Ward was extremely bullish, and the banks were talking about our reputation, and he latched on to that. I said if we went ahead I would have to insist that Ward stayed here, in London. I couldn't cope with the "tranquillised rhino" on my own. We were bound to have terrific aggro from Argyll, and probably legal action. I pointed out that Ward would want us to make it worth his while financially. Iveagh said we had got the costs underwritten, so what did it matter?

'At this point Seelig entered the room and asked if he could have a word. We went and joined the others, and he made an impassioned fifteen-minute speech in front of them, about the certain damage to credibility. It would have been another defeat for Morgan, at a time when they were having a run of defeats in takeover bids. Seelig said he was confident that we could win. Eventually I caved in. I took a deep breath. By this time it was gone midnight. I said to Ward: "You'll have to stay." He said: "You'll have to make it worth my while."'

On February 20, the day after the DTI had allowed Guinness to let its first bid lapse, the company announced a new offer worth £2.35 billion – just ahead of Argyll's – and coupled with a commitment to sell off five whisky brands. The package had a predictably hostile reception from the media, stirred up by Argyll, who launched into a phase of legal moves. They applied to the courts for a judicial review of the MMC decision, arguing that the new bid was not sufficiently different from the old.

Ward had to work very hard with David Connell of Distillers to get him to agree which brands would be sold off, because it was going to be mainly their brands which would have to go. Distillers had a lot of Scots backwoodsmen on the board, some of whom belonged to families whose brands were being discussed. They agreed on a list of brands, of which the major ones were Claymore and John Barr, which had been invented only a few years previously to fill the gap left by the decision to stop selling Johnnie Walker Red in Britain after a European Community decision had gone against Distillers. Another was Haig, but only the rights to its UK sales. There was no shortage of would-be buyers.

Swift was in negotiation with Borrie and Elizabeth Llewellyn-Smith. My father embarked on another round of high-level lobbying to support the OFT's review of the second bid. Meanwhile, Distillers had to find a suitable buyer for the five brands in good time to persuade the OFT that there would be no need to go back to the Monopolies Commission. One plan was to 'park' the brands with Morgan Grenfell as a temporary measure, but the word quickly came through the Whitehall grapevine that this was not on. Lonrho quickly emerged as the keenest and best able to do a deal. They had to show the OFT that their purchase would not just be a put-up job. It was being suggested that the obvious and simple thing would have been for Guinness to sell Bell, but there was no way that my father was going to do that. He saw tremendous potential in everything to do with the company, from the Bell's brand to the sales force and the operation in Perth. It was far more impressive than Distillers' UK sales operation based in Surbiton, Surrey.

February 27 was the day of the Guinness annual shareholders' meeting, with Lord Boyd in the chair. At the shareholders' meeting my father urged investors to write to Mrs Thatcher in support of the Guinness case to have the fresh bid cleared.

On March 3 Guinness published the formal document in connection with its offer, and a covering letter from my father and Lord Iveagh. It stated: 'Distillers is a company whose core assets are its international brands. It is the expert management of these assets to create growth in international markets, and the development from that growing base, that will determine the future of both the company and its balance sheet. We know how to utilise research and development, advertising and promotion, production and distribution. Through these marketing skills, we will build this British-owned international consumer brands company into a world-class force.

Under the leadership of Ernest Saunders, we will bring to Distillers this experience, these achievements and our dedication to the establishment of a British export-led consumer brands company.'

Although Sir Thomas Risk was to be appointed non-executive chairman, there was no doubt who was going to run the company if the bid was successful. The letter added: 'The proposed new board will have a strong Scottish representation. We shall take the necessary steps to make the holding company a Scottish registered company and will move the group headquarters to Edinburgh, where the group chief executive's office will be located.' And the new holding company would change its name.

For once my father held a mass press conference to discuss the document, instead of his usual one-to-one briefings. 'We squeezed them all in the boardroom at Portman Square, and it was the most awful meeting I had had to cope with. You would think that I was facing the Argyll press corps. They were downright insulting. I was treated to a barrage of hostile and critical questions. It was most depressing.'

As Lonrho had agreed to buy the brands to be divested, Terry Robinson, one of their directors and a neighbour in Beaconsfield, said that Tiny Rowland wanted to meet Ernest, so they had lunch at the Berkeley Hotel. 'Rowland told me that it was the first time that anyone had ever picked up the tab for a lunch with him.'

At about this time Argyll added injury to insult by running a press advertisement depicting Guinness's main brands in a dustbin full of broken bottles and cigarette butts. This incensed Ernest even further. 'I thought to myself, they can attack me and my policies, but if they attack the brands they attack the very fabric of the company.' On the advice of Sir David Napley, Guinness sued Argyll in Britain and the US. Although Argyll refused to do anything about the ads, the Takeover Panel laid down very stringent rules on the type of advertising that could be allowed in future.

There was also a big boost for the chances of the revamped Guinness bid gaining official clearance when Argyll's judicial review case was rejected by the High Court and the Court of Appeal in March, because the press reported the decisions as if the courts had given credibility to the fresh bid, which seemed to make it all the more difficult for Borrie to have it referred.

Ernest: 'But we had nonetheless had to do a great deal of lobbying. Through Sir Jack Lyons I was invited to lunch at Bain and had occasion to sit next to Jeffrey Archer, then deputy chairman of the

Conservative Party. He came straight out and said, "How much are you going to give to the Conservatives? I notice you don't give anything at present." '

On March 11 Gordon Reece held a party in Birdcage Walk, near Buckingham Palace, to celebrate his knighthood. The guest list was studded with members of the Cabinet and editors of national newspapers that Ernest had been having difficulty in getting to see during the bid. It was a heaven-sent opportunity to talk to them. Tim Bell was there, naturally enough. My father also had his first reunion with Kenneth Baker since they had been at school together.

As the time for a Monopolies decision approached, Roux and the Bain team had to begin putting together a presentation for the investment institutions who would have to be persuaded to accept the Guinness bid. Ernest: 'We had to get it right first time, because there was so little time that we would have only one go at most institutions. Argyll had been round the circuit twice and in some cases three times.'

Roux got the brokers to start making appointments with the institutions on the assumption that Guinness would be cleared. He had to fix up between fifty and sixty of these meetings. It began to look a horrendous timetable, even at a punishing rate of four presentations a day. Some would have to be held in Scotland and others elsewhere round the country. There was intense public interest in what was going on, because of the Monopolies referrals and non-referrals, and the court cases brought by both sides.

Ernest: 'I was hardly ever in the office and the lists of unanswered phone calls began to mount again. All sorts of people were phoning. The extraordinary thing was how many people got hold of my carphone number, my ex-directory number at home, and the direct lines in the office as well as in whatever hotel room I was staying. In most cases these calls started on some sort of pretext such as football, interest in our hotels, Distillers' properties, just looking for business, or offering gratuitous advice. But there was one common factor: sooner or later they were all fishing for information on what I was thinking. Some were very skilled in detecting one's mood from the way one talked. A lot, I am convinced, wanted information so they could deal in the stock market. A lot I fobbed off: I really was not too pleased to be called at home at 8 a.m. on a Sunday by the likes of Robert Maxwell, or have Gerald Ronson on the phone in the office demanding to speak to me.'

While the rest of us at home were getting fed up with the constant interruptions at night and at weekends, my father's working life was becoming more and more disorganised. He had to keep changing appointments to fit in the vital lobbying. He used to find people sitting in the boardroom or in his office, writing, talking or using the phones. 'It was like a railway station – and that was only what I could see. But when I walked down the corridor there were all sorts of other people standing around and chattering or whispering. I asked who they were and they were always supposed to be working with Roux, Ward or Davidson. And there were two lots of back stairs in the building, as well as the main lifts. Complete strangers were coming and going all the time.'

Borrie cleared the second Guinness bid on March 21, prompting Argyll to step in immediately with an increased bid valuing Distillers at £2.5 billion. My father had advance notice of the clearance late the previous day, and that led to a series of consultations at Portman Square to decide whether they should respond with an improved offer. Seelig was adamant that Guinness should not do so, explaining that the market would just take it all the way down again by knocking the Guinness share price.

Ernest: 'I got the feeling that Seelig, on behalf of Morgan Grenfell, also felt that the market would not take the underwriting of another huge offer. Ward and I wanted to raise the bid. But Seelig was an extremely powerful advocate, and he persuaded us not to.'

On March 21 Ernest went to Scotland, returning the next day for the QPR-Watford match. The 23rd, a Sunday, was my sister Jo's twenty-first birthday, and we had a celebration lunch at Penn. The Sunday press was beginning to come round to the idea that Guinness might actually win the battle after all, although the *Sunday Telegraph* was more concerned to vent its spleen at the OFT for not giving Argyll the field to itself.

The next week Ernest fitted in one or two important functions. On the Tuesday he sat next to Lord Forte, the catering magnate, at a meeting of the Scottish Council of Development and Industry at the Caledonian Club in Belgravia. On Wednesday he had to fulfil a long-standing promise to give a speech at a product development conference at the Barbican in the City. That was also the day when the board members were together for the Extraordinary General Meeting, chaired by Lord Boyd, for Guinness shareholders to approve the increase in its share capital to enable it to make the bid, and the first closing date of its offer. The EGM used up valuable time, but the proposals were nodded through. The offer deadline produced acceptances of only 3.05 per cent of Distillers' shares, but together with the 10.45 per cent Guinness already owned it was within one per cent of Argyll's holding in Distillers. The rivals were neck and neck.

Then my father embarked on the final round of lobbying the media. Among others, he met Neil Collins of *The Sunday Times* and Brian McArthur and Mary Ann Sieghart of *Today* on the Monday, Ivan Fallon, Kenneth Fleet and the Scottish press the next day, and John Bell of the *Sunday Express* the day after that. On Thursday, March 28, he met Richard Lambert of the *Financial Times* and Ian Watson of the *Sunday Telegraph* – 'I was not going to give up on him!'

Apart from the serious issues the press gave considerable coverage to what they termed 'dirty tricks'. Certainly there had been burglaries, electronic eavesdropping, the suspicion that one was being followed. The press seemed to know what was going on at Guinness even before the people at Guinness did.

Roux finalised the institutional presentation with the help of the Bainies over the long Easter weekend. Ernest: 'Our research had suggested that we had to be entirely positive. We had to spell out what we would do, both in the short term and in the long term. It was recognised that we had the long-term marketing skills, but could we make the profits in the short term? Gulliver had a reputation for being able to handle the short term very well. And we had to avoid knocking Argyll. They had been knocking us, but this was what the institutions wanted to hear. They wanted to be able to judge the two companies on their management capabilities. I was going to introduce the presentation, Roux was going to do the financial side, and Steel would cover the marketing aspect because he was going to run the group beverage division, so it was important for the institutions to see him in person. We had a back-up team in case any of us fell sick, especially after we got into doing more than four presentations a day.'

That Friday Ernest managed to join the family in Switzerland for a weekend's skiing. The next working day was Tuesday, April 1. During the succeeding seventeen days Ernest, Roux and Steel fitted in fifty-five investor presentations, to institutions, brokers and others in the investment community. In London they used a 230 Mercedes limousine to carry the three men and all their display charts. Roux was constantly on the phone to the brokers while they were in transit, finding out what was going on. Ernest: 'He talked a lot to Anthony Parnes, David Mayhew, Roger Seelig and Wood Mackenzie. Roux had told me that he found Parnes particularly useful because, unlike the company's official brokers, he knew the jobbers in the stock market and what they were doing and thinking. Roux's briefcase telephone would ring in the middle of briefings, which did not please the fund managers too much. Our job was to win by persuading the institutions at our presentations. I would have liked to end my summing up each time in a good salesman's manner, clinching the order, but the brokers stopped me and said that such exhortations were their job and would follow our presentations.'

The questions after the presentations were normally aggressive. After a while Ernest and the others twigged that there was something going on, because their initial questions were always identical. Ernest noticed some of the audience flicking to something underneath their papers: it turned out that Argyll had sent them all a checklist of Guinness's alleged vulnerable points to bring up. Ernest: 'We got hold of a copy, and I used to say, "Before we get on to the real questions, shall we get the Argyll checklist out of the way?" We had enormous audiences. They were getting quite blasé, feeling their sense of power. In the past few months they had been wooed by us, Argyll, Hanson, Imperial and United Biscuits. I remember one meeting in Scotland where they wanted to get us out of the way quickly: a girl breathlessly told me, "We've got Lord Hanson coming."' Ernest asked what Hanson's presentations were like. She replied: "He isn't going to give a presentation – he's coming to lunch!'

'At the end of each day, Roux would meet the bankers, brokers and his other City advisers, to plan tactics. Steel and I would return to Portman Square where I would take the opportunity to check up on the progress of the business including new products we were developing such as canned draught Guinness and Kaliber. I continued to see the press for breakfast and in the evening, with the occasional lunch. I saw Sir John Junor of the *Sunday Express*, Jeremy Stone of the *Financial Times* Lex column, Melvyn Marckus of the *Observer*, Alex Murray from the *Sunday Telegraph* and John Bell once more.'

There was talk of there being a stalemate, with no one winning, which would have been the worst possible outcome. Distillers would remain independent, and no one wanted that.

The press were, as usual, personalising the battle, and Gulliver seemed intent on giving them every assistance. The Argyll advertising even included full-page pictures of Gulliver's face. But the indications Guinness were receiving showed that that was not the way to approach the issue. Instead, they plugged the famous household name of Guinness and its reputation in the drinks' business.

Ernest thought very carefully about the marketing of the bid to investors and the public. To reach everybody in the investment institutions, not just those who had attended the presentations, Guinness left behind an excellent video that demonstrated Guinness's capability in the world drinks market, for people to take home. The video was also available to members of the public who wrote in. Distillers used a company specialising in telephone sales to contact small shareholders. Frank Lowe devised an attention-grabbing television advert centring on the worldwide marketing expertise of Guinness, and slotted it into the middle of the ITN News at Ten, *Spitting Image* and the sports programmes. They put posters on taxis and buses. 'In the last three weeks our media campaign was incredibly intense, and had enormous impact. There could not have been a single investor who did not see our advertising in this vital period.'

Argyll were naturally doing everything possible to thwart Guinness. They revamped their presentation when they heard that Guinness's was going down well.

The last Guinness board meeting of the campaign was held on April 10. Ernest, Roux, Ward and Steel could not attend because of bid business. At the end of the first round of presentations, after my father had more or less seen all the top people once, he made a list of half a dozen key people whom he thought might not be convinced and required a second visit, including the Prudential and the Post Office Pension Fund. In one or two cases they were very nice and said Ernest need not have bothered, because they were going to vote for Guinness anyway. Then came the big break. Against their tradition, Norwich Union announced early-on that they would back Guinness. That started a bandwagon rolling, and a few others followed suit. On April 15 Guinness had thirty-two per cent of Distillers shares cast in their favour, and two days later it was forty-six per cent. On the Friday, April 18, Ernest claimed 50.7 per cent – enough to give control and victory.

My father declared: 'We are very pleased with this clear result. We are delighted that Distillers' shareholders have shown such confidence in Guinness. We now have a British-owned international consumer brands company able to compete on even terms with the foreign-owned giants. This is a most exciting opportunity for shareholders, employees and management. We are determined to revitalise the fortunes of the Scotch whisky industry and establish our brands in pre-eminent positions throughout the world.'

Gulliver said he was very disappointed, but 'Argyll's judgement last autumn, that Distillers needed a change of direction and new management, was fully vindicated.'

At five o'clock that evening there was a victory party in the Portman Square office. Ernest: 'We invited a number of Distillers people, who behaved most peculiarly under the influence of the champagne. They kept making indiscreet remarks on the lines of "Thank goodness we've escaped from Gulliver, now we can carry on as before." I was not impressed.'

But it was entirely consistent with the feeling that Ernest had picked up during the bid that the Distillers people were all the time hoping for a stalemate, and thus to escape from both bid contestants. 'Working with Distillers, supposedly our partners during the bid, was one of the most frustrating experiences that I had ever had. Distillers used the Takeover Code to the maximum effect to keep information to themselves, and they were simply not used to the need for action.' Ward and Spengler had managed to establish the minimum relationship necessary to avoid disaster, but everyone at Guinness was getting the feeling that working together to deliver the expected profits would prove extremely difficult.

That Sunday, Queens Park Rangers were appearing in the Milk Cup Final at Wembley. The opponents were Oxford United – where the chairman was Robert Maxwell. Ernest was exhausted, but Maxwell revelled in the occasion, especially as Oxford won the match.

11

PROFITS, PRIORITIES AND PROTOCOL

The problems of working with Distillers during the bid had warned Ernest that there were going to be real difficulties in bringing together the two operations and their managements. The Distillers people were not used to action, and indeed made any excuse for inaction. Over the Cup Final weekend Ernest worried about how he could deal with this. At the pre-match reception he had heard the first rumours that Distillers had been loading sales to the US – making sales to the US distributors which were far in excess of what was justified by actual consumption. This had made the Distillers sales figures look good, but not for long, since the distributors had simply stockpiled the surplus. Ernest had also heard that the Distillers people in Scotland had been saying there did not need to be further significant production closures: this turned out to be a gross exaggeration.

Bill Spengler, the American on the Distillers board, had commissioned PA Strategy, a management consultancy made up of former Bain employees, to do a study outlining the company's recommended future strategy and reorganisation. They had been unwilling to share this study with Guinness during the bid because Takeover Panel rules would have meant it would then have had to be available to Argyll. The week after the bid was over, Ernest immediately asked to see it, hoping to speed the process of fact-gathering, as with Guinness in his early days. He already saw that Distillers might need a Guinness-type cost-saving programme to secure the necessary profits in the immediate future, and the PA study would help.

Based on his work with Distillers during the bid, Ernest had come to the conclusion that he would never get action unless Guinness executives had and were seen to have the necessary authority immediately to take executive decisions at Distillers. He discussed the matter with Lord Iveagh, Ward and Vic Steel. Ernest: 'It seemed the only thing these people at Distillers would understand was a military style command structure. We had to focus on the ability to get things done: put two Guinness people in charge. The two were to be Steel on the beverage side and Shaun Dowling covering non-beverage activities. I myself had to become chairman of Distillers, simply so that we could operate on a line basis, with someone at the top giving the orders.'

Ernest and Ward went to see John Connell on April 22 and told him what they had to do and why. Ernest explained that he feared that Distillers was unlikely to make the profits that had been forecast during the bid campaign unless an action-oriented command structure was put in place immediately. Ernest would have to be the effective boss, but Connell could be president. 'He didn't like it, but he accepted the situation. Ward told Charles Fraser from Morgan Grenfell and Sir Thomas Risk, the incoming group chairman, who did not demur. A lot of other things could wait until we had the facts. But we had a major worry about delivering those profits to the shareholders. That was, after all, why they had put us in charge.'

Anxiety about the results was already beginning to grow, because the first announcement would have to be made in November, little more than six months away. Ernest: 'All my experience told me that if you don't have someone in charge saying "I want this done", nothing happens. I thought we could deal with the board, the administration and the location of the offices later. That was all to do with corporate structure and administration. I was concerned with the ability to take executive decisions, because I was troubled by the fact that we had gone out with presentations making promises for the short and medium term, and now we had to deliver. My fear was that a "Fortress Distillers" would be set up in St James's Square. All the signs were that they were going to do their damnedest to carry on as before. I wanted to make sure that would not happen. It was an essential, immediate act.'

The PA report argued for radical streamlining and rationalisation, and pinpointed obvious cost-saving areas. It was not comprehensive, but it was well done and gave Ernest a good basis for action. PA wanted to carry on with it, but Roux objected and Bill Young from Bain, the man who had done the analytical work on Bell, was drafted in. Steel, Young and Phil Rhodes, the Guinness controller, got down to finding out the detailed costs of the various Distillers operations, as had been done with Guinness in 1981–82. 'It takes time to turn brands around, so you have to get at the costs first and stop people spending money. I organised a meeting with the Distillers management at Distillers House. I gave them a talk about how we did things at Guinness, and we continued over drinks. I sensed tremendous resentment at the realisation that they really were going to have to change. A number of Distillers managers came up with the most extraordinary, aggressive and arrogant remarks to me about how I would never get the changes through, and I didn't know what I was up against. The editor of the Distillers in-house magazine talked to me about his fear that others in the company might use guerrilla activities to resist change. I was staggered. I said to Vic Steel that apart from getting a programme agreed with Bill Young and Phil Rhodes, he would have to get some sort of task force around him to deal with the issues requiring immediate attention.'

Ernest and Carole then went to New York for a meeting with the influential American licensed trade media. 'They were very flattered that I should come over right after the bid was over. But the time off I was to have in Florida after that was ruined by the confirmation that there had been a large amount of Distillers stock loaded into the US market, and that the marketing effort had consisted of little more than discounting. It suddenly dawned on me how Distillers had managed to come up with such good figures.'

The alarm bells were soon ringing. The editor of *Impact*, the most powerful drinks trade paper in the US, asked Ernest if he knew about the government's plan to put a penal duty on imported Scotch and gin. After just two days of much-needed rest in Florida, Ward said my father had to come to Washington immediately because the US Trade Secretary was about to announce the new duty as part of a squabble with the European Community. The Distillers and Bell people in the UK had done nothing. The same applied to the Scotch Whisky Association. Ernest had talks with the Trade Department and said he would get on to the UK Department of Trade and Industry when he got back to Britain. The problem of sorting out Distillers was only just beginning.

Back in London on May 12, Ernest called a comprehensive control meeting to get to grips with Guinness again. He felt he had to return to the routine of weekly control meetings which had served him so well, enabling him to keep his finger on the pulse of all the various activities round the group. 'I had a long talk with Lord Iveagh, and I had previously arranged to ask Vic Steel to bring me up to date with his thoughts on the beer business – he had only joined the company in October, so we had had little chance to sit back and take a view on where it was going. I saw all the other managing directors, so that I got a feel for the state of the business.'

Meanwhile, Steel had set up an office at Distillers' head office in St James' Square with a small group from Guinness until a clearer picture of management requirements could be formed. They enrolled Ed Kappus, an organisation specialist whom Bain had often used. Steel was getting concerned: overselling and overcapacity had been confirmed. My father arranged to see Sir Brian Hayes, permanent secretary at the Department of Trade and Industry, about the US duty threat.

Ernest: 'It was against this background that I started getting heavy breathing from Risk, who had gone on holiday after the bid. When he returned he wanted to know about reorganising the board, and when was the company going to be registered in Scotland, and so on. I had to go back to the US for some prearranged investor relations meetings, so I suggested to Risk that since we had been in control of Distillers for only a few weeks we should discuss what we had discovered. As Ward, Steel and I had to be in the US anyway, I asked Risk to come over to meet us in Washington. Steel was going to be present as the boss of Distillers. However, a philosophical difference was already manifesting itself between Guinness and Risk. We saw our priority as making profits for our shareholders: he seemed to be concerned with corporate matters and administration.'

As the date of the Washington meeting approached, the difficulties Steel was experiencing in getting things done became clear, and doubts began to grow as to whether the two-tier board structure was going to get in the way of the smooth and efficient running of the combined group. Ernest: 'And moving the head office to Scotland, lock, stock and barrel, could not be contemplated at that moment. It would have resulted in chaos. We needed more flexibility in implementing the timing of these changes. The question was, would Risk agree and what would happen if he didn't? Peter Keehan on the Guinness board was protesting violently about not being on the board of the new holding company, to maintain the Irish representation. Other Guinness directors were making similar noises. Worst of all, Lord Boyd's name was left off the list of holding board directors as a result of a printer's omission. He was to resign from the board, and at a board meeting on May 9. I was elected deputy chairman in his place.'   The third week of May was to prove crucial.

Ernest and Steel flew to the US with Rhodes. They saw the major businesses over there, including Somerset Distributors and Renfield, and had a series of meetings with investors. Their session with the Somerset people did not fill them with confidence. It was clear that top management would need to spend a lot of time in the US, and the group would have to appoint an American supremo. They briefed a headhunter and eventually recruited a top executive from Unilever. 'I thought that maybe I should do what the managing director of Nestlé had always done, and supervise the US myself as it was going to be so important to the overall future of the combined company. It was a country of stark contrasts, between massive opportunities and massive immediate problems, particularly from increased duty and parallel imports. We had no top-level contacts. It is in this context that one needs to look at Ward's recommendation with regard to our $100 million investment with one of Boesky's investment funds that summer, as a means of having a high-level financier taking an interest in the company: he could put us in touch with key people and help us with our eventual US acquisition programme. I had a half-hour breakfast meeting with him, and he impressed me enormously. We were always getting propositions for acquisitions in the US, but only after everyone else over there had seen them. Boeksy was a high-flyer, and maybe he could help us.'

Steel had dinner with Risk on the Saturday night, May 17. Ward and my father arranged to meet Risk for lunch the following day, at the Ritz Carlton Hotel in Washington.

'On Sunday morning, I called Vic from my car. He was tired. He said that my meeting with Risk would be difficult, as he was irritated at having had to come to the US at all. Ward and I met him in his room at the Ritz Carlton at 11 o'clock: his tone was frosty, and maybe he was still jet-lagged from the previous day. But he said that this was the only time he had available. He didn't have a suite, so we were all sitting round his bed. I started talking about the problems of working with Distillers, the management lethargy, what we had found, about the overselling, the fact that Distillers had obviously misled us about production rationalisation, and how I was very worried about the profits against that background. I said that the major issue we had to resolve was how to make things happen at Distillers in order to keep the shareholders satisfied. On June 16, only a month away, we had to announce the Guinness half-year results, and I would certainly be asked what I had found at Distillers. The analysts and press would be probing, and they would be clued-up to look for any weakness or hesitation. We would have to appear confident in what we were doing, but at this stage I lacked the facts to be confident.

'Risk appeared to be listening for a bit, and then he interrupted: "That is very interesting, but my concern is to ensure that the legal sanctity of the listing particulars in the offer document is adhered to, to the letter. When are we going to move the head office to Scotland and change the company name?" If production in Scotland was going to be further rationalised, he would have to be convinced that it was justified, and the same went for other matters. He was going to see to it that everything was implemented to the letter. He kept banging on about the fact that the listing particulars were legally binding.'

The three men went to lunch, all feeling ruffled. Ernest was put out that Risk constantly talked about himself and his own views. The pair of them were clearly taking very divergent views of what needed to be done, and what was most important. Ward was cautiously trying to hold the middle ground.

'Over lunch Ward asked Risk how he saw his role as non-executive chairman, the term which had appeared against his name in the Distillers offer documents. This has been subsequently presented as a provocative question, but it was sparked off by this "I" monologue we had endured from Risk. The response was unexpected. With a smile, he said: "In company law there is just a chairman, and the chairman is the boss." I could propose, but he would dispose, and he would be the conduit with the non-executive directors. I had always seen the board of Guinness and the management as members of a team. He was saying that he would organise the non-executives. He would chair investor meetings, which had not been the practice at Guinness. He would determine the board meeting agenda, and he would determine how executives would run the company. The role of the executives was merely to implement, no more and no less.

'I said, choking on my soup, "That is not at all the spirit in which we had discussed the role of the non-executive chairman in this case." The success of Guinness to date had been at least partially based on the harmonious working relationship among members of the board and management. This had enabled the management at all times to move very quickly and take decisions. Before every board meeting I had taken Lord Iveagh through the agenda, so he was well-briefed, but he didn't tell me what to do. The offer document had said that the company would be run under my leadership, which was totally different from my being merely the implementer. Ward was provoked into remarking that the proposed board structure, against the need to move fast, was top-heavy and would be an impediment to action on Distillers. He thought there was a real danger of this being seized on as an excuse for inaction by people at Distillers who didn't want change. If they felt that the chairman and chief executive were separate and apart, they might slip through the middle and make it virtually impossible to implement the decisions Steel would have to make.

'At this point Risk said: "Are you saying that you don't want a separate chairman?" Ward said that that was not what we were saying. We had a separate chairman and chief executive now, but we needed some flexibility and time to set things up so that we got it right for the business. We didn't want to make mistakes simply because we were being driven by the wrong priorities. For example, it was impossible that we could just tell everyone in the Portman Square office that they would be in Scotland on Monday morning.

'At the end Risk was poker-faced. I said, "Your views on the chairman's relations with the management, and in particular me, are so different from my understanding and intent when we got into this that I will have to discuss it with Lord Iveagh before we go any further." At that, the meeting ended and Risk took a plane home.'

Ernest insists that he never claimed Risk 'thumped the table' during this confrontation. Instead, his recollection is that Risk was icy and at times sneering. 'It seemed to be a matter of Scots pride: we may have lost the battle, but we will run the company. He would also be seeing off the Irish. Risk denigrated the family aspect of Guinness and the Irish dimension, although I pointed out that Guinness had taken drastic steps to rationalise production in Ireland. He kept repeating this phrase about "the legal sanctity of the listing particulars".'

When Ernest returned to London, his immediate priority was to catch up with the progress that Steel and Young were making in getting the facts on Distillers.

Steel had decided he had to hold review meetings of the Distillers companies. He asked Ernest to sit in on these when he could, to get a feel for what was being discussed. Ernest also attended reviews of the beer business and the retail and health groups. The Distillers reviews confirmed the need for immediate cost savings to protect the profits, but also the difficulty of doing this. Rhodes was pushing, and the Guinness auditors, Price Waterhouse, wanted to be allowed to get at it, so did Bain. There was still considerable foot-dragging at Distillers. Like the Guinness Irish operations in Ernest's early days, they would ask to be told what Steel and the others wanted to know, but would never themselves volunteer anything in return.

Ernest: 'The nightmare began to envelop me, and so did Risk's insistence on instant implementation of the structure of these boards and sub-boards, which were now looking more like an impediment than a basis for action. There was a real danger of loss of control from administrative constipation. This is why companies often turn in poor results after a takeover. But Risk and Charles Fraser were determined to pursue their legalistic, bureaucratic line. Steel and I and the others were working flat-out, and we were tired and worried. Fraser and Risk were orchestrating a campaign involving Distillers directors and advisers, including Lord Rockley of Kleinwort Benson and Sir Nigel Broackes. They were starting to create a crisis.'

Ernest met Fraser on June 3. 'He was quite reasonable to my face, but a new worry was beginning to bother me. All these people had some sort of special interest in addition to their ostensible concern about the letter of the law. Risk was interested in the group's banking business, Fraser the legal business, Broackes had talked to Ward about his own company, Trafalgar House, supplying shipping services.'

My father discussed these problems at length with Steel, Ward and Iveagh. It was a conflict caused by a clash of timescales and priorities. Risk's concerns had sown real worries in Ernest's mind.

The whole issue was formally and exhaustively discussed by the Guinness board on June 12, at a meeting in the Portman Square office attended by every director except Ward and the Marquess of Dufferin and Ava. Iveagh recalled that the bid for Distillers had been approved by the board in January on the basis that Ernest and his team would manage the businesses in every sense of the word, along the lines that had been so successful over the previous four years. And this was precisely the basis upon which the institutional investors had supported the bid. The outline board structure suggested at that time had seemed to be appropriate, he added, based on the limited amount that was then known about Distillers. Now that the bid had been successful and more was known of Distillers, said Iveagh, Guinness had to be very careful to ensure that the ultimate board structure was totally appropriate to the needs of the business, and was not such as to be likely to operate against the company's interests. 'The executive directors have a tremendous task ahead to achieve the profits needed,' he pointed out. 'It can be done, but the management needs an unimpeded road to do so, removed from business politics, special interests, or other difficulties. This, of course, has been the secret of Guinness's success in the past four years, and indeed over as many years as I can remember.'

Iveagh declared that a study had to be undertaken now, to decide how the board structure should evolve to support the management and the interests of shareholders. In the meantime, those board members whose names were not on the list of directors discussed for the new holding board should send him their offers of resignation for him to hold and exercise at the appropriate time.

It was one of the few occasions where Iveagh clearly wanted to take an active part, and he gave every impression that he had discussed it with the family. Ernest then reported that information coming through on the situation at Distillers suggested that the 'inflexible attitude to an evolutionary process' by certain individuals could pose difficulties. The board formally endorsed Iveagh's views.

There now developed an intense political struggle, the like of which the Guinness board had never encountered. Risk and his allies were continuing to agitate. Christopher Reeves, chief executive of Morgan Grenfell, was pressing my father to go along with Risk. He and Risk had gone on a trip to Moscow, and afterwards Risk had written him a letter which had been a model of how a non-executive chairman should act, and not at all consistent with what had been talked about in Washington.

Ernest: 'They also saw their opportunity to become pseudo-heroes and get control over me. In their lobbying of the merchant bank and stockbroker advisers, and of Robin Leigh-Pemberton, Governor of the Bank of England, they were calling it "a test of the new City". It was no longer a question of the timing of the changes to the board and administration. They were blowing it up into a real threat to the whole self-regulatory system. Risk was seeing Leigh-Pemberton at least once a month, in his role as head of a clearing bank – the Bank of Scotland. They were meeting behind our backs.'

Guinness consulted Freshfields, the solicitors, who were also lawyers to the Bank of England. Their opinion was that fiduciary duties required the directors of the company to consider what was in the shareholders' interests at all times. It is easy to forget in the midst of all this turmoil that the Distillers offer document contained no timetable for the implementation of the various changes. Freshfields said that the board of Guinness had to do what they thought was right for shareholders *at that time*. If they believed that the intentions stated in the offer document were not going to work, they had a duty not to implement them.

Ernest talked to Sir Gordon Reece, Howard Hughes of Price Waterhouse, and David Walker of the Bank of England – who had been lobbied by Risk, and did not go along with the line my father was taking. He suggested that Ernest should have a final attempt to sort things out with Risk.

On June 16 Guinness announced its interim results, which were well received. Ernest was able to handle the Distillers questions without overclaiming or understating, cautious without giving cause for alarm. He said: 'We have been in control for only eight weeks, and there is a great deal to do.'

Risk and Ernest met for dinner in the Grill Room at the Savoy Hotel in London on June 26. They had what my father describes as a perfectly polite conversation, in which Risk nevertheless would not budge on his insistence about the listing particulars, and the latest theme about this being a test of City self-regulation. 'He was immovable. I said, let's be sensible, we need time and what's a month or so anyway? It was turning from a worrying situation into an internecine war. I mentioned the Freshfields opinion, but it made no impression. He informed me that it would not be long before the press were told about the whole situation. In the middle of the meal, Risk took a telephone call. It turned out to be from Broackes. I subsequently found out that Risk and Broackes were organising opposition to a number of resolutions at the next day's Distillers board meeting. They knew that Guinness representatives didn't normally turn up to those meetings. However, on this occasion a number of us turned up in Spengler's office in time to ensure that the resolutions were passed without difficulty.'

A succession of City people started paying visits to Portman Square to deliver their views on the situation to Ernest. 'Reeves and Rockley were worried about their reputations in the City.' On July 2, Seelig had indicated that a compromise might be reached. He said that Risk might not feel so personally uptight about the need for flexibility, and might accept a compromise, such as choosing another non-executive chairman, whom Risk would approve. But at their next meeting on July 8 the rest of the Guinness board reacted badly to what they quickly named the 'rent-a-chairman' concept. They felt that if they had got themselves into this mess by appointing someone they did not know, then choosing someone else they did not know would only compound the problem. Iveagh clearly did not want to face the impending City aggro, and told Ernest that he would opt for the presidency. Thus the only logical candidate for chairman was Ernest, who was already vice-chairman and chief executive. Ernest and Iveagh agreed that there would be no change to their working relationship: only their titles would change.

They endorsed Iveagh as president. Ernest: 'I had it in mind that Vic Steel could become managing director of the group eventually, and I could just be chairman. If I had wanted to be chairman all along, the time for me to have said so would have been at the beginning of the Distillers bid.' The board endorsed this scheme for implementation at the right moment.

On July 10 Risk and his friends had a meeting at Morgan Grenfell's offices with representatives from Cazenove, Wood Mackenzie and Kleinwort.

'We had a real feeling that the whole thing was rapidly running out of control. Steel said Distillers was becoming unmanageable, because a number of their senior people knew what was going on. It would have a disastrous effect on the shareholders if it broke surface. John Chiene, senior partner of Wood Mackenzie, a close friend of Fraser and still resentful at Cazenove being brought into the takeover battle, was against any compromise: he wanted Risk installed with as much power as possible.'

Later on July 10, Iveagh asked Risk to see him at Portman Square. Risk had said on June 26 that he wanted to see Iveagh, and Ernest had promised to fix it. The two of them were there to greet Risk, who without hesitation told Iveagh he wanted Ernest out of the room before any more was discussed. He said: 'I am not speaking to you with him around.' When they were alone, Iveagh told Risk that the Guinness board could not accept him as chairman. Risk left.

The next day Wood Mackenzie said they were against Risk stepping down, or any other compromise. Chiene went to see Ernest and Iveagh, and fired a few shots across their bows, including a threat to resign the Guinness account and make the row public. Risk and Fraser had previously made similar threats. Ernest: 'The battle with Risk was taking up too much time. We were now convinced that the whole thing was out of control, and would be seen to be out of control. It became inevitable that we could not delay the board's agreed plan to remove the uncertainty and to be seen to be in control of our own affairs.' On the Friday, there were rumours from the Guinness public relations department that Risk, Fraser and co. had briefed the Scottish press as they had threatened, with the aim of making a pre-emptive strike. Iveagh and Ernest went to see Ivan Fallon of *The Sunday Times*. 'He used to call every Thursday to see if there was anything new he could latch on to. We gave him a background briefing on the situation, so that he had an understanding of Iveagh's philosophy and mine. He was the only City journalist Lord Iveagh had met in years, but he wanted to make sure Fallon didn't think it was just me who was behind our point of view.'

That night at Knoll House my parents held a party with the intention of getting the senior Guinness and Distillers people together socially. They erected a marquee on the lawn, which was also used the next night for a combined twenty-first birthday party for Jo and myself and on the Sunday for a fête to raise money for roof repairs at the village church next door. When my mother introduced herself by saying, 'I'm Carole Saunders, I'm so pleased to see you,' John Connell's wife replied, 'I'm *Mrs* Connell,' and proceeded audibly to criticise the seating arrangements, the decor and the food. She had obviously decided to take her revenge for the changes at Distillers, despite the fact that they still had their company Bentley.

On Sunday Ivan Fallon wrote: 'Saunders needs an unfettered hand, and there is just a possibility he won't get it. The key man was to be the august Sir Thomas Risk, Governor of the Bank of Scotland and Distillers' principal banker. On paper and in the heat of battle that sounded fine. Events since have changed the perspective, however. Lord Iveagh's willingness to step aside should permit Saunders to assume the role of executive chairman; no "rent-a-chairman" would be needed.' Fraser briefed the Scottish press on the Sunday, and the Monday papers were full of rumours. Ernest called Iveagh and said they must make an official announcement immediately, to remove uncertainty.

On 10 a.m. on Monday July 14, Guinness announced that Ernest had been appointed chairman as well as remaining chief executive, with Iveagh as president. There was to be no holding board structure, and no place for Risk. After the announcement Ernest called a number of major shareholders to inform them of the news. They had no reaction, but thanked Ernest for letting them know.

Shortly afterwards, Robin Leigh-Pemberton's office called the chairman to a meeting at the Bank of England. Ernest, Iveagh and Ward saw the Governor at three o'clock, with George Blunden, the deputy governor, and another official. 'Leigh-Pemberton was very uptight and brusque at first. He said, "What's going on?" Ward and I explained the problems with Distillers, and the dilemma we faced. We had asked for flexibility. It had become impossible to work together with Risk, and there was a danger of losing control. We had to deliver the profits to the shareholders, and to do so required flexibility in terms of timing and implementation, but Risk had refused to see the point, and we had taken legal advice about where our fiduciary duties lay. We had no desire to ride roughshod over City regulations, but the action we had taken was absolutely necessary. Leigh-Pemberton gradually calmed down, but Blunden was angry and kept interrupting. Finally the Governor conceded that we had legal right on our side, but gave me a lecture on handling sensitive Scottish issues, how to be a good chairman and the need for damage limitation. We had had a serious talk, although Blunden was still unhappy. We left feeling that Leigh-Pemberton basically accepted the situation. There was no mention whatsoever of City self-regulation.'

The following morning's press was largely critical. The *Financial Times* commented that my father had lost a great deal of goodwill in the City in one day. He had used the promise of a holding company to swing the Scottish institutional vote. Explanations so far had been 'so vague as to be insulting'. The *Guardian* believed that Ernest had chosen the wrong approach: 'the effects will linger for a decade'. Ernest: 'They were fed all sorts of stuff by Risk, Wood Mackenzie, Fraser and Argyll. The idea seemed to be that with sufficient press pressure the Guinness board would feel obliged to compel me to retract. I would lose face and resign.'

On July 15, Reeves, Seelig and Graham Walsh from Morgan Grenfell visited Portman Square in very solemn mood. They pronounced that the best way to calm the situation would be for Ernest 'to have the courage of his convictions' and put the issue to shareholders at an Extraordinary General Meeting. They said: 'If you get their endorsement, no one can say anything against you.' It was an idea that Ernest had not thought of, and he immediately said he was perfectly happy to go along with it.

Ernest also got a message from Malcolm Rifkind, the Scottish Secretary, who wanted a meeting. Ernest went on his own, and found Rifkind accompanied by Sir William Fraser, his permanent secretary. 'I got one hour of personal abuse, clearly intended as a public relations exercise for the Scottish press. It was later referred to as a dressing-down. I didn't get a word in edgeways, and I eventually walked out in disgust. I said, "I'm not putting up with this." Every time I tried to explain something, he said he was not interested. He was so unpleasant, and I have never been talked to like that in my life. He had no conception of the practical problems of trying to run a business, or the need to adapt one's priorities when the situation has dramatically changed.'

A multi-dimensional battle was developing, quite as intense as the takeover campaign, involving the City, Whitehall and Scotland. It would inevitably interfere with the process of revitalising Distillers. Guinness was lurching from one major confrontation to another. Ernest told his management at Guinness to keep their heads down while he dealt with the public crisis.

Wood Mackenzie resigned as stockbrokers to Guinness in a message sent by facsimile machine on July 15. Cazenove said they were not going to resign but were not going to do anything. Roux was nevertheless against firing them. 'To resolve the situation, we needed some new merchant bank advisers. I had a long-standing meeting with Sir John Nott, the chairman of Lazard Brothers, arranged by one of their corporate finance directors, Marcus Agius, who had been wooing us for some time. The idea germinated that we should ask Lazard Brothers to act as special advisers to Lord Iveagh, and to help us through the EGM phase, which we did.'

Ernest was then thrust back into the tedious routine of lobbying and explaining to all and sundry why the board changes and the related EGM were necessary. 'I had to go back to the US and explain the situation. They couldn't understand the fuss. The most noise came from the Department of Trade and Industry, pushed by Blunden, Rifkind and Alex Fletcher, the former DTI Minister who had joined the Argyll payroll. We saw the Takeover Panel – I went with Anthony Salz from Freshfields. The Stock Exchange was closely involved in the circular calling the EGM. Lazards consulted the Bank of England. Towards the end of July Guinness was summoned by Michael Howard of the DTI, who threatened us with a DTI inquiry if we did not implement the provisions of the Distillers offer document to the letter.

There was then a process of negotiation with the DTI over a period of weeks, led by Nott with Salz and Ward. No one was arguing about Risk any more. The goalposts kept changing. First, Risk had been mainly concerned with 'the legal sanctity of the offer document'. Then it became 'a test of City self-regulation'. Now it was fundamentally about the sanctity of offer documents, and above all that there should be a non-executive chairman. A compromise emerged to create a non-executive committee of the board, which would have power to appoint and remove the chairman. It was to be a committee composed entirely of non-executive directors, and there had to be a certain number of new appointees, of whom a certain number had to be Scottish. It became known within Guinness as the 'sack the chairman' committee.

The plan was put to the full board of Guinness on July 31. Ernest was not present for the discussion of Item 4, Board Structure. Ward explained to the meeting that the combination of the roles of chairman and chief executive was apparently considered to be too great a concentration of power and the DTI were, therefore, pressing for the separation of these appointments under threat of a formal investigation into the bid for Distillers. The rest of the board expressed their wholehearted support for the action taken so far, and for Ernest, as the present prosperity of the group was very largely due to his efforts, and it would be 'a major setback if his motivation were reduced in any way'.

Ernest: 'It was reported that I had enormous difficulty in getting people willing to fill the non-executive posts. On the contrary: there were plenty of offers, but I specifically wanted people who could bring valuable expertise to the company. We had no one on the board who knew about retailing, so I phoned Ian MacLaurin (now Sir Ian), the chairman of Tesco. He agreed. We wanted to expand in luxury goods, so I approached Anthony Greener, managing director of Dunhill Holdings. He was delighted. Lord King, chairman of British Airways, had agreed to let me invite Colin Marshall (now Sir Colin), his managing director, whom I had met and who knew world markets. But his appointment was blocked by Robert Henderson, BA's deputy chairman, who was a director of Kleinwort Benson. Lazards pushed for Sir David Plastow, managing director and chief executive of Vickers, a favoured Lazards client.

'Sir Ian MacGregor, who was just leaving the National Coal Board, was also suggested, and I was very keen on him. We consulted Angus Grossart, our Scottish merchant bank adviser during the Bell bid but who had been against us on Distillers. He proposed Sir Norman Macfarlane, whom I had met during the Bell bid. When I suggested to Macfarlane the additional appointment of MacGregor to make up the Scottish numbers, he violently objected. I had ultimately to choose between the two, and Lazard, Grossart and the Scottish Office said Macfarlane would be the less controversial of the two. Later I thought of Ian Chapman, then of William Collins the publishers, as we had a publishing business with *The Guinness Book of Records*.

'It was quite thrilling to interview these famous people. The problem was getting them accepted by the DTI, the Bank of England, the Scottish Office, a group of major investors led by the Prudential and all the others who seemed to have a special interest in the future of myself and the company. It was very clear that a double game was going on: the first was to agree an acceptable compromise with the authorities, and the second was to ensure that behind the scenes a structure would be in place to reverse any EGM decision in my favour by boardroom tactics. I was surrounded by political sharks, but I didn't realise it at the time.'

When he left the room during the board meeting on July 31, Ernest went straight to the Fitzroy Nuffield Clinic in nearby Bryanston Square. Carole had had to have an emergency operation. For much of August he directed Guinness from her bedside. Because of the controversy my mother was at a low ebb, and had not recovered by the following year. Her popularity was as great as my father's unpopularity: the same people who were sending her messages of goodwill were firing missiles at Ernest.

The notice calling the EGM was sent to stockholders on August 22, accompanied by an explanatory circular signed by Lord Iveagh and a letter from Ernest, Steel and Edward Guinness paying tribute to Iveagh and recommending that his contribution should be recognised by electing him president.

The circular recounted the circumstances leading up to the vote, declaring: 'It is important to restate the fundamental objective underlying the offer for Distillers, namely the creation of a new British-owned international consumer brands group able to compete with the great consumer companies of the world on equal terms. This would only be achieved through a revitalisation of Distillers based on strong financial management and international marketing skills. Guinness offered Distillers' shareholders the opportunity of realising this objective through the expertise of the Guinness management team led by Ernest Saunders.

'The board of Guinness is committed to achieving its fundamental objective and is convinced that, to achieve it, the management must be supported by a board structure entirely suitable for the very substantial task ahead. Your directors believe that, if Guinness is to achieve its objectives for Distillers, decisive action must be taken as soon as possible and a streamlined organisation structure must be established in order to implement the necessary rationalisation of the whole Distillers business. Your directors believe it is essential that the board of the company should be structured in such a way as to give the executive management team sufficient authority to take swift and decisive action, while at the same time ensuring that management receives direction and support from non-executive directors.

'In view of what is now known about the situation at Distillers, it has become apparent that the two-tier board structure proposed at the time of the offer, which involved a holding company board and two subsidiary operating company boards, was misconceived. The board of Guinness has, therefore, decided not to establish the two-tier board structure as it would have been too unwieldy and unresponsive to provide effective direction and control.

'Since April, certain members of the board have held discussions with Sir Thomas Risk, who in January had agreed to become non-executive chairman following the acquisition. These discussions covered various matters, including the manner in which it was felt that the company should be run. In the light of these discussions and the situation at Distillers, the board of Guinness concluded that it would not be in the best interests of the company and its stockholders for Sir Thomas to be elected chairman. Given the decision not to implement the two-tier board structure, your board has also decided not to proceed with proposals to appoint certain Distillers directors to the board of Guinness.'

Then Iveagh broached the nub of the matter: 'There should be no doubt that the board of Guinness recognises the importance of statements made in connection with an offer and the board unequivocally confirms that statements made in connection with the offer for Distillers fully accorded with its intentions at that time. But the board faced a serious dilemma. In its clear view it was commercially imperative to implement without delay the board structure required to direct the revitalisation of the Distillers businesses. It concluded that simply to have gone ahead and implemented the statements relating to the board appointments and structure in accordance with their precise terms would have jeopardised the achievement of the fundamental objective underlying the acquisition. The board of Guinness was most reluctant to depart from statements made in connection with the offer, but in the light of its responsibilities in the exceptional circumstances in which it found itself, the board sought advice as to how it might resolve its dilemma. The board was advised by its solicitors that its continuing fiduciary duties to Guinness and its stockholders required it to consider what was in the company's best interests at that time.

'The decisions relating to the board structure having been taken, Ernest Saunders's election as chairman (from being deputy chairman), while retaining his responsibilities as chief executive, was, in the board's unanimous judgement, required in order to secure the best interests of Guinness and its stockholders. The board strongly believes that Ernest Saunders should combine these roles at this important time in order both, internally, to reinforce the authority for implementing the necessary re-organisation of Distillers and, externally, to ensure the coherent representation of the company's policies internationally at the highest levels of industry and government.

'In reaching its decision, the board recognised that the combination of these roles provides a successful working basis for a large number of major British companies, including British Telecom, BTR, Burton Group, Cable and Wireless, Dee Corporation, Dixons, Fisons, Jaguar, Marks and Spencer and Sainsbury. It is also a familiar feature in the United States, a market of great importance to the group.'

The circular explained the need for a strong body of non-executive directors, listed the proposed new appointments and stated that they would have the power to elect and remove the chairman. The document went on to reaffirm that the group's registered office and designated head office would be transferred to Edinburgh. The meeting was set for 10 o'clock on the morning of September 11, at the Mount Royal Hotel in Bryanston Street, a couple of minutes' walk from the Portman Square office.

There were only three voices against the proposal in advance of the EGM. David Hopkinson, then the chairman of the M & G unit trust group and a personal friend of Risk, spoke out. Ernest went to see him and he was totally reasonable but said he could not change his public posture. But he did not vote against Ernest at the EGM. And Raymond Johnstone of the Glasgow fund managers Murray Johnstone – another close friend of Risk – wrote to the *Financial Times* criticising the Guinness board's stand and alleging that the non-executive committee was 'toothless'. How wrong he was to be! The investment manager of Scottish Amicable also came out against the Guinness board. But most institutions backed Ernest, and his position was strengthened when it emerged that the apparently spontaneous Risk press statements had in fact been orchestrated by Good Relations, a London PR company. In advance of the meeting, one or two major institutions announced that they would be backing the Guinness proposals, and this produced a snowball effect.

With the help of another brilliant television advertisement by Frank Lowe to ensure that the public understood Guinness's commitment to rebuilding the Scotch whisky industry, Ernest had the proxy votes he needed to win well before the meeting started. 'But, although I already had enough votes to carry the day, I wanted to win the debate on the floor of the meeting.'

There was a huge flood of press comment running up to the morning of the meeting. On the Monday, three days beforehand, the *Financial Times* pronounced: 'No one is irreplaceable.' Kenneth Fleet came thundering in from his Wapping eyrie to tell *Times* readers: 'A clever, finely orchestrated campaign by the Scottish commercial establishment will reach its crescendo in the Mount Royal Hotel, London, tomorrow. The clans in Glasgow and Charlotte Square are baying for blood and the Scottish media bathe daily in mass hysteria. The blood in particular they want is Ernest Saunders', who has been subject to malign and racist insults of a despicable kind. It is important for Guinness shareholders to recognise fully what the Scottish clique, in alliance with Kleinwort Benson, the closely related M & G and other southern supporters, are asking them to do when they vote tomorrow. They are being asked to undermine the position of Ernest Saunders and the Guinness board and senior management to the point where the group would become unmanageable.

'No one may be irreplaceable, but at risk here is an entire board. Therefore the effect on the Guinness share price if shareholders were to reject the first resolution (setting up the non-executive committee) would be painful. For that reason alone it would be inexcusable if any investing institution did not consider its obligation to those whose savings it holds and voted for the Guinness board. The voting ought to, and I believe will, go in Guinness's favour. One of Guinness's difficulties in defending its corner is the contrast that has been skilfully drawn between the ambitious and abrasive Saunders and the dignified and constructive Risk, who has wanted "to keep away from personalities" but has been astute in the timing of his interventions – and even in his use of a professional public relations adviser.

'Though Sir Thomas has seemed to keep a low profile, leaving much of the campaign against Guinness to his close aides, Raymond

Johnstone, chairman of Murray Johnstone, and Charles Fraser, the Scottish solicitor who left Morgan Grenfell with a great flourish on Monday, his role has been crucial, notably in contesting the truth of Guinness statements about the course of his dealings with Guinness directors from the time the Distillers bid succeeded up to the final break in July. For the chairman of a major bank, he has taken an extraordinary chance. Guinness insists that there are gaps in Sir Thomas's version which, if revealed, might shake some of the confidence placed in his account of events.'

On the morning of the EGM my father was woken in his hotel room by Robert Maxwell, who was launching a magazine that day and had flown in from the USA to use the EGM for his own promotional purposes. He also received a letter from the Rev. Muspratt, the vicar of Penn, telling him to fight the good fight. 'If you continue to stand rock-like and unfaltering, brushing aside all unworthy accusations of foul play, I believe that you will win the day – although somewhat battered by having to run the gauntlet of hostile opinion whipped up by your opponents.'

Queues formed outside on the pavement well before the meeting was due to begin. Ernest and Maxwell had a banter before the start. My father refused to allow TV cameras, which did not please Maxwell. Almost as soon as the proceedings opened, Maxwell in his red braces did his best to reduce the whole thing to a farce.

'The night before, Carole and I decided that if I lost the vote I would immediately resign. I told her that I reserved the right, if I won, to do the same thing. I said, "I have had enough. Guinness will never be the same again after this. I am a creative marketing man, not a politician and not a City figure, so don't be surprised if I resign."'

Iveagh made the speech of his life. He outlined the problems and the dilemma. He supported Ernest. He took his glasses off and said: 'I deeply resent the unfair personal attacks that have been made on Ernest Saunders. It has been totally unfair, and we admire him for standing up to it.'

For the next hour and a half Ernest took questions and speeches from the floor. He answered every point without a note. The red-bearded Graeme Knox of Scottish Amicable, who had been belly-aching for months, got his attack in first. However, he was completely upstaged by a Mr Gillies, a maverick who had been suing the Royal Bank of Scotland, and who made a long speech congratulating Ernest for routing the Scottish mafia. It began to turn into a hilarious event. Maxwell kept getting up to make remarks. The ever-faithful O'Hegarty talked about 'the brigands of Broad Street'. But he also asked: 'What about the cost of the bid?' Roux said it had been £2.5 billion. O'Hegarty: 'No, the lunches, the fees.' Roux did not want to answer, so Ernest turned and asked him. He said to Ernest, 'Say £100 million.'

Then Maxwell got up again, looked around and boomed: 'It's quite clear that we should all support Mr Saunders. I just want to ask him, "Will you abide by the decision of the shareholders?"' Ernest replied yes.

'I knew there were enough votes in the room to defeat me, if any proxies were withdrawn, because there were a lot of important fund managers there. The sympathy of the room was with me, so I thought I'd bring matters to a head. I asked the company secretary to read out the proxy count and then to put the resolution to the meeting. "All in favour?" We had a very considerable majority on a hand vote. Knox asked for a poll, but nobody supported him. So we closed the meeting. When everybody had left the room, I realised that now was my opportunity to resign and inform the press waiting outside. I packed my papers very slowly. It would have been a sensational thing to do. But the shareholders had supported me, and I felt I could not resign. So I didn't. I walked slowly out of the room and was then besieged by the Fleet Street press, and I could see the Scottish press leaving with their tails between their legs. We had a board meeting immediately afterwards, when I was congratulated on my handling of the meeting, and the board pledged support.'

Ernest wanted to hold a meeting of the new board in Scotland as soon as possible, but the first date they could all get together up there was February 10, 1987. The first full meeting they could have anywhere was in London on December 2. There was a lunch for directors at Portman Square after the Mount Royal meeting, but it is significant in the light of later events that neither Macfarlane nor Plastow stayed for that.

After lurching from one major drama to another for the past fifteen months, Guinness was at last able to get down to business. Ernest organised a get-together for the team who were going to run the group. Brian Baldock had come from Imperial Group after the takeover by Hanson that year, joining Dowling, Roux and Steel. A weekend seminar was fixed at Champneys for early October, to sort out administrative procedures and the decision-making structure for the enlarged group. 'We had to forge a new entrepreneurial style, now that we were so large. I had finally got the people I needed, so I wouldn't have to run the operations myself. The only remaining personnel task was to replace Roux, so that he would be free to pursue his plans in the City. We also started to rethink the strategic balance of our product groups. Now that we had Distillers we had a marvellous portfolio of beverage brands. We also had superb brand assets in Gleneagles, Champneys and Hediard. We were in luxury products as well as being in the beverage business. We would inevitably now have to rethink our corporate positioning and priorities.'

The Distillers reviews were gathering pace and a programme of cost-saving was implemented to protect profits. A strategic brand review was started with the aid of Lowe Howe Spink, and its findings began to be put in place. Production was centralised in Scotland. A centre for worldwide brand development was set up in Hammersmith. New arrangements to improve and control distribution were being planned overseas. Bell was to become the UK trading company, taking over the UK Distillers brands, and it would continue to be run from Perth. Ernest agreed that White Horse should sponsor the British entry for the America's Cup as a way of giving that brand a fillip: it worked well. Guinness was working with the DTI on reaching an agreement with the Americans on spirits imports. As part of his desire to establish a fresh working relationship with the Scots, Guinness gave Royal Bank of Scotland some of the business Distillers had taken away from it. Sir Michael Herries, the bank's chairman, gave valuable advice on how to improve the group's relationships in Scotland. Plans were announced for the Mark Phillips Equestrian Centre at Gleneagles.

Ernest met Garret Fitzgerald, then the Irish Prime Minister, in Dundalk. Fitzgerald urged him not to forget the Irish role in Guinness.

As had been agreed, it was necessary to extend the company's international shareholder base beyond the UK and into Europe, the US and Japan. Furer had talked about this before the bid, and Roux and Ernest went to Japan to talk to investors there, as well as holding a one-week roadshow in Europe. Plans to have the shares listed in the US had been under way since the summer.

On October 29 the board held its first formal meeting since the EGM. Furer, MacLaurin and Plastow could not make it. The non-executive committee was approved, but it was noted that the proposed powers and procedures of the committee were very poorly drawn and could be regarded as potentially divisive. The board decided to review the committee's constitution when the necessary amendments to the company's Articles of Association were considered. The Distillers share registrar in Edinburgh would be asked to take on the whole group register, but Roux reported that more time was needed to sort out the business of registering the company in Scotland.

Ernest: 'I felt that, with a couple of months free from corporate trauma, we were rolling again.'

12

SCAPEGOAT

The shareholders' meeting concerned with the Thomas Risk affair was a pyrrhic victory for Ernest. He now had a whole new board, many of whom did not know each other, including a powerful and ultimately fateful Scottish presence on the non-executive side led by Sir Norman Macfarlane, who immediately had himself elected chairman of the non-executive committee. Sir Norman was personally and professionally extremely well-connected in Scotland. His friends, he claimed to my father, included the Scottish Secretary of State, Malcolm Rifkind, the merchant banker Angus Grossart, James Gulliver's adviser Sir Alex Fletcher and many, many others.

The non-executive committee, which had been given the power to remove the chairman, was intended as a safeguard to prevent the chairman and chief executive from abusing his powers. Its very constitution provided the Scottish group with a tailor-made means to get rid of Ernest Saunders.

He had routed the Scottish Establishment, taken back across the border what many saw as the crown jewels, Arthur Bell, and then the crown itself, Distillers. He had taken on the Secretary of State and he had in their eyes spurned the Governor of the Bank of Scotland. Perhaps most dangerous of all, my father had defeated James Gulliver, the Campbeltown grocer's son and a champion of Scottish industry. Scotland may have lost the battle, but they could still win the war!

Even after the landslide victory for Ernest at the shareholders' meeting in September 1986, the Scottish press continued their vitriolic attack on him. As the shareholder channel had been closed by the EGM, in Edinburgh, Glasgow and London various Scottish factions plotted to find other means. The *Sunday Telegraph* wrote in January 1987: 'Is there, as some believe, a Scottish Mafia at work behind the fall of Ernest Saunders at Guinness?' The article went on: 'Those who know Scots will appreciate that there can never be one Mafia, but at least two: east and west.'

Macfarlane became both Trojan horse and standard-bearer for Scotland. He would inevitably become Lord Macfarlane of Glasgow if his valuable services to that city could be rounded off with the chairmanship of a company as substantial as Guinness.

Ernest, on the other hand, had only one objective – to be allowed to get on with the reorganising of Distillers and make the company perform as he had said he would. It was a massive job, and Bill Young of Bain & Co. and Vic Steel worked continuously on this with my father. They had decided to change the group's year-end to December 31, but still had to produce results for the twelve months to the end of September, 1986.

On November 20 Malcolm Bruce, Nicholas Fairbairn and four other MPs put down an Early Day Motion in the House of Commons. It contained a horrifically personal attack on Ernest:

'That this House deplores the conduct of the chief executive of Guinness-Distillers plc (sic), who has brought the business world and the City into disrepute (sic) by wilfully misleading Ministers and Members of Parliament, by making promises to move the head-quarters of the Guinness Distillers group to Scotland in order to influence public opinion in advance of the takeover bid while clearly having no intention of doing any such thing; regrets that a major British company has at its head a person of such low integrity; and calls on the Secretary of State for Trade and Industry to introduce measures to penalise severly (sic) companies and persons who pursue such blatantly dishonest practices to promote takeovers.'

Other Scottish MPs added their names to this motion. As far as Ernest was concerned, the issue had died at the shareholders' meeting, but the Scots had not given up. If they could paint Ernest in a bad enough light, then with intense lobbying against the background of the government's weak electoral position in Scotland, the demand for an inquiry could succeed. Alex Fletcher, then a Scottish MP and adviser to Gulliver, was continuously pressing Michael Howard, the then Under Secretary of State for Trade and Industry, to investigate Guinness.

On Saturday November 22, just before Ernest went north to watch Manchester United as a guest of Professor Roland Smith, an odd message came via Roux from Anthony Salz of Freshfields, the solicitors. Ernest: 'Salz was saying that we should do everything to make ourselves "useful" to the Department of Trade and Industry, who might always reopen the inquiry that had been threatened earlier. I found this hard to contemplate, since the shareholders' meeting had to my mind closed this matter once and for all. The shareholders had supported us, and I thought we had a deal with the DTI, the Bank of England and the rest of the regulatory authorities on this point.' As it happened, Young, Steel and Ernest were already in close contact with the DTI regarding the problem of whisky tax in Japan, threatened gin quotas on imports into the US as a result of a dispute with the European Community, and other matters including an agreed minimum standard for Scotch. 'These were all items in which we felt we should take a lead, since we were now the dominant producer in the whisky industry.' In some of these cases Ernest felt that the government did not correctly understand the issues and faced the potentially embarrassing prospect of having to rebrief representatives at negotiations. 'The DTI officials were most appreciative of our help and said so.' Ernest thought relations were good.

Suddenly a meeting he had arranged with the permanent secretary at the DTI, Sir Brian Hayes, was inexplicably cancelled, just before the end of November. Ernest did not understand what was going on. He asked around and discovered that Gulliver had suddenly become what was described as 'hyperactive' at the House of Commons, freqently being seen lobbying MPs. Brian Basham of Broad Street Associates was also active behind the media. Gulliver is now chairman of Broad Street and a major shareholder.

By the end of 1986 the mood in Britain was turning against takeover activity. The boom had peaked with two mega-bids running concurrently. United Biscuits had battled with Hanson for Imperial tobacco, and Guinness had defeated Argyll to win Distillers. There were three companies involved in each bid, bankers and brokers representing all of these, and the amount of money involved either in underwriting the bids or paying advisers' fees was incredible. There were fears that the merchant banking machinery was breaking down under the strain of increasingly aggressive tactics. Both United Biscuits and Guinness had got bids de-referred from the Monopolies and Mergers Commission when they agreed to sell off brands, thus setting a precedent in competition policy. Meanwhile the government was becoming increasingly alarmed at excesses in the City. There had been scandals at Lloyd's insurance market, involving millions of pounds. Johnson Matthey Bankers had crashed in October 1984 and had to be rescued by the Bank of England, and the government was still reeling from the Westland crisis at the start of 1986.

Although some of these issues dated back several years, they were unresolved and seemed to be getting out of hand. And the City was grappling with the strange new world ushered in by the stock market's Big Bang, where the old jobbing system was discontinued and share trading vanished from the floor of the Stock Exchange and instead took place on the telephone with prices posted on computer screens.

Self-regulation in the City was perceived as being threatened, insider dealing was rife, and Labour MPs were calling the City to order. Bryan Gould, Roy Hattersley and Denis Skinner warned that Mrs Thatcher's popular capitalism was giving way to a 'casino economy' and draining industry. 'City greed', 'white-collar fraud' and 'insider dealing' were phrases of the moment.

On the other side of the Atlantic, the American Securities and Exchange Commission was in the process of busting Ivan Boesky, the legendary Wall Street arbitrageur, for insider dealing. He had agreed to name names as part of his plea bargaining: the effect on the takeover scene was dramatic. The world of mergers and acquisitions shut down almost overnight. The other arbitrageurs retreated to their lairs. Everyone was agog to know whether Boesky's confessions would have a ripple effect in Britain.

Above all, the government was making plans to ensure a favourable political climate for the likely general election in the summer of the following year, 1987. The Conservatives could not be seen to be going easy on City or commercial crime. They knew that the long-awaited House of Commons insider dealing debate was due to take place on December 2, and they were open to opposition attack over the lack of City prosecutions.

Malcolm Rifkind, the Scottish Secretary, was applying pressure of his own on Howard to take action over Guinness. The Tories knew that if they alienated the Scots at this stage they would lose even more seats north of the border than they already feared. Paul Channon, then Secretary of State for Trade and Industry, was powerless to resist pressure. He could not lift a finger in Guinness's favour for fear of being accused of bias, since he was a member of the Guinness family by marriage. He stood aside and Michael Howard came into the front line.

On December 1, Roux went into Ernest's office and told him that the DTI had sent two officials into the Portman Square headquarters, and others to other Guinness offices, carrying a letter of authority to investigate the affairs of the company. Ernest told Roux to get Salz of Freshfields to come round as soon as possible. Ernest informed Lord Iveagh, and the Guinness company secretary advised the rest of the board. Without warning the DTI issued a press statement which included a very damaging phrase, subsequently withdrawn, alleging 'misconduct by members of the board'. Withdrawn or not, the damage had been done. Trial by innuendo had begun.

Guinness put out a statement to press and staff which contained virtually no comment on the investigation, but told everyone in the company to proceed on the basis that the show must go on and people should get on with their jobs. But Ernest was devastated.

'Davidson rushed up to tell me our shares had plummeted and all hell was breaking loose on the stock market. I was deeply shocked and totally dumbfounded. What on earth was this about? Why did they do it? It subsequently became clear that a number of forces had put pressure on the government for different motivations, and that Guinness/Saunders would be an ideal scapegoat for a demonstration by the DTI of its determination to "clean up the City".'

The City Establishment and the regulators, angry at the Risk affair and investor support for Ernest, were very aware of the public's increased awareness of City practices, insider dealing and bid manipulation since BTR/Tilling had set off the mega-bid era, followed by the highly publicised battles involving Dixons/Currys, Burtons/Debenhams and the various deals of Lord Hanson. Now with Big Bang, the size and scale of bids was enormous. Yet the Establishment wanted to maintain control by self-regulatory action. They needed a visible example.

'I was not part of the Establishment, so an attack on me would not damage City credibility. I was considered to have achieved very big success too fast. I was very visible and totally identified with Guinness, making me the perfect fall-guy. The government wanted to demonstrate and broaden reciprocal working arrangements with the US authorities. The Boesky scandal provided the opportunity and the incentive. Guinness had put $100 million into one of Boesky's investment funds in the summer of 1986, at a time when he was still being hailed as a genius. But by December any links with Boesky aroused suspicion and the association with insider dealing.

'One big attack on a high-profile company, identified with one high-profile person, was the ideal strategy. It might be all that was necessary to remove potential electoral embarrassment concerning City scandals. There was a general election to come in 1987, and

Thatcher wanted the decks cleared.'

Guinness had planned a reception at the National Gallery on the evening the DTI investigation was announced. At the initiative of Jacob Rothschild, the company had lent the famous Scottish painting, *The MacNab*, for the new Barry wing of the Gallery. A large number of influential guests had accepted invitations, including a number of Roux's City contacts, some old, some new, as well as a few leading financial journalists. That same evening there was to be a dinner hosted by Sir David Plastow for the new non-executive committee of Guinness. The idea was that the new non-executive directors were to meet informally with the other non-executive directors left over from the old board: Lord Iveagh, Jonathan and Edward Guinness and Tom Ward.

Ernest: 'It struck me as odd that there was to be a pre-meeting of the new directors on their own. From the outset they seemed to be setting themselves up as a board within a board. There was also no suggestion, in the interests of harmony, which was what Sir Norman Macfarlane had kept stressing to me after the shareholders' meeting, that the executive directors or even the chairman should be asked in for a drink. Tom Ward was briefed by me to explain the Boesky investment to his new colleagues. He was the originator and the architect, and so was in the best possible position to do so. There was to be a full board meeting the next day, December 2 – the first occasion when all the directors could get together since the changes wrought by the shareholders' meeting.'

The press were waiting for Ernest at the National Gallery that evening. Ernest did not know why the inspectors had been appointed, so he had nothing to say to them. They even decided to forgo the planned speeches, where Ernest was to be thanked, as the company's representative, for lending the painting. One or two senior Ministers cried off, including the Secretary of State for Agriculture, Guinness's sponsoring ministry, but the recently appointed Minister for Scotland, Ian Lang, did attend and appeared to know nothing, as did Sir Gordon Borrie.

The next day, December 2, Ernest asked Ward how his presentation at the Sir David Plastow dinner had gone. He replied that they were all very supportive, and he had explained the Boesky investment. But Ernest instantly sensed trouble brewing at the board meeting that followed their conversation.

'Macfarlane was the leading player. It was clear that the new directors, under the leadership of Macfarlane, were in the forefront and were ignoring the other non-executive directors. Macfarlane started to act most aggressively from the outset. No one was interested in the forthcoming results or other agenda items. I was attacked personally over the Boesky investment, which was stoutly defended by Roux and Ward. The new guys would look out of the window, or scribble on their pads, while I was speaking. The term "error of judgement" came up over and over again. Sir Norman was extraordinarily rude and hostile: this was the first time any director had ever criticised me in that way. Ward and Roux gave a detailed account of the Boesky investment. Both, expecially Roux, were most emphatic in denying any suggestion that the investment had anything whatsoever to do with, or was in any way a *quid pro quo* for, Boesky assenting his Distillers shares to Guinness. Roux was most eloquent and gave an excellent rationale for the investment.

'Macfarlane started talking about "City greed" and "avarice", the sort of words that were being used by Michael Howard and other government Ministers.'

There was discussion about when to make the Boesky investment public. Ward counselled that the responsibility of the directors was to get back the investment intact, and that from his information there was a good chance of this happening, but not if Guinness mishandled the matter and acted unilaterally without considering the other investors. Ward was in touch with lawyers representing the other investors. 'We had to be very careful,' he said, 'about what we said publicly.' This strategy was agreed on the day.

Ernest: 'The rest of the meeting rambled on with aggressive questions from the new directors regarding the DTI investigation. They asked me if I knew anything I had not told them. Since I did not there was no difficulty in answering that question. What I resented were the innuendoes right from day one that I was somehow responsible for the DTI inquiry itself, and I could not believe the death wishes that I could feel around me from Macfarlane and his other new directors. He was not only acting as leader of the new non-executives, but as the lead Scot, now on the inside. The *Sunday Express* claimed that the board wanted me out, but Macfarlane was quick to call me at home to deny it and pledge his full support. Against enormous media pressure and shock inside the company, I tried to deal with this new crisis, even though I was already exhausted from the Bell and Distillers campaigns and the Risk affair.'

Ernest promised to keep the board advised of developments. Howard Hughes of Price Waterhouse was also at this meeting, and when he was asked about the interim financial statement he confirmed that Price Waterhouse had been fully consulted in its preparation and had reviewed the figures and were satisfied. Meanwhile, Freshfields were working with Roux and setting up a team to work with the DTI inspectors on document collection. There was to be a room in Freshfields' offices where Guinness's documents would be collected. Ernest was very concerned about company morale, and he told Roux to ensure that he and Alan Scrine, the company secretary, handled the operating people and other executives very sensitively.

Ernest: 'Not for the first time I emphasised what I believed to be the first principle of the law in this country – that no one is guilty until proven to be so – and we must not have the company people, who had a daily job to do, feeling somehow that they were under personal suspicion. It was shattering enough for them to have to live with constant uncertainty, but I was adamant that, even though the press innuendo was totally irresponsible on this issue, they should not feel any sort of guilt. One of our recently recruited executives reported being frightened stiff by lawyers asking him questions when he was unprepared. This was just one of the problems we were going to have to face. I was frantically busy trying to keep the company going, giving guidance to Davidson on the media, and we also had our results to announce.'

On December 9, Ernest took the precautionary step of re-appointing Lazard Brothers, the merchant bank, to advise Guinness on the handling of the DTI inquiry. Ernest: 'Calling them in again was not without some misgivings, considering their strong relations with Plastow in particular.' Lazards would be working with Freshfields, Roux and David Wynne-Morgan of Hill & Knowlton, the public relations firm. Brian Baldock had recommended that Wynne-Morgan be co-opted on to the team as the external PR adviser.

The situation was becoming inflamed, however. A company called Schenley, part of the Rapid American Corporation owned by Meshulam Ricklis, which distributed Dewars whisky in the US, had at some stage exceeded the five per cent shareholding in Guinness beyond which it was required to declare its stake under UK company law. But it had not declared it – Ricklis claimed ignorance of the legal requirement – and people had begun to talk about such stakes being used to bolster share prices during bids. Roger Seelig of Morgan Grenfell told *The Times* that his bank 'had no knowledge of any contact between Guinness and Schenley during the bid'. The situation was very unstable. What else was going to emerge in the press?

Ernest and Roux gave the usual results presentation on December 10, and made it clear that they would not discuss the DTI investigation. The results were very well received by the press, as indeed they should have been. Guinness was showing record pre-tax profits for the year to September 1986 of £241 million. The original Guinness group had easily met its profit target of £130 million, with profits of £132 million. Sales of draught Guinness were up seven per cent by volume in the UK and Bell's long-term decline in domestic market share had almost been arrested. Even the Distillers group was producing more profit in the five and a half months since the takeover than in the comparable months of the previous year. And everyone agreed that the real benefits from Distillers would not be seen until the rationalisation of the company had been completed. Already things were looking very good.

Unfortunately, the press took more notice of the DTI inquiry than of the results. The company share price reflected this. *The Independent* concluded: 'If it were not for the DTI, shares on a current p/e of 10 would be undervalued. But only those prepared to speculate should move in at the moment.'

Then Ernest and Roux went to New York and Boston to repeat the presentation as part of the publicity exercise leading up to Guinness obtaining a share quote over there.

Ernest: 'On arriving back at Heathrow airport on December 13 I went straight to the office, where I received a call from Sir David Napley, the solicitor who had helped me with the defamation actions against Argyll, and whom I had informally consulted on the DTI issue because of his wide experience in this area. He asked to see me straight away. I drove out to his home in Burnham, Buckinghamshire. He told me of a conversation he had had with Hugh Peppiatt, senior partner of Freshfields, who had said in effect that they might be facing a conflict of interest. Napley presumed he was referring to Anthony Salz, as Salz had been our main legal adviser and worked intimately with Roux and Morgan during the Distillers bid. Napley also told me Freshfields were very uncomfortable about their situation and had been consulting numerous counsel about it, presumably at Guinness's cost. It was the first that I had heard about this. He also told me that Freshfields had some thoughts about splitting the board and certain executives, notably myself, in terms of legal representation which he, Napley, said in his experience was a very dangerous and unnecessary step to consider. It would weaken the company's ability to act coherently as one unit, which was essential.

'In fact, at a brief meeting I had had earlier at Freshfields' offices the question of my needing a lawyer myself, in addition to the company, was casually raised. I had said I would think about it, believing that if this was going to be necessary I could always have Sir David act for me. Carole had in fact already asked him to look after her affairs and the children's. Napley asked Peppiatt if he could relay the conversation to me. Peppiatt agreed. Napley and I then discussed in concept the position of Freshfields and whether they ought to act for us in the DTI matter. Was there not a conflict regarding Salz's close involvement with Roux and the company during the bid? I actually saw Salz early the next week. He came to see me at the Inn on the Park, the first time we had really talked since the DTI had arrived on the scene. Salz talked in vague terms about the general situation and the need, he felt, for me to have separate additional representation.

'He left a note with me from Peppiatt which was long, detailed and quite specific. It made certain demands along the lines Napley had told me of, suggesting separation of the company, myself and others in terms of legal representation, and gave an indication of the advice Freshfields had received from counsel. There were many aspects which I quite frankly did not understand, so I called Tom Ward in his capacity as the Guinness director with overall legal responsibility, and arranged to fly to see him in Brussels, where he was attending to other business. I also suggested that he should see both Napley and Freshfields, as clearly we needed a decision on how to handle our legal representation. I asked Roux to come with me, but he refused. On December 17, when I showed Ward the Freshfields letter and told him about my conversation with Napley, he felt that we should not compromise ourselves, given Salz's potential difficulties. He advised that we should straight away ask Napley to handle the DTI work, of which he had much experience, and let Freshfields or someone else continue to handle UK commercial matters, but keep Salz available for consultation. Ward had also been led to believe that Freshfields represented Boesky's main UK company, Cambrian and General Investments.'

Early on the morning of December 18, during Ernest's visit to Ward in Brussels he received a telephone call from Davidson in London, to say that *The Independent* was running a story about the

Guinness family being major investors in Boesky. Davidson added that all our advisers insisted that we would immediately have to issue a company statement about the Boesky investment. A draft had been prepared by Lazard Brothers.

After Ernest put the phone down on Davidson, he and Ward discussed the potential damage to their chances of recovering the money in the Boesky investment as a result of it being disclosed in the press, but the London team were insistent. Ernest told Davidson to advise the board in advance of a notice going out. He apparently passed this responsibility to Scrine, who had difficulty in contacting everybody before the press release was published.

Ernest: 'Macfarlane and co. blamed me for that as well. I returned immediately to London and called a meeting of as many directors as I could get together, for an update. It took place in my room at the Inn on the Park on December 18.'

There were seven directors at the meeting, including Lord Iveagh, Macfarlane and Plastow. Ernest told them about the problem of legal representation and they discussed the Boesky announcement, which inevitably they did not like. Macfarlane described the wording of the press release and the decision to issue it as 'disastrous'. He and Plastow did not like the idea of Freshfields being replaced, but others saw the point and were in favour. Ernest: 'What we did not know at the time was that Macfarlane and his group were already consulting independent lawyers: Lord Goodman and, later, Herbert Smith.'

Ward came to London the next day, December 19, on his way back to the US. He called Macfarlane and told him that in his opinion Freshfields should not handle the DTI matter, but that it should be handled by Napley, who had all the right experience. According to Ward, Macfarlane did not disagree.

Ernest, Ward, Iveagh and the company secretary, Scrine, met later that day at the Inn on the Park to discuss the question of legal representation. They acknowledged the conflict of interest that Freshfields had, and Ward again suggested that Kingsley Napley be appointed, and that they should work alongside Travers Smith Braithwaite, the long-standing lawyers to the company and the Guinness family. Salz should also be available to give assistance. Towards the end of the meeting, John Humphries, senior partner of Travers Smith, arrived with Alan Keat, another partner. Humphries outlined a possible conflict his firm had: it had in the past acted for Boesky's British company, Cambrian and General Investments, but this connection had been severed when one of his partners had left the firm in early 1986. Humphries added that the matter was being looked into urgently, but he subsequently bowed out.

On that Friday night, wild rumours started circulating in the press that Ernest was resigning over the Boesky investment. The company immediately slapped them down, but the pressure on him did not go away, especially as Macfarlane and the new non-executive directors were becoming scared stiff of their position.

A follow-up meeting took place the next day, Saturday, December 20. The Guinness executive directors were all present, and Sir David Napley. It was agreed that the company should appoint Kingsley Napley, but that Freshfields should be asked to continue to handle commercial aspects. 'Roux was absent, but it was well known that he was strongly against his close friend and associate, Salz, being taken off the DTI team.'

At that Saturday meeting Napley said that, from his discussions with Freshfields, it appeared also that they wished to take instructions from a person in Guinness other than Ernest, with which he did not agree. My father was very concerned about this.

As the other directors at the meeting were unanimous about replacing Freshfields, they asked Macfarlane to come over to discuss the proposition, although they were not strictly obliged to do so. He agreed it.

That afternoon, Napley and Ernest went to see Hugh Peppiatt of Freshfields at his home in Wimbledon. After a prolonged discussion Peppiatt agreed that Freshfields should stand down from acting for Guinness on the DTI inquiry.

The DTI inspectors were informed on the Monday, and Napley took over.

After Freshfields was asked to step aside, Ernest did not see Roux again until January 6. Ward never returned to Britain and Iveagh went sick. Iveagh did not participate in any more board meetings during the rest of my father's tenure of office. Sir David Napley immediately tried to get into the situation properly. Ernest had it in mind that at each meeting of directors Sir David would provide an objective update on all relevant matters concerning the DTI. He was to have access to everyone, and Ernest wanted to know what was going on, as chairman.

Napley laid out how he wanted things done. He objected to two assistants of Ward's who had been sent over to 'assist the understaffed Guinness legal department'. Napley sent them back to the US. Ernest brought his former personal assistant, Ian Cheshire, back from the Guinness Health group to help him.

Sir David wanted to see Roux, but had great difficulty in doing so as Bain had appointed lawyers for Roux. The lawyers happened to be Denton Hall and Burgin, where one of the partners, Henry King, had been our family lawyer for many years.

Ernest had attended one meeting briefly with Roux at Napley's offices shortly after returning from the USA. Roux never attended a second meeting, but eventually agreed to a formal interview with Napley on December 30. An alleged transcript of the interview appeared in *The Sunday Times*. There was a fuss initially over who had authorised the leak, and later over claims that what was printed was incorrect.

At a pre-Christmas meeting of directors on December 23, Sir David outlined very concisely how things stood on all DTI matters. Roux was not present.

Ernest: 'It all seemed most odd. Sir Norman Macfarlane was extremely rude to Sir David Napley. Whilst Napley was giving his update, Macfarlane was fiddling with his pencil, clearly demonstrating that he was not in the least interested in what he had to say.' He had even asked Ernest what Napley was doing at the meeting in the first place. 'He then started to attack me again on the Boesky investment, and each of the new directors in turn had a go at me about something as if cued in by computer – either the reappointment of Lazards, the content of the Boesky press release drawn up by Lazards, or for failing to consult them adequately. Macfarlane was again talking about "errors of judgement". He and his group were not at all interested in what the executive directors had to say about what we were doing to keep the company going, keeping up morale and making profits, or protecting our position.'

'One of the proposals that we had wished to discuss involved a formal representation to the DTI of the need to broaden the inquiry to include all the parties to the takeover, notably the Argyll Group. It was patently unfair, the executive directors felt, that Guinness alone should have been singled out for alleged improprieties. To everyone at Guinness, it smelt like a one-sided plot.'

Napley specifically asked the board to stop leaking stories to the press. It would harm the company. No further statements should be made to the press unless they had been cleared by his office.

During the meeting Sir David Napley was called by his office: Roux's lawyers wanted to know if they could hire Michael Hill, a criminal barrister, for Roux. The problem, they said, was that Hill had been approached by Freshfields to act for Guinness.

Previous to this meeting, the last before Christmas, two other events had occurred.

In an attempt to create harmony between the new directors and the old, Ernest had asked Iveagh, Macfarlane and his wife to join Carole and himself for dinner on December 8. Unfortunately, on the night before the dinner was to take place, my brother John had a horrific accident at his boarding school. My parents were woken in the middle of the night by a phone call from John's school, saying that John had put his hand through a window and lacerated his wrist, cutting all the arteries and severing the tendon and part of his thumb. He was in hospital, and after a six-hour operation his life was ultimately saved. Carole had immediately gone to be with him, and so could not attend the dinner. My mother had not been completely well herself at this time. But the dinner went ahead, and it was, superficially, a perfectly pleasant evening.

Secondly, on December 22 Ernest, Iveagh and Howard Hughes of Price Waterhouse had a pre-Christmas dinner at the Inn on the Park. Ernest: 'During that dinner, as we reviewed the DTI matter,

'Saunders of the River up the creek.' JAK of the *Standard* was one of Fleet Street's most regular commentators throughout my father's five years at Guinness.

including Sir Norman's behaviour, the conversation quite spontaneously turned to Roux.'

Roux had had mixed emotions about his future position with Guinness, and Hughes knew this, being one of those who were helping to find candidates for the job of permanent finance director. Roux was known to be under pressure from his wife, who expected him to be home at hours that were incompatible with life during a major takeover bid. He was actively considering going into the consulting or investment management business with other Bain partners who had become resentful of Theroux. They felt they were doing all the work and he was getting all the glory.

Security had been a major concern of Ernest's since the kidnapping of Freddy Heineken and his warnings to Ernest about industrial espionage. My father remembered the dirty tricks during the Distillers bid and the constant press leaks. Now he was certain that there was something going on within Guinness itself. 'I consulted the new head of security that I had insisted on appointing on the recommendation of Brian Baldock. It was he who gave special security instructions to the Inn on the Park.

He was also very concerned at the number of people who were now milling around the chief executive's suite and using the many telephones. An area where there should have been so much tight control had become like a railway station. There were lawyers from Guinness, Kingsley Napley, Freshfields and from Ward's office in Washington until Napley sent them home. There were numerous people from Bain, replacement secretaries because of the enormous workload, and personal assistants as well.

'And who knows who else, and who was getting at the cleaners and other service personnel not on the payroll. To my dismay one night when I was leaving the office very late, I stumbled across the security guard at reception who was dead drunk and had left the office keys on the desk in front of him. I also began to notice people I did not recognise in the conference rooms on the corridor down to Roux's office. When I asked who they were I was told that they were "connected with the DTI inquiry".

'It would have been very easy for documents to have walked out of my office or been tampered with. I had our head of security check again and again whether we were being bugged. These checks did not result in anything, although I saw cars parked suspiciously outside the building with aerials of various sorts that suggested we were being listened in to. And I am sure that I was being followed. Who by? And why?'

At about this time a disturbing dialogue took place between David Wynne-Morgan and Rupert Faure-Walker, one of Gulliver's bankers at Samuel Montagu, who were absolutely terrified of being drawn into the inquiry. Wynne-Morgan was convinced that Gulliver's people were stirring things up for Guinness.

Ernest: 'Certainly they contributed to publications that emerged in 1987, and to the DTI inquiry, with antagonistic and self-serving comments, all hostile to Guinness in general or me in particular.' Wynne-Morgan told the bankers that if they did not desist, he would push for the DTI inquiry to include Argyll as well.

By Christmas Ernest reckoned he had never felt so exhausted in his life. My mother and brother John flew to Switzerland ahead of the rest of the family. Coincidentally they met Sir Jack Lyons's son, Jonathan, on the plane, and Tony Parnes was at Geneva Airport.

Ernest: 'Jonathan Lyons phoned me a couple of times over the holiday, offering a social dinner, but each time the dinner was called off at short notice and we never met again. In a similar vein, Carole had called Sir Jack Lyons at home. Lady Lyons answered the phone and said Sir Jack was not in, but Carole could hear him telling his wife to say that he was out.'

The Saunders family and Ernest's aunt, Mina, had their usual social dinner with the Furers at the Hyatt Hotel in Montreux. Dr Furer was interested and disturbed by my father's accounts of the hostile attitudes of the new directors, and encouraged him to take heart and stand up to them. He asked if Ernest felt the DTI inquiry might prejudice the timetable for the planned introduction of Guinness shares in the US, Japanese and European stock markets, but Ernest said he didn't know how long it would take to sort out.

But the phone kept ringing from London, and my father was getting no rest at all. He had left Brian Baldock in charge of public relations over the holiday, but the press was full of rumour.

Ernest: 'I decided that I must get away and I took a plane to Washington to seek Ward's opinion about the board and how to handle them. Tom was very busy. I stayed around for about thirty-six hours before flying back on New Year's Eve. His attitude, like Furer's, was that having got the massive endorsement from share-holders in September, my duty was to see the company through this crisis and not be swayed or blown off course by Macfarlane. It would be as if we had lost the shareholders' meeting, as opposed to winning

Left: Bill Bain, founder of Bain and Co., the management consultants called in by Ernest to help save Guinness

Below left: Olivier Roux, the Bain 'controller' who went on to become director of financial strategy and development at Guinness

Below: Lord Iveagh, Chairman of Guinness, became President of the Company in 1986

Left: Raymond Miguel, Chairman of Bell's. They had a smart sales team but were no match in a contest with Guinness

Below: Jimmy Gulliver, Chairman of Argyll Foods, already in 1984 had his eyes on Distillers

Left: John Connell, Chairman of Distillers before the takeover in 1986

Below: David Connell, Ernest, Sir Thomas Risk and Charles Fraser toast a new partnership at the launch of the DCL bid in Edinburgh

Right: Sir David Napley, of Kingsley Napley, the solicitors brought in by Ernest in December 1986 to get to the bottom of the DTI inquiry

Below: Sir Norman MacFarlane, the Chairman of the non-executive committee.

Above right: Paul and Ingrid Channon. He was Secretary of State for Trade and Industry in 1986. Unfortunately he was not only a Guinness himself, but his wife had previously been married to Jonathan Guinness

Right: Thomas Ward, U.S. attorney at Ward Lazarus Grow and Cihlar, was a director of Guinness until he resigned in May 1987

Above: Arthur Furer, ex-managing director of Nestlé S.A., resigned from the Guinness board in January 1987

Right: Roger Seelig, Morgan Grenfell's most entrepreneurial takeover specialist until he resigned in December 1986

Above: Gerald Ronson, the multi-millionaire boss of Heron Corporation

Right: Lord Spens, corporate financial director of Henry Ansbacher and Company until 1987

Knoll House in Penn, Buckinghamshire, the family house which had to be sold after Ernest's dismissal in January 1987

Below: Ernest, Joanna and myself in March 1988, leaving the High Court after winning the right to draw living expenses and buy a small house out of frozen funds

Ernest tells the Press he is being made a scapegoat after the 26/9/88 Bow Street remand hearing

it so handsomely. I also had the opportunity of having a brief word on the question of gin quotas with H. P. Goldfield, an assistant secretary of commerce in the Reagan administration.'

Late on Monday night, December 29, a story broke in the press that Guinness was the beneficial owner of a block of shares held in the name of Down Nominees. Morgan Grenfell released a statement saying it would no longer be advising Guinness. The announcement also contained the news that Roger Seelig, the man who master-minded the Distillers bid at Morgan, had resigned. The first head had rolled in what had become known as the Guinness Affair.

13

BOARDROOM COUP

If 1986 had ended in a thick, baffling fog, 1987 was quickly to unleash a hurricane. Within days, my father found himself fighting for his business life

Ernest returned to the London office on Sunday, January 4, 1987. The next day he called in Baldock, Cheshire and the rest of the team to give him an immediate update. At this meeting Baldock gave a résumé of developments since Christmas. In the light of the adverse press, Sir David Napley had been asked to review the previous Sunday's newspapers to identify inaccurate and defamatory articles. Ernest was adamant that such reporting should be halted for the company's sake, and legal action should be initiated if there was no alternative. An approach to the Press Council was suggested. They also discussed the need to demonstrate to staff, customers, the DTI inspectors and others that the company was ready, if necessary, to take steps to protect itself, and agreed that a letter should be sent to staff, setting out the company's position. The question of organising special briefings for senior executives was raised, and Ernest proposed to brief as many directors as were available the next day at the meeting to be held at Napley's office.

None of the executive directors still had any specific idea what the DTI inquiry was about. 'We couldn't understand why Argyll was not involved. No information was coming from the DTI: there were only "revelations" in the media.' But the fog was about to lift dramatically.

Ernest's secretary knocked on the door and brought in a letter marked 'private and confidential' from Sir David Napley. It was a bombshell. It contained a letter from Roux, addressed to Napley, with a copy for Macfarlane. No copy was addressed to the chairman of the company – Ernest.

The letter outlined what Roux described as 'certain basic information' known to him, which bore upon the subject matter of the DTI inquiry. And he implicated Ernest.

Ernest: 'This all came as a complete surprise and terrific shock to me.' The effect of these allegations was to be devastating. At a time when everyone was desperately looking for someone to blame, they had seemingly been handed the ideal way out.

Sir David Napley's office asked Ernest to meet Napley right away, which he did. Ernest had previously arranged a lunch for Napley to meet Hughes because he wanted to make the auditors available to Napley to assist his inquiries. Hughes turned up with John Salmon, who had been directly responsible for the Guinness audit for some years. 'When Sir David outlined the contents of the Roux letter, Hughes and Salmon were clearly shaken. Of course, Price Waterhouse had an enormous amount at stake here. It was PW executives who had been working hand-in-glove with the Guinness finance group, including Roux and Bailey, throughout the year and throughout the bid.'

Towards the end of the lunch Hughes, having recovered his composure, said he would need to see the board to review the implications of Roux's letter in terms of the company's borrowing powers and the closing of the accounts.

Ernest called a meeting of directors on Tuesday at Napley's office in Long Acre, to discuss the Roux letter. Iveagh, Ward and Roux himself were absent. All the new non-executives had clearly had a copy of the letter in advance, and my father could not help wondering how long it had been in their possession. None of the executive directors or Guinness family representatives had seen it before.

The object of their attending the meeting, as far as the new directors were concerned, was to get my father to immediately resign, or be suspended. Macfarlane asked him if he believed what Roux was saying about his involvement.

'When I said I categorically denied Roux's allegations concerning myself, it was as if he did not even want to hear my reply. He and his group had made up their minds.

Ernest: 'Macfarlane kept asking me whether this was a full board meeting or not. He knew he needed only a simple majority of non-executives to get me removed and he was continually counting his supporters.'

Ernest asked Napley to give the board an update. Napley said that he had seen Roux on December 30. He read out a draft of the statement which Roux was prepared to sign, which Napley believed to be true. Napley said Roux had declined to discuss any other matters. Sir David said he had tried to see Roux again, but Roux had refused via his solicitors.

Napley then returned to the Roux letter, saying he saw no grounds for my father's suspension. He referred to a letter that Ernest had signed on January 5 to send to Bain on his advice, asking that Roux should not attend at the company offices. Sir David had also told Ernest to have Roux's office locked to prevent unauthorised entry and any papers from going missing. A chain was put on the outer door of Roux's suite.

Macfarlane appeared not to listen to Napley. He had his own surprise to spring. He said he wanted to telephone Roux and ask him to attend. Napley warned that Roux should not be subjected to cross-examination by the board. Roux was in fact already waiting downstairs, as arranged privately with Macfarlane, and came straight up. Macfarlane, showing no respect for the one person who ought to be present, demanded that Napley, the acting company solicitor, leave the room. Sir David was so shocked that he abandoned the meeting in disgust.

Roux then read a prepared speech, by way of contrite apology. He said he had worked for Guinness for five years, and in that time had developed a strong sense of loyalty to Mr Saunders and the company. Over the past twelve months he had been worried by some situations in which he had been involved, but had carried on with his duties because of that loyalty, and in order to resolve matters.

However, when the DTI investigation was announced he realised that the situation could not continue, and he had opposed the replacement of Freshfields by Kingsley Napley. He said he felt that during the meeting with Napley an attempt to cover up certain matters was being made, and he would not participate in this. He added that he had also been aware of concern expressed by Price Waterhouse regarding the closing of the company's accounts at December 31 1986, and had therefore concluded that he must seek independent advice regarding his own position.

Baldock asked Roux about the Price Waterhouse aspect, and Roux replied that he had reported to others the concern made known to him by PW, but he refused to say precisely to whom he had passed on this information. He then revealed that his solicitors were acting jointly for Bain & Co. and himself, and perhaps three senior people at Bain knew of the contents of the letter.

Ernest: 'The meeting listened in silence, but what Roux said did not appear in any way new to the new non-executives, Sir Norman and Co. Roux left, and there was then pressure on me to resign or be suspended. I said that this was a matter for the whole board, not just for a group who were largely imposing themselves as a board. By this time Macfarlane was behaving as if he was chairman, and I had to remind him on several occasions that I was chairman; I had the unanimous support of the executive and Guinness family directors, who all subsequently wrote letters to Sir Norman complaining about his behaviour, the way his non-executive colleagues were acting like a self-appointed junta and his antagonistic and unhelpful attitude, pointing out that the pressure on me to resign was unjustified and terribly damaging to the company.

'Sir Norman, aided and abetted by Sir David Plastow, nevertheless said he had no confidence in me as chairman, repeating the original campaign words of "errors of judgment". They added that they would come to me tomorrow to pursue the matter again. They also wanted a special audit carried out by a firm chosen by them. I thought this was crazy. We needed an audit, and quickly, and Price Waterhouse, who knew the company inside out, had been working with the finance department all along. They should be allowed to do the job with Napley as I had already suggested.'

At this point Sir David Napley was allowed to rejoin the meeting. He said that as the letter was not a privileged document, it should be disclosed to the DTI inspectors. It was, however, very important that the letter should not be disclosed to the press. Indeed, he asked the directors to desist from speaking directly or indirectly to the media. Macfarlane announced that he would personally take a copy to the DTI.

The meeting then discussed my father's possible suspension. Vic Steel perceptively pointed out that although the facts had not yet been established suspension would be seen as a judgement of my father's guilt. Sir David Napley said he shared this view, adding that the inspectors would probably be adversely influenced, too. In fact, of course, this adverse effect was intended. But it was finally agreed that neither Ernest nor Roux should be suspended for the moment.

Sir Norman hurried off after the meeting to take a copy of Roux's letter to the DTI, although this was unnecessary since Sir David Napley had already said that he would do so in his capacity as the company's solicitor.

The next day, January 7, after fending off the press yet again,

Ernest tried to get hold of Macfarlane to discuss the special audit.

'He was unavailable, but I found out that he was at Lazards. Clearly Lazards had been pressured by Sir Norman and Sir David Plastow to side with them over plans to get me out. Indeed, I subsequently received a visit from Sir John Nott, chairman of Lazards, urging me to resign voluntarily. Eventually Sir Norman arrived, bringing Plastow with him. I had Sir David Napley with me, and Alan Scrine. Macfarlane and Plastow agreed to the audit being carried out by Price Waterhouse, whom they had obviously seen. They again stressed that they wanted me to resign. I replied that this was a matter for the whole board, and that a board meeting should be called, with proper notice so that everyone could attend. Macfarlane and Plastow argued aggressively against this, but Sir David Napley and Alan Scrine supported me. As usual when I needed him, Lord Iveagh was away sick. I especially wanted him to be at a board meeting at which matters of such gravity were discussed. I would also have liked to have Arthur Furer and Tom Ward there as well, to give balance to the non-executive board.'

A board meeting was fixed for the following Wednesday, January 14, and a press announcement was made saying that an emergency board meeting had been called for the following week. The announcement included a statement that directors had been briefing themselves on the affair through a series of meetings. On January 10 the *Financial Times* commented that announcements from the Guinness camp this week 'have left little doubt that he (Roux) played a key part in the events now being investigated by the inspectors of the DTI'.

It is hard to overstate the pressure building up on my father. He was trying to hold the company together and keep up morale, in the face of constant attacks on him by members of the board, not to mention the relentless pressure from the media.

The press were now on the rampage. Brian Basham of Broad Street Associates was spreading rumours about my father's imminent departure. David Wynne-Morgan had to remind the Basham team that if they persisted in muddying the waters for Guinness, the response would have to involve a reciprocal attack on Argyll.

The new non-executive directors of Guinness were leaking information from their meetings to the media. Ernest: 'Sir David Napley had actively accused them of this, and we had evidence from Wynne-Morgan that it was happening. It was damaging the company of which they were directors but, as part of the process of destroying my reputation, it was clearly seen as being in a good cause.'

Ernest was understandably keen to deal with the Roux letter, and asked Alan Bailey from the finance department to meet him at the Inn on the Park to go over it.

On Wednesday evening, my parents had dinner with Jonathan Guinness, whose position on the board Ernest had fought hard to retain for him and whom he naïvely thought could, in Iveagh's absence, help the board arrive at a sensible solution. They had come to the conclusion that life was intolerable. Ernest: 'The company I had rebuilt was being torn apart. I was exhausted and increasingly unwell. Carole was deeply concerned about my health and that of our son, John. She was still far from well herself. So I decided to recommend to Jonathan Guinness that an independent chairman of unimpeachable integrity and above all a peacemaker, not interested in fuelling scandal, but in getting the facts with the minimum of damage, should take over my position. I would remain as chief executive.'

Jonathan apparently thought this a good idea. Ernest called Lord Iveagh, who reluctantly agreed. Ernest began to consider possible candidates. Extraordinarily, the next day Jonathan gave an interview

'Are you certain they're not vultures?'

to the London *Evening Standard*, saying that Ernest would be resigning. Ernest telephoned him immediately he saw the front-page banner headlines. Jonathan denied giving the interview and persuaded the *Evening Standard* to drop the story. But more damage had been done.

'The attitude of my executive colleagues, who had been so supportive, now changed. It became apparent later why. When I received a visit from Sir John Nott, chairman of the Lazard Brothers merchant bank, urging me to resign, I got the impression that Lazards had seen the executive directors and indeed other Guinness board members, with the intention of forcing their hand.' It is in fact believed that Herbert Smith, the solicitors who had been advising Sir Norman Macfarlane had warned the directors that unless they dissociated themselves from Ernest they and their families would be liable to be personally sued on various grounds and at very least for breach of fiduciary duty to Guinness shareholders. Naturally, their attitudes to Ernest would have changed in the light of such a threat. Especially since the executive directors, with the exception of Dowling, were not used to standing up to corporate lawyers.

Ernest arranged to see the executive directors, his closest colleagues, on Friday evening to review his decision along the lines agreed with Carole. He had heard rumours during the day that Roux, though he had not reappeared in the office, had been in constant touch with his team, notably Simon Duffy, his associate. Roux was claiming that Ernest would be 'gone by Monday. Macfarlane had said so'. Ernest also picked up on a rumour that Plastow had already commissioned a firm of headhunters to look for a successor.

At 6 p.m. they met in the boardroom at the Portman Square office. Edward Guinness immediately made an uncomfortable prepared speech, saying that they had all individually seen Lazards and Herbert Smith and had been told of the risk to them and their families if Ernest stayed on. They were therefore asking Ernest to 'step aside completely' during the DTI investigation. Ernest: 'This was one step further than I intended, but I had had enough: provided the terms were fair, I said I would agree.' He said he presumed he would continue to receive his salary, benefits, etc., and get every help to clear his name, including legal costs.

Vic Steel, who was in tears, agreed that that was exactly the situation – Ernest should be given every assistance to vindicate himself. My father said he would have to consult Carole and Sir David Napley. In any case, he wanted an announcement drafted that he could show them. A press statement was prepared which talked about Ernest's decision to stand aside in the interests of the company and his family. A board minute was also prepared, covering the terms and conditions which were to apply. Ernest was to retain all his benefits. This was extremely important, as he had previously been persuaded by a combination of the Guinness personnel department and Price Waterhouse not to cash certain share options that had become due earlier, so that he would be seen to be supporting the company.

They discussed the prospect of appointing an independent, conciliatory temporary chairman. They were all, however, so frightened by the pressure put on them by Sir Norman Macfarlane, Lazards and Herbert Smith, that they made it clear, between the tears, that if Ernest did not agree to stand down – and agree by 9 p.m. that evening – they feared Lazards would issue a statement which would make Ernest's position untenable. They also feared that the Roux letter had been leaked to the press.

Ernest called Carole and arranged to meet her at Napley's office in Covent Garden. Napley called Steel to confirm the conditions, including the payment of legal costs, which Steel duly did. On that understanding Napley told Steel the announcement could go ahead.

Ernest: 'I went back to Portman Square to say goodbye for now. I had a drink in the bar, and Ian Cheshire offered me a few days' rest at Champneys, which I accepted. At this point Dowling sheepishly came into the room with a photocopy of the board minute and the announcement released at 9 p.m. It was only afterwards that I noticed that there had been an addition of which I had been unaware. A sentence had been added to the minute stating that "These Committee minutes are subject to ratification by the full board, in accordance with normal practice." I immediately suspected what was going to happen: The deal would not be approved by the full board and I would be left without the means to defend myself.'

The next day, January 10, the press reported Ernest's 'standing aside' announcement, which stated: 'I feel personally that because of the uncertainty and disruption that has been caused to the business as a result of the Department of Trade and Industry inquiry, this action would be in the best interests of the company, its shareholders, its employees and my family. It is my personal view that it is of paramount importance that this fine company's progress should be allowed to proceed, and that the action I am taking should enable this to be achieved.' *Today* commented: 'Last night's move followed reports, later denied, of behind-the-scenes moves to oust 51-year-old Mr Saunders. Main board director Mr Jonathan Guinness described as an "outrage" newspaper reports that he planned to force Mr Saunders to step down as chairman ...' Ironically, the article went on to say that Jonathan Guinness 'pledged the support of the Guinness family in the difficult times ahead for the brewing chief'. The *Daily Express* and the *Irish Times* carried similar stories. *The Times* went further: 'A subsequent statement from both Lord Iveagh and Mr Guinness only half denied these reports, and significantly contained no statement of support for Mr Saunders.'

That day, Saturday, Ernest flew to Geneva to see Arthur Furer. He had arranged the meeting during the week to consult Furer on his, Ernest's, position, but now it was to say goodbye rather than to consult. He then flew to Dublin to see Lord Iveagh – the man who had hired him, and with whom he had worked over the entire period at Guinness. Lord Iveagh, who had been unavailable, apparently through sickness, for all the recent critical directors' meetings, seemed in good health when he came to Dublin Airport to meet Ernest and Carole. They went to Iveagh's house at Farmleigh for the night. Ernest: 'He was most kind, as was his eldest daughter, Emma. He was speaking boldly about using his position as president to chair the company himself for the time being, to maintain continuity and rebuild stability.' The two men spoke to Hughes of Price Waterhouse. Iveagh told him of his plan to step in as chairman, and Hughes was very supportive. Ernest then asked Hughes whether he had found anything in the PW report that implicated him. Hughes said there was nothing.

Finally, Ernest asked Iveagh, in the presence of Carole, about the arrangements for his standing aside, showing him the minutes. Ernest said he trusted that Iveagh would not allow the company to renege on any of the promises. Iveagh said he would on no account allow this to happen, and he also volunteered that the family would never let Ernest and Carole down after what Ernest had done for the company. 'He said he would insist on my financial arrangements being honoured. Erroneously I took some comfort from Lord Iveagh's remarks. I believed he was an honourable man. Then I had a brief word with Ward, who had flown in to see Iveagh: Tom denied all the allegations out of hand, including those directed at him.'

On Sunday Ernest and Carole returned to England and went to Champneys, where the staff did their very best to take care of them. My father was exhausted.

The contents of the Roux letter, if not the letter itself, were reported in *The Sunday Times* of January 11. Macfarlane and co. were talking to the press, as was the company, probably Roux as well and others, especially Basham. A new type of comment was emerging, though: the papers, fed by my father's enemies, had embarked on a campaign against him.

There was a plethora of stories along the lines of 'the rise and fall of Ernest Saunders', giving the impression that he was to blame for anything that had gone wrong at Guinness.

On Sunday evening a Guinness board meeting was held to which Ernest was not invited, and for which he was not sent an agenda, even though he was still a director. At this meeting Macfarlane was appointed acting chairman. Still at Champneys, Ernest was far from well and unable to sleep.

On Tuesday he called some of his ex-colleagues at Portman Square. Carole spoke to Colin George, the personnel director, who confirmed that the financial arrangements that had been made for Ernest were all in order. Macfarlane had told him so. Ernest also wrote, constructively despite everything, to Macfarlane about the responsibilities he was passing to him in his capacity as acting chairman.

Carole took Ernest to the doctor, who immediately had him admitted to the Lister Hospital, Chelsea, under an assumed name, where he was put under heavy sedation and a regime of pills to reduce his extremely high blood pressure. Ernest: 'The doctor told me that the only positive thing he could say about my situation was that if I had gone on any longer in the way that I had been living, he and I would not be talking and I would most likely be dead.'

On Wednesday, January 14, Guinness held a full board meeting. Macfarlane refused to ratify the conditions that Ernest had agreed with the executive directors. He was dismissed without pay, and deprived of the means promised to clear his name. Predictably, instead of hoping Ernest would vindicate himself and return to the chairmanship, Macfarlane wanted him not merely out but down and out. It was a most brutal and unnecessary step. 'I received a brusque letter from Macfarlane via my doctor in the Lister Hospital. He couldn't wait even until I had been discharged to mount his coup. He didn't even tell me what was going to happen – my children heard it on the radio before I was informed.' None of us can still quite believe the callousness with which the deed was done. The letter said:

Dear Ernest,

I am writing to you following the meeting of the Board of Guinness PLC held this afternoon at which your position was discussed. I regret to have to tell you that it was the unanimous view of the Directors present that all connections between the Company and yourself should be terminated.

Although on Friday you agreed to stand aside as Chairman and Chief Executive pending the outcome of the DTI inquiry, it was felt that the developments since then have rendered that arrangement no longer appropriate. Accordingly it has been decided that, with immediate effect, you will no longer be Chairman and Chief Executive of the Company. Steps will also be taken to remove you as a Director from the various subsidiary company boards on which you sit. I am afraid that all your remuneration and other perquisites will cease forthwith.

In addition, it was decided that the various arrangements which exist between Guinness PLC and your wife will also be terminated immediately.

In these circumstances, I hope you will agree that it is no longer sensible for you to remain as a Director of Guinness PLC and I should let you know that the Board therefore urge you to tender your resignation.

A statement is being made to the press tonight following this afternoon's Board meeting and reference to the above will be included.

Yours sincerely
Sir Norman Macfarlane

In the letter Macfarlane referred to developments since Friday having rendered the agreement to let Ernest stand aside on full pay with legal costs 'no longer appropriate'. In fact there had been no damning revelations against Ernest: the only developments that took place between Friday and Wednesday had been the resignation of Roux and the election of Macfarlane as acting chairman.

It took Ernest's solicitors until February 26 to obtain from Herbert Smith & Co., Guinness's new solicitors, a written statement of the reasons for his dismissal. Not until the annual shareholders' meeting in May did Macfarlane publicly disclose any reasons, and even then he merely referred, in an answer to a question, to the board 'having reason to believe that Ernest was in breach of his fiduciary duties to the company'. There was to be no corporate responsibility as far as Macfarlane was concerned.

As a result of this action Ernest's integrity was given a shattering blow. By the time the media had finished with the story of his sacking, few remembered Ernest Saunders the rebuilder of Guinness.

They only remembered the man who seemed to be responsible for all sorts of increasingly murky deeds. So effective was the adverse publicity that in the coming months the only person in the country who spoke out on Ernest's behalf was the courageous local vicar of Penn, the Rev. Oscar Muspratt.

Also on the Wednesday, as a result of the board meeting, Arthur Furer resigned as a director of Guinness. Tom Ward too was asked to resign, but like Ernest refused. Roux had already resigned, on January 12, two days earlier.

Perhaps most sickening of all was the attitude of the Guinness family, notably Lord Iveagh. He, who had personally assured Ernest only the weekend before that all his financial arrangements would be honoured, did nothing to ensure this would happen. On television that night, and in the press the next day, he was quoted as saying, 'Once a friend, always a friend, but I do feel let down.' What he should have said was, 'Thank you, Ernest, for making me a rich man again.'

Two more changes emerged from the Wednesday meeting. Sir David Plastow was appointed deputy chairman and Sir David Napley was replaced as legal adviser by Herbert Smith & Co. Guinness had seemingly purged itself as far as the public was concerned.

14

PROSECUTION

The first two weeks of 1987 had been traumatic. My father's confusion at the reasons for the DTI inquiry had suddenly been intensified by a ruthless power struggle, in which he had inevitably been the victim. And worse was to come.

At the end of the fateful week of his sacking, Ernest left the Lister Hospital and returned to the family home at Knoll House in Penn, Buckinghamshire. He was still unwell. For days he just lay in bed and slept. My mother and sister had to feed him and dress him. When they took him anywhere he would just curl up on the back seat of the car and go to sleep.

The house was under siege from the media. Sturdy white-painted wooden gates kept prying eyes away, but every time a car went in or out, or someone went for a walk, the press leapt into action. For long periods the leafy country lane outside would be quiet, its grass verges lined with an unusual number of parked cars, all with bored people sitting in them. But if one of the white gates opened, like collapsing dominoes a string of car doors would be flung back and reporters, photographers and TV camera crews would fumble with their various bits of equipment in a frantic effort to get a statement or a few pictures. Mercifully for him, it was never my father who came out of the front gates: my mother and he would always slip away quietly and unnoticed by walking through our garden and out via the Penn Church graveyard next door.

The house was to remain constantly under siege for the next two months, and then intermittently until we sold it in June 1987. We used to pity the reporters camped outside in their cars waiting and hoping for a glimpse of my father. I don't think they ever got one. The best they usually got was a few pictures of me, and many more of my sister. One particular photographer turned up so many times that after a while he would bring his latest pictures to give to Jo, and then take a few more to please his boss.

I remember one particularly wretched Sunday when the whole family were at home for lunch with a few friends. We sat at the table with the curtains closed as a stream of reporters came and banged this time on the front door to try to get us to open up: it was a contemptible invasion of privacy. They would have photographed us through the window if they had had the chance. After lunch I went up to the first-floor landing, which looked out over the lane. There were plenty of cars there, but no one in sight. We had planned to go for a walk, without my mother and father of course, so we walked out of the gates and started off down the lane, past the cars with the church on our left. We were fifty yards down the road when we spotted a small army of photographers and men with microphones talking to the Rev. Muspratt under the porch of the church. I saw the vicar look over in our direction. The press instantly spun round and a cry went up: 'The Saunders!!'

There followed a scene worthy of a Monty Python sketch. The reporters and photographers, lenses falling out of every pocket and cameras jangling round their necks, began to run towards us, jostling each other, dropping things and shouting 'Stop!' Not minded to stop, we walked calmly back into the house. Just as we closed the door, the desperadoes tore through the gates and started banging on the outside, imploring us to come back out with cries of 'Just a few pictures! Just a brief statement!' No chance.

Later the same day, as I set off to drive back to Cambridge, an over-enthusiastic photographer jumped out into the road in front of my car. He was practically on the bonnet before he realised that it was me and not my father at the wheel. I had to swerve to avoid him. As we continued down the road I saw him in my mirror, standing forlornly like someone who has just missed the last bus.

My mother remembers seeing another spectacle around this time. Several photographers had climbed on top of the garden wall behind the house, and were standing there trying to see in, when a number of outraged old ladies from the nearby Penn Mead old people's home tried to hook their legs down with their walking sticks as they went past.

After Ernest's return to Penn from the Lister I took a few days off university work to help my mother find lawyers for him. He was heavily sedated and in no fit state to choose a lawyer for himself. We went to see Sir David Napley at his home a few miles away in

Burnham, and he advised us to get in touch with Henry King of Denton Hall and Burgin, who had been our family solicitor for years. Napley feared that he himself would be barred from acting for my father because of the help he had given Guinness during the Distillers bid on libel actions against Argyll and because he was the lawyer subsequently appointed by the company for the DTI inquiry. He said he thought he would not be able to represent Ernest on civil matters, but he reserved the right to act on criminal matters if it ever came to that. Carole wrote to Henry King, but never received a reply.

Since Napley could not act and King would not, we had to look elsewhere. It was surprisingly difficult to find a lawyer in London who was free to act. Every firm we contacted seemed to have some connection with Guinness, Distillers or Argyll or their advisers, or were on retainer to another company, notably one who had been involved in recent takeovers, or indeed were advising the City self-regulatory authorities. Everyone in the City was understandably nervous, and had rushed to retain a law firm. In the end we went to a firm called Payne Hicks Beach in Lincoln's Inn Fields. Stephen Ralph was the partner who would be in charge of Ernest's case. He immediately retained as counsel Philip Heslop QC, Edwin Glasgow QC and John Mathew QC, before there was no one left in London. Ralph immediately asked for money on account of costs, so we gave him whatever cash we had and the proceeds from selling shares. Guinness was holding on to all my father's stock options and share certificates, and refused to let him realise them.

From the date of Ernest's sacking his name hardly ever appeared in the papers without the prefix 'disgraced'. At every opportunity his name was linked with whatever illegalities were under discussion, even Boesky and insider dealing. Of course, the public confused all three issues. It was trial by innuendo, and as a result Ernest became associated in readers' minds with anything dirty in the City. This was especially ridiculous, as he had never been a City man.

The media campaign took another turn on January 21 with the handing back, in a blaze of publicity, of the £5.8 million that had been paid by Guinness to Gerald Ronson, chairman of Heron Corporation, one of Britain's largest private companies. Ronson had written a letter to Sir Norman Macfarlane, who had penned a reply with the media in mind in which he thanked Ronson for his honesty and openness. The press shouted excitedly, 'Ronson names Saunders in £5.8 million payment,' and went on to make such comments as

'Yesterday's statement provides clear indication of Mr Saunders's involvment in the Guinness share price support operation.' My father has always denied this.

By the time the press had devoted a few more weeks to this one-sided coverage, who could even remember that there had ever been another side to the story? On top of this, Ernest was in a serious state of shock and unable to counter personally the media campaign. 'I had no publicity machine, no office, no real money and no means of correcting anything even if anyone had been willing to listen.

'Those involved in the bid, both within Guinness and outside, did nothing to redress the balance. They either had their jobs to protect or they were suppliers who wanted to retain company contracts, or were individuals who wanted to play down their role in order to minimise their own potential liability.'

Further, Ernest was convinced the DTI could not have been uninfluenced by the press. A convenient picture had already been sketched for the inspectors which portrayed Ernest as the centrepiece of the Guinness jigsaw. They now only had to slot in the other pieces of the puzzle.

On January 16 Macfarlane sent a letter to the Guinness shareholders explaining the Boesky investment, and various share purchases. In addition, the letter stated that Price Waterhouse had uncovered £25 million of mystery invoices, representing fees paid to third parties 'for advice and services believed to be in connection with the Distillers bid'. On January 22 the BBC TV news named the companies involved in the ten invoices allegedly relating to the £25 million payments.

At the end of January 1987 Lord Spens resigned from Henry Ansbacher & Co., the merchant bank, Sir Jack Lyons was dropped by Bain & Co., and Alexanders Laing & Cruickshank severed links with Parnes.

As a result of January's developments Ernest had been left at another tremendous disadvantage. Far from Guinness fulfilling its promise of giving him 'every assistance' to help clear his name, they had cut him off from all his papers, and had told employees not to talk to him, and to report any contact he made. After the first criminal charges were heard in court against my father in May 1987, his bail conditions forbade him from having any such communication with current or past employees. Ernest: 'Everyone else was free to examine documents, talk and share thoughts, while I was deliberately isolated. It all seemed part of a plan to disadvantage me and make it impossible for me to get at the facts for the forthcoming DTI inquiry interviews. I was unable even to talk to personal friends of long standing, who had had absolutely nothing to do with the Distillers bid, simply because they had worked for Guinness.'

He attended his first meetings with Payne Hicks Beach with Carole in support. Ernest was far from well, heavily sedated and basically in no condition to argue with lawyers. But Stephen Ralph strongly advised that Ernest should start to brief them in anticipation of the DTI hearings. A great many hours in February and early March 1987 were spent answering solicitors' questions in a most unco-ordinated way. This had to be worked into a statement, a time-consuming process. Ernest: 'When the DTI announced they wanted to see me in February, a number of my friends recommended that I should not attend – I was not up to it. Carole asked Payne Hicks about this, and they advised us that I must go.'

There followed a number of interviews with the DTI inspectors. Payne Hicks decided it was necessary that my father should be accompanied by an army of solicitors, assistants and counsel, although Ernest could not see any benefit to him from such a large and expensive representation. 'The attitude of the DTI and the form of the questions was in the manner of an inquisition. They refused to give advance warning of questions or documents that would be referred to, which was particularly important to me, since I had no documents from which to refresh my memory. Unlike everyone else summoned, I could not even go back afterwards to consult documents held by Guinness because of the company's hostility and their hand-in-glove relationship with the DTI.

'The sessions with the DTI inspectors were really unpleasant. I was still under sedation and feeling unwell. I kept having to ask for a break to take my pills or get fresh air. They did not stop me, but insisted that I was accompanied every time I went to the loo or outside. David Donaldson QC asked all the questions and tried every means of getting me to give the answers he wanted to hear. When I made points that the inspectors did not want to know about, they listened briefly, then reverted to their original line of questioning.'

The inspectors' recently acquired powers and procedures are draconian in the extreme, as many others interviewed by them have testified. Witnesses have no right to silence: the inspectors can compel answers, on pain of imprisonment for contempt. Ernest: 'They operate completely outside the principles of normal justice. I do not think the public understands what a DTI inspection involves. It is doubtful to me, having talked to others who have been involved in these investigations, that they are a matter of getting at the whole truth: they are more about getting answers to prove a point of view that suits the inspectors.'

It had meanwhile become impossible for my parents to live at Penn: the DTI interviews and the round-the-clock media siege of the house had created intolerable and unremitting pressure. They decided that they would have to sell Knoll House as they could not keep up the running costs if Ernest was not working and had huge legal fees to pay. This decision was taken with enormous regret, as we all loved the house dearly. In mid-February my parents called in estate agents and Landau and Landau, the solicitors, were briefed to undertake the conveyancing. When he arrived at their offices Ernest was greeted by Gerald Landau, whom he had not met since their days in National Service.

In an effort to get away from the constant media attention, Ernest and Carole started staying with friends. My parents also bought an answerphone to screen incoming calls. My sister's and my respective universities were superbly protective. At my Cambridge college, friends would call to leave messages and the porters would deny my existence. My brother's school also did a grand job of fending off callers.

Ernest: 'Carole was increasingly depressed and tearful. Inevitably, she could not keep up the bold front that had sustained her since early January. In any case she had not been able to recover fully from a major operation the previous summer. She was particularly upset by the attitude of some friends who – believing what they read in the papers – made tactless remarks without thinking. The Guinness machine seemed to be getting at me even through my family, who had been so supportive of my work for the company and had often helped directly in Guinness matters.'

I myself was not at home much for the first two months of 1987, as I was in my last year at university, preparing for my Law finals. I came down once every few weeks, but never stayed long enough to appreciate quite how ill my father was, and how ill my mother was becoming. But by the end of February she had lost an enormous amount of weight, looked exhausted and cried a great deal.

My sister Jo did a marvellous job, spending practically all her time at home, when she should have been back at university as well. Jo: 'I remember she went to her regular aerobics class in Penn once and came back in floods of tears because Jan Leeming, the TV announcer who had recently had acid thrown in her face, said to Carole that she sympathised with her, as Carole's situation was much worse than hers. Carole was gradually being worn down. It got to the stage when she could not even decide what to have for supper.'

Early in March my parents, Jo and a friend went one evening to see a play at John's school. They took him out for the weekend, but could not take him to Penn because of the press. They went to stay with our good friends, Gaston and Paula de Chalus. On the Sunday morning they were again greeted with the usual dose of Sunday press, including a huge picture of Knoll House in the *Observer* under a headline speculating that it might be up for sale.

Ernest: 'We had had enough. We needed a real break from the lawyers, the DTI, the media, the lot. I asked Paula to take care of John and get him back to school, and asked Carole to pack a few things. We were going to get away for a few days. We drove to Victoria, bought two train tickets and travelled overnight to Lausanne in Switzerland. We were going to seek peace in a country where we had friends, a small flat and the prospect of not being disturbed so that we could regain our strength and stability. I had of course told Stephen Ralph, our solicitor, where we were going.'

They had an awful journey. Neither slept. At the 6 a.m. change of trains at Basel in northern Switzerland Carole was disorientated by the weirdly dressed people celebrating Faschings Night who were leaping out of shadows and dark doorways. Ernest and she arrived at Lausanne Station shortly after eight o'clock. At this point my mother collapsed.

Ernest immediately called Dr Eric Rochat, who had been Carole's doctor when we lived in Switzerland. He came at once. Dr Rochat decided that Carole was having a serious breakdown and must be moved to a clinic in Nyon at once. He said that Ernest must check himself in as well, but separately. They were taken to the clinic and spent most of the next few days asleep under medication, interspersed with psychotherapy.

The only interruption was a visit from Ralph, who insisted on seeing my father at the clinic, because he apparently had to assure the DTI inspectors that Ernest really was ill.

Dr Rochat discussed with the clinic's psychologist, psychiatrist and head of medical services what should be done when Ernest and Carole were discharged. They all felt that my parents should stay longer, but Ernest told them that they no longer had the money to do so. Dr Rochat agreed to a compromise: they should continue to recuperate in their small flat in Les Diablerets, in the mountains above Lake Geneva, but under no circumstances should Carole be left alone. Fortunately my brother John was about to begin school holidays, and Jo left her university and drove him out to be with them.

Alas, the press discovered where my parents were. The continual harrassment began all over again, replicating what they had suffered at Penn. When I flew out to join the family for a short break between revision for my finals they had had to move yet again. In the midst of their illness Carole and Ernest were being literally driven from their home.

Back in London, Guinness had gone on the legal warpath against Ernest. Herbert Smith & Co., their new solicitors, famed for their aggressive approach to litigation and clearly with an unlimited budget and a mandate to pursue every available remedy, had set about trying to recoup the £25 million of allegedly illegal payments made during the Distillers takeover. One invoice concerned £5.2 million paid to a Jersey-based company called Marketing and Acquisitions Consultants. They claimed that no one at Guinness knew who this company was, or what services had been provided to justify that sum. Guinness started legal action in Jersey to find out, and discovered that the payment was made for the benefit of the American lawyer Tom Ward.

The press got very excited. Before Ernest had an opportunity to explain what, if anything, he knew of this matter, Guinness issued writs against him and Ward alleging that Ernest had breached his fiduciary duty to the company by authorising the payment without telling the board, and without Ward having done anything to earn it.

Guinness wanted to litigate and recover the money. If they could not get it from Ward, they would try to get it from Saunders. Ward had admitted that he had all the money and had already offered to put some of it into an escrow account, so the matter could be settled by arbitration, but Guinness had refused.

On March 25, Guinness's lawyers were back in the High Court seeking a 'mareva' injunction to freeze Ernest's assets in the UK. More facts emerged which Guinness used to paint my father in the worst light. Coincidentally, he had lent Ward the use of an old bank account he had inherited from my grandfather in Zurich.

A mareva order was granted, freezing Ernest's assets in the UK up to a value of £5.2 million. A similar order was granted against

Ward. It was a ridiculous piece of litigation. The claim was ludicrously in excess of Ernest's assets, and Guinness knew this. He had been their employee and they knew what his salary had been. Certainly his stock options, which Guinness had reneged on, would have provided him with capital, but still nothing like £5.2 million. Herbert Smith had apparently seen the picture of Knoll House in the *Observer* and apparently feared that Ernest would sell and move the proceeds abroad. Ernest's lawyers vigorously denied that he had benefited in any way from Ward's £5.2 million, and told the court that Ernest would be applying for all court orders against him to be struck out.

Two weeks later his lawyers returned to the High Court to get the mareva injunction lifted. At least, this is what Ernest understood to be the intention. In fact, it had been decided to use this opportunity additionally to clear up a number of the misconceptions that Guinness had been perpetuating about Ernest's involvement in the affair. The press held its breath. 'Court to be told Saunders's side of takeover story' was the headline on Lawrence Lever's story in *The Times*. Ernest was not going to be present at the hearing as he was still very sick, but he would be submitting affidavits which were expected to contain answers to the Guinness allegations.

Guinness put its case first. This was clearly intended to blacken my father's name before the court. The Roux letter was read out, thus presenting Ernest's involvement as unfavourably as possible, even though the letter's accuracy had not been established. Next came an aggressive, sensationalist affidavit from Shaun Dowling, one of Guinness's executive directors. Ernest was most surprised when he heard later of Dowling's involvement in the proceedings: he had not been a director of Guinness at the time of the Distillers bid. Guinness was presumably using him to front the attack on account of his personality.

The Dowling affidavit said: 'Guinness suspected that Mr Saunders and Mr Ward were at all times agreed that £3 million of a £5.2 million payment made to a company in the Channel Islands should secretly go to Mr Saunders.' The next day, the *Financial Times* headline read: 'Saunders in secret £3 million deal'. Fortunately the *Daily Telegraph* countered: 'Ex-Guinness chief denies "secret deal".'

My father's forty-eight-page affidavit, rushed by Payne Hicks Beach to Ernest while he was ill in Switzerland, was read to the court and the highlights were printed in the *Telegraph* the next day. In it he claimed that he was not a man versed in financial and City matters, and he insisted that the £5.2 million was a fair payment to Ward for, amongst other things, thinking up the arrangement whereby Distillers would pay Guinness's costs in mounting the takeover, win or lose. Ward also secured Distillers' agreement to the plan, which would have saved up to £100 million had the bid failed. He added that Ward was an extremely successful Washington lawyer who effectively gave up his practice and moved to London for the duration of the bid. He had told Ernest that if he were to remain in Britain, he would expect to be paid handsomely for his services. 'Quite frankly, I recognised at this time that Mr Ward had Guinness over a barrel,' Ernest said in the affidavit.

On the next day of the hearing Ward's affidavit was read to the court. He blasted the Guinness allegations that Ernest had secretly received £3 million of the £5.2 million as being 'scurrilous and insupportable'. Ward spelt out how the legal action against himself and Ernest was part of a 'co-ordinated worldwide effort' to give the impression 'of a desperate international hunt for money alleged to have been secreted mysteriously by its American director'. Ward said that the simple truth of the £5.2 million payment was that it was fair remuneration for his services during the Distillers takeover. He accused the new board at Guinness of attempting, by using courts in three jurisdictions, to rewrite history and to question in retrospect the former management's business decisions. He added that he now held the entire £5.2 million, less tax, in the US and Ernest had not benefited from it in any way.

Herbert Smith, however, were running a public relations campaign as well as a legal case. The affidavits in support of Guinness were being turned out thick and fast, and each one made more sensational reading in the papers.

Just before lunch on the third day, the Guinness lawyers produced a rabbit out of their hat – an affidavit from Margaret McGrath, Ernest's former secretary at Guinness. The judge, the Vice-Chancellor, said he would read it over lunch and then rule on its admissibility. He was to comment that the mud-slinging by Guinness was merely fodder for a scandal-hungry press and was not clarifying the mareva issue. But he returned from the break and allowed the McGrath affidavit.

In it, Mrs McGrath claimed that Ernest had asked her to shred a diary and other documents after the DTI investigators walked into Guinness. After this submission, the court learnt to its surprise that Guinness was withdrawing its allegation that there had been a secret deal between Ward and Ernest. One of my friends, who had sat in on the whole case, said it was like an episode of *Dallas*, with Ernest painted as J. R. Ewing.

Stacked on top of that was a further damaging affidavit from Howard Hughes of Price Waterhouse, and even a statement from Charles Fraser, the Scottish lawyer, put together in such haste that it was submitted covered with handwritten corrections. To cap it all, the Guinness team decided that Roux should put in an affidavit to counter every one of Ernest's arguments which had been presented earlier in the week. They were on the spot, and able to react immediately, while my father of course was stuck in Switzerland, ill and out of touch. *The Independent* wrote on April 11: 'Mr Roux challenged Mr Saunders' version of events in almost every particular, describing large chunks of it as "completely untrue".' Roux, naturally, was backing his original letter, and having heard Ernest's version of events earlier in the week, was ideally positioned to challenge it.

Payne Hicks Beach finally decided that Ernest should respond to these attacks. Ralph was on holiday, so they sent another lawyer and a barrister to Switzerland. Ernest got out of bed and was driven to Lausanne to compile an affidavit.

Since one of McGrath's allegations concerned a Mr Heuberger, whom she alleged had held some secret meeting with Ernest in Zurich connected with the £5.2 million payment, and that Ernest had told her to conceal it, Payne Hicks felt an unequivocal rebuttal from Heuberger was required. By now it was the weekend and Ernest had enormous difficulty in locating the man, a friend of his father's whom he had not seen for several years, but when he did track him down, Heuberger kindly agreed to meet Ernest at the British Consulate in Zurich on his way to Spain. Ernest and Carole then took the train to Zurich, and Heuberger signed an affidavit stating categorically that he had not met Ernest since September 1984, nor had had any plans to do so. Ernest sent the affidavit to London by air courier, and went back to his sickbed.

How was the Vice-Chancellor going to decide? He resolved the case by strictly applying a section of the 1985 Companies Act, and the mareva remained intact.

He did say that Guinness were not now alleging that Ernest had benefited from any of the £5.2 million. But the judge could not have been uninfluenced by the Guinness propaganda and hugely adverse press coverage, as he went on to say that Ernest had worked in Switzerland, and there was a strong possibility that Ernest might transfer his assets out of the court's jurisdiction to defeat any claim by Guinness.

We only later appreciated that the Vice-Chancellor's remarks about my father, as reported in the press, set an unfavourable precedent that was to create an undeniable bias in subsequent judicial processes.

This 'mini-trial' was anything but beneficial to Ernest. He had agreed to the hearing in an attempt to get the mareva order lifted and had come out of it in a worse position than when he had gone in. He had spent substantial sums in legal fees and been slandered by everyone at Guinness. With hindsight, he would never have agreed to the mini-trial had he been fully fit. He was still in a state of shock, a complete novice to legal wrangles, and was wholly dependent on his legal advisers.

Ernest's opinion of the judicial process was not strengthened in the next few weeks by the fact that another judge – against the Law Society's advice – permitted Denton Hall and Burgin to continue to work as Roux's solicitors. It seemed unfair that although Henry King had been Ernest's family lawyer for years and was intimately familiar with much of our private affairs, his firm should now be allowed to act for Roux.

The media had not finished yet. The continuous description of him in public as 'the disgraced former chairman of Guinness' was serving to reinforce prejudice. Ernest: 'Repetition, as Goebbels taught, is one of the key elements of propaganda. You take emotive words like "disgraced", "theft" and "steal" and pummel readers with them until they believe the message. It is insidious.' It was depressing to see how easily people were led to believe something simply because it was printed in the newspapers. *The Times* confirmed my worst fears. It ran a half-page advert for its sister paper, *The Sunday Times*, containing a large picture of the singer, Boy George, under the caption 'Coming Clean'. Next to this was an equally large picture of Ernest under the caption 'Playing Dirty'.

Ernest and Payne Hicks began work on his claim for wrongful dismissal against Guinness. He duly filed his counter-claim, which still stands. But this did nothing to ease the family's critical financial position, now that all assets had been frozen. If anything, Guinness became more determined to pursue their £5.2 million claim. They saw Ernest fighting back and decided they must show they were as serious as he was. Of course, it did not cost the directors of Guinness anything to chase every available remedy.

Out of the blue towards the end of March, Ernest received a phone call from Tiny Rowland, the charismatic chief executive of Lonrho, the international trading group. He left a message on the answerphone at Knoll House saying he would like to talk to Ernest, who was in Switzerland at the time. The message was passed on, and my parents arranged to meet Rowland and his wife in Geneva. Ernest: 'He was very sympathetic about our position.'

It was now May, and Ernest had been ill in Switzerland for two months. The DTI inspectors, in contact throughout with Payne Hicks Beach, were beginning to apply enormous pressure for Ernest to return for further interviews. They claimed they had urgent deadlines to meet for their report (though it took a further two years before even an interim report emerged). Dr Rochat was adamant that he did not want Ernest to go. He felt that Ernest was not mentally or physically fit enough to withstand another round of interrogation. Payne Hicks Beach told Ernest that if he did not return to the UK the DTI would take proceedings against him. Ernest reluctantly agreed to the solicitors' request to return. Interviews with the DTI were arranged for early May.

On May 6, Ernest went to see the DTI inspectors at the office of Thompson McLintock, the big firm of City accountants. He was questioned as before, but curiously there was an unusual adjournment at the request of the inspectors, and Ernest saw his diary disappear during the interview. 'Someone came in to get it,' he remembers. He returned to Payne Hicks's offices in New Square, Lincoln's Inn, at about 6 p.m. They have two offices in New Square, Nos. 1 and 10, on opposite sides of the small square. Stephen Ralph left Ernest alone in No. 1 while he went to No. 10. There was no one else left. Even the secretaries had gone home.

Suddenly there was a loud knocking on the large oak door. Ernest opened it and two men rushed in out of the night and grabbed him and the briefcase he was carrying. One of the men announced himself as Chief Inspector Wooton, and said he was arrresting Ernest for 'attempts to pervert the course of justice'. My father was stunned. He had come over voluntarily from Switzerland to London, against doctor's orders, to continue to co-operate with the DTI. Ernest: 'My solicitor had arranged it all, and yet here were the police arresting me without any warning.' He insisted on waiting for Stephen Ralph, who was still at No. 10. Ralph came back to find Ernest and the two police officers waiting for him, and he immediately phoned John Mathew QC, Ernest's criminal counsel on retainer.

Ernest was then taken to Holborn police station in a police car, where he was asked to sign for his papers. He did so, and a policeman took his briefcase away. He was ushered to a cell, where he was told to wait.

A short time later, Stephen Ralph appeared, saying that John Mathew would be following. He did, however, say that he feared that it was too late in the evening for Ernest to avoid spending the night in the cells. There was no hope of going to court to be bailed that evening. Ernest remembers the arrest with some gall, because it caused him and the family the maximum possible distress.

Ernest had spent the previous night with our friends, Gaston and Paula de Chalus. When Ralph told them the news, Gaston came straight over with clothes for Ernest. He also undertook to call Carole in Switzerland, and Paula phoned Jo, myself and John's school. Carole was in Les Diablerets, being looked after by Ernest's aunt. When she heard what had happened she had a second nervous collapse and was immediately put under sedation.

Ernest spent a sleepless night in the cell, which he remembers vividly. 'Despite my sleeping pills and two visits from doctors, I did not sleep a wink because of the jangling of a policeman's keys as he stomped up and down the corridor. They left all the lights on, too, just like in the movies. I was told that I was to be questioned in the morning by Detective Superintendent Botwright, who was in charge of the Guinness criminal case. By the time he arrived, Ralph was there with me. It was quite clear that I was to be charged with a number of offences.'

Ernest was then taken to Bow Street Magistrates' Court, opposite the Royal Opera House in Covent Garden. Mathew visited him in a cell under the court. Despite his state of shock, Ernest found himself interpreting for a German in the cell opposite who spoke no English and could not communicate with his solicitor.

Bow Street is the local Magistrates' Court for London's West End. Ernest stood at the back of the court waiting his turn to be heard alongside an incredible menagerie of characters: pimps, prostitutes, burglars, indecent assaulters and the usual sprinkling of drunk and disorderlies. And then there was E. W. Saunders in a blue round-necked jumper, unshaven, hair tousled. The police had told Ernest to smarten himself up, or people might think he had been mistreated. 'I refused to do anything about my appearance, I was so angry at the way I had been treated. I was feeling ill and had had no sleep.'

When his case was called, Ernest stood in the dock, which at Bow Street consists of a bench long enough to seat five people, surrounded on three sides by a waist-high iron railing. The charges were read. He was accused of intention to pervert the course of justice, and with destroying and falsifying documents. The alleged evidence must have come from Margaret McGrath's allegations three weeks before.

Chief Inspector Wooton was questioned by the magistrate. 'Are the police opposing bail?' Wooton said 'Yes,' and gave his reasons. These appeared so outrageous and without any substance to Mathew that he stood up, cross-examined the policeman and demolished his case. The magistrate said he would grant bail, but it was fixed at the exorbitant figure of £500,000. It was a tycoon's ransom, that Ernest would have great difficulty in finding. If he could not raise the money he would not get bail, and would be kept in custody. Ernest did not know where he could get sureties for such a large sum, so Mathew asked for an adjournment to discuss the matter with Ralph. In the end the magistrate agreed to release my father into the custody of Ralph while attempts were made to find the sureties. For six days until the following Tuesday, when the bail hearing would be reconvened, Ernest would have to stay at Ralph's apartment and remain with him at all times. Jo immediately rushed to London from university in Exeter to stay with my father.

Despite her state of shock, Carole immediately got on the phone and made desperate pleas for help. Many friends were frightened off, labouring under the misconception that putting up bail actually meant handing over the money there and then, and also because of the prevailing paranoia about the City. Carole called me from Switzerland and asked if I would call a few parents of my friends to ask for help. Again wary, they were reluctant to get involved. My mother also contacted Tiny Rowland at his home, even though she had met him only once. He immediately agreed to help. She also called Herbert Heinzel, an old family friend from my parents' Loudwater days, whose wife had been a patient of my grandfather, and he said he would help, too.

Ernest returned to Bow Street, still in Ralph's custody, on May 12. Rowland and Heinzel stood as sureties to the tune of £250,000 each. To the amusement of everyone present the magistrate, Geoffrey Breen, asked Rowland if he would have any difficulty in raising the money. 'None at all,' said the multi-millionaire.

But that was not the end of the matter. There were conditions: Ernest must surrender his passport to the police and not apply for any other travel document; and he must not directly or indirectly contact any past or present employee of Guinness.

'Now I was completely cut off from my wife and former friends and colleagues at Guinness by this action. In the future Guinness were to use this ban to prevent suppliers and other sympathisers from communicating with me. They might have been inclined to help me with legal defence funding, but they all backed off after threats from Guinness.'

After the hearing he went to the offices of Payne Hicks and issued a statement to the press, denying the charges and vowing to expose those who were really responsible.

The statement said: 'I have spent a considerable amount of time this year in co-operating with the DTI inspectors. Unfortunately, as a result of my wife's health and my own, there was a break in my attendance with the inspectors, although they were kept fully appraised of the position by my lawyers at all times. My wife is still in Switzerland, unfortunately most unwell. I myself returned against strong medical advice on Monday of last week to continue the meetings with the inspectors – and found myself arrested and my passport confiscated. Quite frankly, I am astonished at the timing and the manner and the fact of my arrest. As you will know I have spent a number of years, at considerable personal and family cost, building Guinness into one of the leading British companies in the world. I think you will understand that I am, of all people, determined to see all the true facts emerge and those responsible for any wrong-doings brought to account, whatever steps are necessary to achieve this.' I want to make absolutely clear that I have not had any interest in the alleged improper payments to others, nor any knowledge of, or part in, any unlawful share support operations, as I am confident will emerge when all the true facts are known.'

The headlines the next day were sensational. *Today*'s front page read: 'I'LL EXPOSE GUILTY MEN – Ex-Guinness chief warns wrongdoers.' *The Times* recorded: 'Exposure threat by angry Saunders.' In their book *Takeovers* (Hamish Hamilton), Ivan Fallon and James Srodes wrote: 'They (the Fraud Squad) began work just as Margaret Thatcher called an election, one where the opposition had hoped to score points over the issue of corruption in the City and the numbers of rich capitalists, some of them Tory supporters, who had become involved in the widening Guinness affair. In the event, however, financial scandals and Guinness scarcely featured in the election campaign: the arrest and charges against Ernest Saunders early in May saw to that. There were reports of an unnamed cabinet minister warning that unless "we get the handcuffs on quick", financial scandals and insider trading were going to be a serious embarrassment to the government in the election. Now government Ministers could and did plead that the matter was *sub judice*, and if pressed further could point to the Saunders's arrest and the punishment of insider trader, Geoffrey Collier. Action was being taken against financial abuse, alleged or proven, arising from the takeover boom and the rise in share prices; what more was there to talk about? The subject as an election issue sputtered and died in the first week of the campaign.'

My father was arrested on May 6. The date of the 1987 general election was announced very soon afterwards.

Ernest: 'All this was totally unnecessary – it was a deliberate attempt to humiliate me. The police had known exactly where I was when I returned from Switzerland, they knew I was with the DTI, they knew who my lawyers were. All they had to do was to make an appointment to see me.' It should be noted that none of the other people later arrested in connection with the Guinness affair had to spend a night in a cell, with the exception of Anthony Parnes, who was arrested under different circumstances in California. 'This demonstrates how victimisation, oppression and mischievous innu-endo were deployed against me. If you are sacked and arrested, then everyone automatically assumes you have done something wrong!'

On May 19 Ernest's barrister applied to have his bail conditions varied so that he could visit my mother, who was still very ill in Switzerland. The magistrate allowed him to have his passport back on condition that he gave the police written details of all travel plans and surrendered his passport within twenty-four hours of his return. Ernest immediately left to see my mother.

Ernest: 'Carole was understandably in a terrible state. Her doctor had even sent a letter to the court in which he made comments about his – and, for that matter, the rest of the world's – opinion as to how British justice was going about this whole business. Our lawyers insisted that the letter should be toned down – but the doctor was right! We were left in peace, other than by periodic attempts by the gutter press to bother us.'

But there was to be no rest for Ernest back in London. The Guinness board, under the influence of Sir Norman Macfarlane, had been calling for Ernest's resignation since his dismissal in January. At the company's Annual General Meeting on May 27, one of the proposed resolutions was that he should be removed as a director. Ernest knew that if he did not resign he would provide Macfarlane with another media platform to humiliate him in front of the stockholders. He decided therefore to resign, which was in any case a formality.

On the eve of the AGM he sent a two-paragraphed letter to Macfarlane via Payne Hicks, tendering his resignation. Accompanying it was a detailed two-page letter which Ernest asked to be read to the shareholders at the meeting. It said in part:

> ... I have throughout sought to co-operate fully with the DTI inspectors, and indeed was doing so at the time of my arrest, having returned voluntarily from Switzerland, where my wife is still very ill, and against firm advice of my own doctors, to attend meetings arranged with the inspectors. This co-operation has involved an enormous amount of time and effort on the part of myself, my family and my lawyers, and substantial expense.
>
> In its explanatory memorandum, the board states that, arising from investigations made into certain matters disclosed in early January 1987, at a meeting on 14 January it unanimously decided to ask me and Mr Ward to resign as directors. I do not know the nature of these investigations. The only matter of which I am aware is the letter of 4 January from Mr Roux, whose references to my involvement and/or knowledge are categorically denied.
>
> I have strived to achieve moderation. I declined to participate in any public debate on these matters until such time as I was forced into the public arena by the proceedings brought against me by the company. I had been advised and considered that to do so might impede the course of the DTI investigation and could further embarrass and damage the company. But I can no longer hide the fact that I feel incensed at the lies which have been told about me by others. I am also distressed by the way in which I have been treated, particularly by my former colleagues on the board, who were my allies whilst it suited them, but now seek to make me the scapegoat. An investigation into the company appears to have turned into a personal vendetta. I can only hope the Guinness board will not treat the fruits of the success they inherited with the unjustified contempt they have shown for the man who produced it.

Understandably, Ernest did not trust Macfarlane to read out the statement, so Payne Hicks took the precaution of issuing it the same night to the press. The next day, the day of the AGM, many papers reproduced the letter in full. The *Financial Times* carried the headline: 'Saunders resigns as Guinness director with attack on board.'

The AGM had all the makings of great theatre. Guinness had hired the Connaught Rooms in London to accommodate the thousand or so shareholders who were expected. This was to be the first AGM since the Distillers takeover, and the organisers did not think that the traditional venue of the Toucan Inn at the Park Royal Brewery would be big enough. It was also the first AGM after the new board appointments, Ernest's dismissal and prosecution, and the DTI inquiry. There were bound to be questions on all these points, and rumour-mongers were speculating that my father would turn up in person. Robin Cook, the Labour Party spokesman on the City, had announced his intention to represent the Labour Party pension scheme at the meeting, and would obviously try to score points. The stage was set, the doors were opened and the shareholders poured in.

Sir Norman Macfarlane announced that, in view of Mr Saunders's resignation the night before, the resolution calling for it would no longer be put. As anticipated, he refused to read Ernest's letter with the excuse that, in the light of his resignation, the letter was irrelevant and contained 'a large number of statements and allegations with which this board disagrees'. Moreover, he continued, 'since the company is in legal dispute with Mr Saunders it would not be appropriate so to do'. A shareholder piped up, 'We want to hear it,' but Sir Norman slapped him down, saying that the statement had been widely reported in the press and copies could be obtained from Mr Saunders's solicitors.

So ended Ernest's five and a half years' service with Guinness. However, as Jeremy Warner wrote in *The Independent*, his spectre loomed large over the meeting. Many of the shareholders' questions concerned the board's treatment of Ernest. When asked why he was dismissed at all, Sir Norman replied: 'The board had reason to believe he was in breach of his fiduciary duties to the company, and this resulted in a loss of confidence in him by the board.'

'You have turned on him in a despicable manner,' said one shareholder, drawing widespread applause. A second added: 'The dismissal of Mr Saunders without giving him a fair hearing was a breach of natural justice.' 'A man is innocent until proved guilty,' chipped in another.

But the comments were inevitably not all in Ernest's favour. His supporters' speeches were greeted by ripples of applause and a few cries of 'hear, hear'. But there was support for a man who accused Ernest of 'bringing shame' on the company. This man turned out to be a former advertising director of Guinness, whose wife had opposed Ernest's appointment at his first AGM.

Macfarlane was obliged at one point to acknowledge Ernest's contribution to the company over the previous five years was 'beyond dispute', but then corrected himself – 'until the Distillers bid'. It seemed, and a company spokesman indeed later acknowledged, that the board had prepared for every possible question. 'In fact, as one of Sir Norman's advisers confided afterwards, there was not a single question put during the meeting for which Sir Norman did not have a prepared answer,' wrote Warner in *The Independent*. 'His only real mistake was to be a little too prepared.'

He had been warned to expect hostile questioning from Declan O'Hegarty, a frequent critic at Guinness shareholders' meetings. 'I have been waiting to speak to you, Mr O'Hegarty,' Sir Norman announced. Unfortunately he had the wrong shareholder. O'Hegarty was the next questioner, and, undeterred, he went on to propose that Mikhail Gorbachev join the board. 'Perhaps then we would get a bit of *glasnost*,' he suggested.

Robin Cook, wearing his Labour Party pension scheme hat, was the only institutional representative to enter the fray. He demanded to know what Guinness intended to do about Cazenove & Co., who were Guinness's brokers during the Distillers bid. Cazenove had ordered an investigation on their role in the bid to be carried out by their own solicitors, Simmons and Simmons, who had awarded them a clean bill of health. Cook was not satisfied.

Other shareholders attacked Price Waterhouse, the company's auditors, and the directors for failing to detect the illicit payments and share support operation. Sir Norman's reply to all questions of this sort was to say, 'That was all to do with the Ernest Saunders regime.'

When the meeting ended a commissionaire and a Guinness official held back the journalists to stop them pursuing the directors as they left the platform and walked out of the room.

Kenneth Fleet handed down his verdict on the proceedings from the columns of *The Times*: 'Ernest Saunders, who rescued Guinness from the shadow of the breakers' yard and added Arthur Bell and Distillers, has been dismembered in public view, not least by those who prospered in association with him – without even the ritual of a trial . . . Thank heaven therefore for the private shareholders. Some of them actually showed some sympathy for their former chairman and chief executive, who may or may not be guilty of the wrongs attributed to him but who, in their view, had been treated with astonishing callousness. But even more to the point, several showed proper concern about the way Guinness's non-executive directors, executive directors and various professional advisers had discharged their responsibilities during the Saunders era. The tendency is to lay all blame at his door and to claim that none of it could happen now. If you believe that, you will believe anything.'

15

THE FIGHT FOR JUSTICE

Ernest found himself in a living hell. He had had to cope with the ongoing Guinness action, criminal charges and the trial by media and innuendo. He had been cut off from his friends at Guinness by his bail conditions. Some outside the company were panicked by what seemed to be happening in the City and avoided him. Others merely met him in order to satisfy their curiosity. Ernest saw only the few people he could really trust, his long-time family friends from Loudwater or Les Diablerets. Not only did he have to defend himself and try to keep the family together, but he was running out of money fast. It is, of course, well-known that the law does not come cheap.

I took my final examinations at the end of May and my father's first public appearance after his arrest and court hearing was at my Cambridge graduation ceremony in June. Ernest: 'My old college, Emmanuel, put me up for the night. I had a good chat with the Master, Dr Derek Brewer, whom I knew well and who was very supportive. Jo came up from Exeter the next day, and the ceremony was as magnificent as ever. Afterwards at the college there was no suggestion of anything but support.'

But that month saw the start of a new problem: where to live? Knoll House was sold, with the court's permission, and in my mother's absence Jo and I packed the furniture into store. Guinness, by their oppression, had effectively forced us to sell the much-loved family home. I had enrolled for a nine-month course at Bar School in London, and my father needed to be in London also, to attend meetings with lawyers and others connected with the case. Both Jo and John needed somewhere to stay when they were not at university or school.

Whilst we were trying to work out where to go, Tiny Rowland

again came to the rescue, offering us temporary accommodation in a flat in London. As the last removal lorry set off for storage, Jo and I filled a transit van with personal belongings and drove to London. Neither of us had any idea how long it would be before we could take anything out of store. Thanks to Rowland's generosity we had a place to stay until late November of that year.

It meant that we had a place to camp, but never a home. My mother remained in Switzerland, Jo went back to university and John to boarding school. My father and I were living together for the first time since I had become a boarder at prep school, aged nine. So the coming months required considerable readjustment for both of us. I valued my independence dearly, but I had given up little compared with my father. As far as I was concerned, there was nothing particularly unusual about my living with my father. Most of my university friends, whose parents lived in London, were also at home whilst they got settled after graduating. I still saw many of them, and began my Bar School course.

However, my father had become a shadow of his former self. He had lost his job, his house, his assets had been frozen and he had been arrested. His wife was ill and former friends from the business world were scared to see him. Fortunately, family friends rallied round, offering meals, weekends to stay, and even to do our washing. But it was conversation that Ernest craved most. He did not want to be left alone in the flat, and when I was there he would often follow me from one room to the next as I went about routine chores. His only real contact with the outside world was through the telephone.

At weekends we would often go for long walks in Regent's Park, or sit and read the papers in the afternoon sun. Sometimes we would stand on the terraces at Stamford Bridge or Plough Lane, Chelsea and Wimbledon's football grounds.

As neither of us was much good as a cook, it is not surprising that we both lost a lot of weight in the four months we were alone together. I used to burn the meat and boil the vegetables dry. Jo would sporadically come up from Exeter with food and, like a saint, set about cleaning up.

To be honest, I did not really know my father before this phase, and I am sure he did not really know me. If it had not been for me having to study in London, we might never have ended up living together. We had always got on reasonably well, but over the previous five years we had increasingly been caught up in our very different lives. I had travelled a great deal since leaving school, and I had been at university. He had been giving Guinness his undivided attention twenty-four hours a day, seven days a week. He paid my bills and let me get on with whatever I was doing. I would not have wanted it any other way: he left me to make my own decisions and mistakes, rather than impose his will on me as some fathers seem to do.

How he coped with the readjustment to his new life, I shall never know. While he was slowing down from the ferocious demands of life at the top of a major corporation, he had to cope with the tremendous pressures of arrest, criminal prosecution, the Guinness litigation and intermittent illness. Over this period I discovered a man with enormous courage and decency. He accepted me, my habits and friends. He became a flatmate and we became friends. If Steven Ralph, his solicitor, shoved a bundle of papers under our front door at 11 p.m. before Ernest's court appearance the next day, we would pore over it together. He listened to what I had to say in a way that nobody had done before, valuing my limited legal knowledge. He also had to put up with a flatmate who was often absent, and when he locked himself out of the flat on one occasion he had to spend the rest of the day in the porter's flat with cats and empty bottles of whisky for company.

In the first week of July 1987 there was more legal pressure from Guinness. Herbert Smith & Co. went to court to try to get summary judgment against Ward on the ground that he had no defence to the action and should immediately repay the money.

The hearing was again before the Vice-Chancellor, who at that time was hearing all the Guinness-related actions. Guinness based its case on the affidavits that Ward had submitted for the April 'Dallas trial'.

On July 17 the Vice-Chancellor gave judgement. He ruled that Guinness was entitled to immediate repayment of the money. Ward was ordered to repay the full amount, even though he had a claim pending for fair remuneration for his services. My father was not involved in this action but, despite never having benefited from any of the £5.2 million, he was held liable to make up any deficit left by Ward's response. Ward has taken the case to higher courts, and at the time of writing it is still unresolved.

Later that month Ernest took his first formal counter-steps against Guinness. On the advice of his solicitors, Payne Hicks Beach, he joined Olivier Roux as a third party to the action, which meant that should Ernest be found liable to repay any of the £5.2 million Ward had not repaid, he would seek to recover it from Roux. Payne

Hicks also formally announced that Ernest had issued a writ against Guinness, alleging wrongful dismissal.

His solicitors were also advising that Ernest should attend more interviews with the DTI inspectors. He thought that, since the inspectors seemed to be more interested in producing a version of events that had Ernest masterminding all the alleged illegal acts, and since he had already been arrested, it seemed pointless to subject himself to more interrogations. Payne Hicks did not share this view.

The dilemma inspired the idea of compiling an accurate account which would give Ernest's version of events. 'We thought there might be one advantage. Maybe we could find a way of presenting the facts so that the inspectors could see them in context, as opposed to following the narrow line of questioning that they had chosen hitherto. That's if they were looking for objectivity at all.'

Over many weeks Ernest worked with an articled clerk on this project in London and even while he was supposed to be resting in Switzerland. It was never finished. Ernest: 'There was another aggressive campaign of pressure from the DTI inspectors which forced on us a deadline for our submission. Payne Hicks decided that the submission would have to be made by a barrister, so Robert Hillyard, a junior to Philip Heslop QC, was selected. Then the poor man had a personal family tragedy which delayed things by weeks and weeks.' They had not even produced a first draft by October.

That was a month which saw a huge resurgence in publicity over the Guinness affair. After five months of apparent inactivity in the wake of Ernest's politically-motivated arrest, Detective Superintendent Botwright suddenly sprang into action. On October 1 Anthony Parnes, the City stockbroker nicknamed 'the Animal' because of his aggressive dealing methods, was arrested as he stepped off an aeroplane in California with his wife and children. Parnes had been in Switzerland and had then travelled to Paris. The French police had let him slip through and board a plane to Los Angeles. In the time it took for Parnes to arrive there the British Foreign and Commonwealth Office alerted the US Justice Department and the FBI were there to arrest him on arrival. This was just after there had been an earthquake in California. Most of the public buildings were closed, but a court stayed open so that Parnes could be charged. He was refused bail and interned in Terminal Island prison.

On October 8 Sir Jack Lyons, the wealthy London financier and UK adviser to Bain & Co. Management Consultants in London, was arrested at his London home. The press even found some humour in these dramatic events by relating the story of how Lady Lyons answered the telephone and pretended to be a French maid. On October 12 Gerald Ronson, multi-millionaire chairman of Heron Corporation, was 'invited to attend' Holborn police station, where he was promptly arrested.

Amid this storm of activity, Ernest himself was again trying to get his passport back from the police so that he could go and visit my mother in Switzerland. His bail conditions specified that he had to apply for it in advance, which he did. But the police, giving very vague reasons, refused to return it. Payne Hicks actually went to court over the matter, where it emerged that the police wanted to talk to Ernest as well as to Parnes, Lyons and Ronson, but not for a few days yet. He had disturbed the carefully-orchestrated timing of their arrests by asking to go to Switzerland. The police then managed to get the paperwork together, and my father was asked to go to Holborn police station the next day.

I went with him and a solicitor to the station at the back of the Aliens Registration Office in Theobalds Road. We were taken to the basement, where the charge rooms and cells were. My father was informed that he was to be charged with a further thirty-seven offences. We were led into a tiny charge room, barely big enough for the three of us and two police officers. The superintendent apologised for the time it was going to take to read out all the charges. The charge officer then began reading. It took him half an hour, stopping only when he had to correct mistakes, or to ask weakly for a glass of water.

Ernest sat impassively, listening to the stream of accusations. He glanced incredulously at me when he heard the words 'theft', 'conspiracy' and the amounts of money involved. He had about as much idea of what he was being charged with as I did. At the end of the reading he signed the charge sheet, as instructed by the solicitor, and took it to Lincoln's Inn to try to work out exactly what these charges related to.

Ronson and Ernest appeared at Bow Steet Magistrates Court the next day, October 13. Ernest was incensed: 'The rest of the Guinness board at the time of the Distillers bid, including the then chairman Lord Iveagh, were apparently not to be involved, at least at this stage. What infuriated me particularly was the use of the Theft Act to suggest to the layman that stealing had occurred, with the implication that I had personally gained.'

The entire press waited outside the court in anticipation. This time, without consulting Payne Hicks, my father made a carefully worded statement, denying the charges and explaining to the public that the use of the Theft Act did not mean what they might otherwise have assumed it did. Lawrence Lever and Joe Joseph reported in *The Times*: 'Outside the court, Mr Saunders vigorously denied the charges. "The mere idea that I have been putting my hand in the Guinness till is absolutely appalling. I have not stolen anything. I have done nothing, and I deny every single one of these charges. I feel very bitter about the victimisation of my family, and I am determined to completely clear my name. I have absolutely nothing to hide. My conscience is clear. The positioning of myself as a scapegoat is appalling."'

Jo and I had suggested to him that this prepared statement would not be enough. He had held his silence for ten months since his dismissal, and it was time to speak out. We hastily borrowed a room in the Waldorf Hotel in nearby Aldwych, and invited journalists to attend. Most City editors of the national newspapers turned up or sent deputies. Ernest sat in front of the gathering, flanked by Jo and me. He proceeded to take the press through the events of the previous ten months, from sacking to the two arrests, commenting on the unfairness of his treatment and the persecution of our family. He dealt with many of the misconceptions the press had perpetuated, both about his personal wealth, the mythical tax haven in Switzerland and the family's circumstances. But, on the advice of his solicitors, Ernest was guarded about what he said about the alleged illegal transactions.

Nick Bunker of the *Financial Times* reported:

'In a colourless, impersonal rented room overlooking a rain-soaked Aldwych, Mr Ernest Saunders held what he called "a family tea-party" in London late yesterday afternoon.

'For more than 50 minutes, Mr Saunders, chairman of Guinness, the international drinks group, defended his past and painted a bleak picture of his financial future ...

'There were "big and powerful forces" ranged against him, he said, and an apparent determination to make him "the overall scapegoat". He spoke of "DTI inquisitions" and "DTI squads" who questioned him.

'Flanked by his son James, a 21-year-old law student, Mr Saunders also said: "We shall tell you what it is like to have a family that has been ripped apart."

'Though addressing "his friends in the press", some on first name terms, he nonetheless condemned "a plethora of horrible stuff" that had been printed in the media about his origins and his role in the Guinness affair.

'These had contributed to his wife's first nervous breakdown, while his arrest on criminal charges in May had precipitated the second, he said.

'Three threads ran through his press conference remarks. Without lawyers present, it had been hastily organised at London's Waldorf Hotel by family friends, his son and daughter Jo within 90 minutes of Mr Saunders' leaving Bow Street Magistrates Court yesterday.

'First, he was a man more sinned against than sinning, who had always placed shareholders' interests first but was now the victim of "an orchestrated vendetta" by former friends and colleagues. "I have nothing to hide," he said, adding: "I deny all the charges."

'Second, he was close to ruin. He said he had never been a wealthy man and he foresaw that the cost of defending himself would leave him "a millionaire in debt terms".

'His third point was the suffering of his family – especially his wife, who, he said, was seriously unwell and living in a small flat in "an unfashionable Swiss village where I used to go skiing in happier days".'

Questions were also directed at Jo and me. What did we think of what was happening? How had this affected our lives? I was quoted in the *Daily Express* as saying that my father 'is nothing more than he ever was: a very good business man who always acted in the shareholders' best interests'. I went on to share one of my beliefs with the press: 'He has never done as well for himself as he should have done. He has always made *other* people very wealthy!'

Two days later Roger Seelig, the most aggressive and entrepreneurial takeover man in the City, was arrested and charged too. There was also a rumour that a warrant had been issued for the arrest of Ward in the US, but no action had yet been taken. Only Olivier Roux remained untouched.

Ernest decided that, since the Crown Prosecution Service had made these fresh charges against him, he would no longer co-operate with the DTI inspectors, supply them with information or go to any more interviews. 'The whole DTI process on their side had been questionable. The DTI had been passing everything to the police, and Guinness in its turn had been feeding the inspectors with information.

By December 1987 he knew that his own resources could not continue to fund his defence in both the criminal case and the £5.2 million civil action. He would have to raise private finance, or go for legal aid.

Payne Hicks were also weighing up the possibility of getting the £5.2 million case postponed until after the criminal trial. Ernest: 'The two cases were unquestionably linked. They both referred to payments of money during the Distillers bid. Roux was the chief prosecution witness in the criminal trial and the chief Guinness witness in the civil trial. Both cases hinged on his word against mine.'

Initially, Payne Hicks's concern was that a full trial involving Ernest in the £5.2 million action, with all the likely attendant press publicity, would seriously prejudice his criminal trial. My father would then go to the Old Bailey even more tainted than was already the case. Furthermore, since Roux was the chief witness for both Guinness and the Crown, the Frenchman would see Ernest's defence to the civil trial in the civil pleadings.

Ernest knew that Guinness would not agree to anything he requested, so if he wanted a stay he would have to go to court to argue for it. He also knew that every step in law would cost more money. 'We had received some suggestions as to how to go about an attempt to raise funds privately for my defence. I spent many months in late 1987 and early 1988 on this matter, and a certain amount of money was donated. But the growing size and complexity of the case made this seem like peanuts. Moreover, the effect of the Guinness and Crown Prosecution Service cases against me meant that no one with existing Guinness business, or hopes of future Guinness business, would help. Secondly, a general feeling was spreading, throughout the business community and notably amongst those who had been involved in takeover deals or other City transactions, that people had better keep their distance. More than one PLC chairman said to me privately that he was ashamed by the attitude of his board. Nobody appeared to have the guts to help, for fear of standing out.' Ernest was being showered with goodwill messages, but no real money. So he reached the conclusion that he would have to apply for legal aid.

In December we had also received word from Lonrho, Tiny Rowland's company, that they needed their flat. We were going to be homeless again. Ernest returned to Switzerland and fortunately met an old family friend, Mary Ledzion, who thought she could help. Her sister had a one-bedroom flat in Vauxhall, south London, which she was not using, and we might be able to camp there for a while. I arranged to pick up the keys and ferried our possessions over the river in several carloads. We stayed there for the three weeks until Christmas, when my father and I went to Switzerland. We both owe a debt of gratitude to Miss Jean Currie for bailing us out.

At Christmas the family regrouped in Les Diablerets. There was no snow, but we took lots of walks in the mountain air. It is one of the most secluded places I know. The pace of life is pleasantly slow, the air has a fresh chill in it almost all year round, and you can believe the rest of the world is a million miles away. My mother, still not strong after her illness, needed this isolation. For Ernest, it was the only respite he could snatch from the continuous pressure in England. Even I felt weary and insecure after the past months in London.

But my father didn't really get much rest that Christmas. Via the newly installed fax machine in the village post office, correspondence was coming from Payne Hicks, asking how the 'stay' application was to be funded.

In the New Year the motion for the stay of the civil case went before the Vice-Chancellor, which was unfortunate in itself: Ernest seriously believed that the Vice-Chancellor had already taken an unfavourable view of him based on the mini-trial affidavits. The application was handled at Ernest's insistence by Philip Shepherd, a barrister recommended by Landau and Landau, who had out of pure kindness been taking an interest in our family difficulties since their involvement in the sale of Knoll House.

In court, Shepherd took on the might of Guinness, whose case was not as strong as the size of the legal team representing them. With its usual no-cost-barred approach to litigation in the share-holders' name and at the shareholders' expense, Guinness had an army of QCs, juniors, solicitors and solicitors' clerks in court to try to steamroller through their case. Shepherd was outgunned but not defeated. The result was a stand-off – no stay would be granted, but there would definitely be no trial before the criminal case was concluded, and all interim civil matters would be heard in private.

Ernest was not at all satisfied with this decision. He could not understand how, from a purely common-sense point of view, there could be no prejudice if the civil matters covered the same ground as the criminal, and were heard first, with the same chief witness in each case. Although he had secured leave to appeal to the Court of Appeal, he now had no funds with which to do so. He would have to apply for civil legal aid.

This led to a parting of the ways with Payne Hicks Beach. Ernest: 'Landau and Landau took over my case with decency, humanity and without funds. They said they would work on legal aid.'

The change of legal representation coincided with a change of family accommodation. Richard and Joanna Bowman, old friends of my parents – Joanna had been one of my mother's bridesmaids and is Jo's godmother – offered us rooms in their house in Putney. For Ernest and me it was the beginning of six very happy months in beautiful surroundings with their happy family, where we felt we had a home for the first time in over a year. Joanna and Richard took a great deal of the responsibility for my father off my hands, just when I needed it, allowing me to prepare in a stable environment for Bar finals due that May.

Nothing was too much trouble for them. Richard even handed over his study for me to work in. The Bowmans provided us with a shield against the events of the outside world. This became all the more important when, early in 1988, Guinness, not content with their oppressive action or litigation so far, stooped to cutting off our financial lifeline.

Under the terms of the mareva injunction, Jo and I had been allowed to draw reasonable living expenses from our frozen trust fund. Out of this we kept the whole family. We had no other money. Then, suddenly, a terse letter arrived at Landau and Landau from Herbert Smith, saying that Guinness would not consent to the release of any more money. We would have to go to court to argue the matter. Guinness knew full well that we did not have the money for litigation, whereas their funds were virtually bottomless. Now the corporate machine was apparently trying to starve us to death.

Jo and I were forced to go to court to ask for the living allowance to be reinstated. We had no money to do so, but the case was prepared by solicitors and barristers who generously agreed to work with no money up-front.

As spring came we were getting desperate. We had been living entirely at the generosity of the Bowmans and we knew they were moving out of London in June, and if we had no money by then we could be both destitute and homeless. My father was effectively unemployable, in view of his other heavy commitments. I was studying for the Bar. Jo was still in her final year at Exeter University. John was 15 and needed specialist tuition for dyslexia. And my mother could not work in Switzerland. But we all needed money to live.

In March we discovered for the first time that there might be such a thing as justice. Through the skill of Philip Shepherd, excellently briefed by Landau and Landau, and in front of the humane Judge Leonard Hoffman, we managed to get our living expenses reinstated. This was a great achievement in itself: but it was perhaps outshone by the fact that Shepherd also got us permission to use money from our frozen trust fund to buy a small house so that the family could at last have a home of its own and stop being gypsies.

For the first time a begrudging Guinness had been forced to be reasonable. We were used to Herbert Smith, Guinness's solicitors, going to battle over the smallest item. Solicitors' letters would be sent back and forth, at horrendous cost to us and to Guinness shareholders, over such items as releasing £9 from the trust fund to buy John Saunders, aged 15, a new grey sweater for school. Herbert Smith were in fact as obstructive as possible. Under their mandate from Guinness they pursued every available remedy and backed it up with the most expensive top counsel. It was and still is a battle between unequal resources.

On March 10 Lord Spens, the merchant banker from Henry Ansbacher & Co., was arrested and charged. On April 7 David Mayhew, a partner in the hitherto irreproachable stockbroking firm, Cazenove & Co., was also hauled in. The City was stunned. The Guinness affair had reached a previously impenetrable inner sanctum of the Establishment. The warning was plain for everyone else in that closed and privileged club: no one was out of reach. In the same week, the Serious Fraud Office officially opened, with teams of barristers and accountants and other experts, working to a brief to speed complex fraud investigations. The SFO took over the Guinness case.

Soon afterwards Landau and Landau submitted a legal aid application on behalf of Ernest to the Chief Metropolitan Magistrate. The application was turned down. No reason was given.

When Bruce Laughland QC appeared for my father at the next Bow Street remand hearing on April 12, he did so therefore without fee. As at the last remand in November 1987, Ernest appeared in court with his co-defendants: Ronson, Seelig, Lyons and Spens were all there with their barristers. So was Parnes, who in March had voluntarily returned to the UK after six months in a Californian prison. Only Mayhew was absent, having been remanded until June after his arrest only five days before.

One by one, the defendants' names were called out. My father, Ronson, Seelig and Lyons filed into the dock and sat down. The Bow Street dock is quite narrow: to his and everyone else's relief,

Spens was not required to squeeze his considerable girth into it, but was told to sit in front on a separate bench with Parnes.

Sir David Hopkin, the Chief Metropolitan Magistrate, came in and the court rose. Victor Temple from the Crown Prosecution Service was asked to give the prosecution's update. He reported that the Crown had been waiting for the new Criminal Justice Act to come into force, as it contained provisions for direct transfer of criminal cases from the Magistrates Court to the Crown Court, without having to hear evidence at the committal stage. A great deal of time would be saved under the new procedure, he claimed.

This was already Ernest's fourth remand hearing since his first arrest almost a year previously. Bruce Laughland got to his feet to protest: 'One does begin to wonder when the time and the opportunity will be found for this important and lengthy trial. The prosecution ought not to be spinning this matter out. The whole conduct of this case means serious potential injustice.' Laughland pointed out that Ernest was in a different position from the other defendants: he was unemployed and effectively unemployable, and his personal resources had been exhausted. His health and that of his wife had been broken, their marriage was under severe and deepening strain, and the family had been 'rent asunder'.

Other barristers made similar complaints, but the magistrate merely remanded until June 1, when the prosecution would be required to give a further update. One by one the defendants left the court, fighting their way through the reporters on the steps outside.

When May arrived I took a day off revision for Bar finals and went with Norman Turner and the Landau and Landau team to the Guinness Annual General Meeting at the Hilton Hotel in Park Lane. A barrister, Jeffrey Littman had offered his services because he was disgusted at the way Ernest was being treated by his former employer, and we met him in the lobby.

Out of courtesy Norman Turner had informed Guinness in advance that questions would be raised about the treatment of Ernest by the board. He had told them that we would force a debate on the company's accounts if all questions were not answered satisfactorily. We took up position in the front row, in full view of the directors' rostrum. The board, led by Macfarlane, filed in and took their places. I noticed each of them glance nervously at our little group.

Macfarlane then opened the meeting, but instead of welcoming shareholders and taking them through the achievements of the year, his opening words were that the board would only answer questions related to the annual report and accounts, and they would not answer any questions relating to Ernest Saunders as the whole matter was *sub judice*. From the outset he was defensive, grey and uncharismatic. All the directors sat there, apprehensive and silent. It seemed to me that this was a completely different company from the one I had found so friendly and accessible in my father's day.

Halfway through the questions from the floor, Littman made his way to one of the microphones positioned down the side of the hall. Macfarlane was taking questions from each microphone in turn. He saw Littman and realised he could not stop him speaking.

He began with questions about oppression. Why was Ernest being sued for £5.2 million when he had never received one penny? Had shareholders been informed of Ernest's claim of £2 million to £3 million against the company for wrongful dismissal? 'We have a right to know what cost the company is incurring by pursuing Mr Saunders, and precisely what benefit can be obtained from placing a man in such a financial plight,' Littman pointed out.

Macfarlane simply blocked the questions. Littman threatened to call a debate on the accounts. Macfarlane said he could not do so. Littman called for a vote. A vote was taken, but by this time most of the audience was bored: they did not like seeing the directors being outmanoeuvred, and they wanted to get out for their usual free refreshments. We lost the vote, but we had made our presence felt to a board which had planned to behave as if the whole Saunders issue was closed. The meeting ended. Bar a bottle to take home, there was none of the traditional hospitality.

Norman Turner was also beginning to lodge serious objections with the Attorney General's office regarding the publication of press articles prejudicial to Ernest's case. The Attorney General, Sir Patrick Mayhew, had seen what could happen when hearings were held in California in March, to extradite Parnes. Even though the proceedings were analogous to a UK criminal committal and over two thousand pages of evidence were submitted to the court, including affidavits from Roux, no reporting restrictions were imposed. Every day there were reports in the British press containing evidence previously undisclosed over here, and commentary on the new material. What was being said about my father had not been verified before it was published in England, yet effectively it became the accepted version. Roux and Parnes could slander Ernest, but as Ernest was not a party to the extradition he had no opportunity to reply.

After a week of this, the Attorney General wrote to newspaper editors, asking them not to report the proceedings. By that time the damage had already been done.

The tide of prejudicial articles continued unchecked throughout 1988. When Ernest was desperately trying to secure legal aid, an article appeared in *Today* entitled 'Guinness was Good to Them', accompanied by a photograph of a large house in St John's Wood, one of the most exclusive districts in north London, complete with a Porsche in the drive. The caption said that this was where Ernest lived now. Of course he did not. The *Sunday Express* printed an article headed 'White Collar Criminals', listing Ernest alongside Keith Best, Rosie Johnson and Lester Piggott – all convicted criminals. My father had not been found guilty of anything, yet he was already being associated in the public's mind with known convicts. He could not defend himself by suing for defamation, as he had no money to do so – and the press knew this. When Ward took his £5.2 million case to the Court of Appeal, Ernest applied for a ban on all reporting of the case, but it was rejected.

Landau and Landau wrote to the Attorney General's office to complain about the effect of individual articles, and about the cumulative effect of such articles over the long period before Ernest's trials. Ernest argued that time would only compound the prejudice, not diminish it. But the Attorney General's office took no notice.

The PR machine behind the other rich and mighty defendants was already rolling to considerable effect. The annual Heron Corporation lunch at the Savoy Hotel was attended by an even more glittering array of businessmen and City figures than usual – all of whom wanted to be seen to show support *for* Ronson, so that they could continue to receive business *from* Ronson. They were all behind him, they said.

This, however, was nothing compared with the extraordinarily favourable press reserved for Mayhew, the stockbroker from Cazenove & Co., when he was arrested. Ernest: 'The supportive behaviour of Cazenove towards one of their partners was the extreme opposite of the tactics employed by Guinness against me. The press, too, was solidly behind the blue-blooded Establishment man. How could an Old Etonian and stockbroker to the Queen have possibly done anything wrong?'

Meanwhile, the City Takeover Panel reopened its files on the purchase of a number of Distillers shares right at the end of the bid. The Panel ruled that Guinness and certain Swiss nominees associated with Bank Leu had been acting in concert.

Guinness took the case to appeal where the Master of the Rolls, Lord Donaldson, upheld judgment against them. The Law report stated that the primary reason the concert party was not dealt with at the time of the Distillers bid 'was because of Mr Roux's false information then given to it.'

At the end of May 1988, one year after my father's arrest, committal papers were at last served on the defendants by the prosecution. But legal papers are no good without legal advice. Ernest submitted a second legal aid application. Again it was rejected.

On June 1, Ernest attended the remand hearing without a barrister. He had taken the view that he could no longer ask lawyers to appear without pay: he decided that he would continue to appear alone until legal aid was granted. None of the other defendants was present, as they had not been required to appear in person. Ernest maintained a silent protest throughout the hearing, in which there was no progress. Afterwards, Norman Turner warned the press that if Ernest was not granted legal aid, there would be such massive delays that the 'jury will probably die off in the meantime, leaving the prosecution to cry into their tea'. He said that serious consideration was being given to the possiblity of applying for judicial review of the decision not to grant legal aid. But emergency legal aid would have to be obtained in order to press for the legal aid, and Landau and Landau would have to obtain this first! Tragedy was turning into farce.

The next remand was on July 11. Ernest presumed that the other defendants would be appearing, but when he arrived he discovered not only that he was to receive two further charges but that all the others had been told by phone that unless they wanted to protest about the delay, or make other representations, they would not have to appear in person. They could send barristers instead. Spens turned up under the mistaken belief that there would be a committal. Ernest again represented himself.

Temple, for the prosecution, asked for yet another remand, saying that if the Criminal Justice Bill became law, the case could be transferred to the Crown Court on September 26. The Bill, on which the prosecution tactics depended, was due to be debated by the House of Lords on July 22. Michael Sherard, Ronson's barrister, complained that because of the delays the seven defendants were being held hostage to the legal system.

Ernest told the court:

The legal complexities of the case drew a foreseeable response from the press's cartoonists.

I wish to protest at the unreasonable delay in bringing this matter to trial. I ask, therefore, for committal proceedings involving the hearing in court of prosecution evidence to begin immediately, for the following reasons.

It is now fourteen months since I was arrested and charged in May 1987 and eighteen months since my arbitrary dismissal by my former employers. During this time my personal and professional life has been ruined; my wife's health broken; and my family have been living under the most enormous continuous stress. This is inhuman!

On top of this, I have had to contend with the continuing burden of oppressive civil litigation; while the criminal charges against me – all of which are strenuously denied – have been reported in every publication in the land, all this giving rise to enormous prejudice.

I am, sir, compared to my current co-defendants – men of the City and substance – in a unique position of disadvantage: without work; without money; without status; and without influence.

My applications for criminal legal aid have been rejected, and I cannot begin to cope on my own with the twenty-five volumes of prosecution papers that have been served on me. The Serious Fraud Office have, I believe, seventeen detectives on the case, and apparently unlimited specialist resources, including top lawyers to carry out investigations. I am a layman, and I don't consider myself, in any way, competent to understand the legal significance of what is involved.

I understand that there exists a perfectly proper and lawful procedure to initiate the trial process, and that I have a right to request it. I believe that after these inordinate delays, committal should not be at the convenience of the Crown, or even this court. I understand that the 'transfer' procedure that the prosecution has been waiting for will not now be available in the immediate future.

The preparation of my defence will take me a long time. I am asking for committal proceedings to begin immediately because I would be greatly assisted in my preparation by hearing the prosecution's opening speech, and their witnesses' evidence, at the committal stage.

I am also concerned that the holiday season is about to begin and I need to make this request now to eliminate even more delays.

May I say in conclusion, sir, that deep down I am really seriously concerned about something very fundamental indeed – having that fair trial that I am entitled to!

The magistrate, Mr Bartle, listened carefully and, once my father had finished, said that he could 'understand Mr Saunders's complaint', but he agreed all the same to the prosecution's request for yet another delay.

The speech appeared on the front page of the *Evening Standard* that day with banner headlines: 'EX-GUINNESS CHIEF PRO-TESTS OVER TRIAL DELAY – I am ruined says Saunders.' The next day the press ran a series of headlines ranging from 'Saunders fails in court bid for immediate committal' in the *Financial Times* to 'Saunders complains of stress over trial delay' in *The Independent*. The *Daily Express* chose a different tack – after the hearing Ernest and I were chased by a photographer down into Covent Garden tube station and on to a train. The *Express* printed a picture of Ernest standing in the train with the headline, 'Down the Tube! Riches-to-Rags Fall of a Tycoon', on a sensationalist story contrasting my father's past and present lifestyle.

By this time Landau and Landau had applied to the Department of Health and Social Security for civil legal aid to hold a judicial review of the magistrate's decision not to grant criminal legal aid. They had also requested civil legal aid to challenge another action, involving the Serious Fraud Office. The SFO had issued a notice ordering Guinness to hand over various documents referring to Ernest's civil and criminal cases. Landau and Landau decided that it was extremely prejudicial to their client's defence to allow the SFO to have them.

It appeared that the SFO, which as a new body was flexing its muscles, might be acting outside the powers conferred on it by the 1987 Criminal Justice Act, as it was seeking to investigate further someone who had already been charged. The court decided that arrest and charging were no bar to continuing an investigation, but Ernest was told he could challenge each request for documents as it arose. Ernest had made his point.

As he says: 'All these concerns contain fundamental issues of basic human rights. I felt that I could not rely solely on the English courts to guarantee these for me. I decided to make a preliminary, informal approach to the European Court of Human Rights in Strasbourg.'

In August 1988, while he was resting in Switzerland, Ernest wrote these notes for his files:

It is interesting to review what the key people involved in the Distillers bid are doing now. Roux has apparently been consulting, earning money, working with two ex-Bain employees in the venture capital area, which was one of his original objectives and one of his preferred tasks, as opposed to staying with Guinness. Indeed, as regards Bain, John Theroux has been given a sabbatical and is out of the country. All the other senior partners of Bain who were otherwise connected with Guinness have now left. Ward has been keeping his cards very close to his chest. We only tend to find out what he is doing when it is already happening. Lord Iveagh – nothing has been heard of him, except for a critical piece in the *Sunday Express* by John Junor, drawing attention to the ir ¬eased wealth that I had been responsible for in relation to the Guinness family and suggesting that Iveagh should pay for my defence, as he once promised he would ...

Roger Seelig continues to advise informally old City contacts, and still sits on the boards of a number of former Morgan Grenfell clients. For David Mayhew, Lord Spens and Gerald Ronson it is business as usual. Morgan Grenfell, of course, resigned from Guinness, but that was just a token gesture since Lazards had effectively taken over in any case. James Gulliver has left Argyll, and amongst other things now owns Brian Basham's PR company, Broad Street Group. His main objective is to keep out of the Guinness affair, and so far he has been very successful in doing so. Last, but not least, there is no question that my phones are being bugged and the police and maybe other private investigators are doing whatever they can to produce even more damaging evidence against me.

Ernest could console himself that now at last we had a home to live in. After the money was released by the court in March 1988, Jo and I went hunting, and we bought a small terraced house in south London. We went to the storage warehouse and collected some of the furniture from Knoll House. We now had a house where Ernest, Jo and I could live permanently, and John could visit at weekends. My mother remained in Switzerland.

On September 26 Ernest was back at Bow Street for the first remand hearing since July. He was again without legal representation. Five of the other defendants were present with their barristers. Only Mayhew, who has asked to be remanded in his absence, was not there.

Victor Temple, for the prosecution, told the court that the new Criminal Justice Act would finally be in force by October 31, and that the case could transfer to the Crown Court any time after that. He suggested that the defendants should be remanded until late November, when they could be sent to trial. He then explained the other purpose of the remand: the charges had been 'rationalised', and several defendants were now grouped under one charge instead of each defendant being charged separately with the same offence. He proposed that the defendants should be recharged in court with the new offences, and in some cases have charges struck out where they were no longer applicable.

For over an hour the defendants sat in the dock, with Ernest on this occasion sitting in front as there was not enough room. The clerk of the court read out a total of 104 offences. Ernest was told he was facing forty-six charges instead of forty-two, Lyons eleven instead of nine, Parnes fourteen instead of nineteen, and Ronson ten instead of eight. Seelig still faced nineteen charges and Spens four. After Ronson's ten charges were read out his barrister, Michael Sherard, stopped proceedings to ask if his client could leave as he had a plane to catch. Like a school headmaster the magistrate, Mr Bartle, said he could be excused, whereupon Ronson sped off in his blue Rolls-Royce.

Robert Harman QC, barrister to Sir Jack Lyons, attacked the prosecution for what he called their 'tinkering to while away the time', and questions were fired at Temple as to whether there was going to be one joint trial or a series of separate trials. Andrew Moor, Spens's solicitor, went one further. 'We are fed up with nothing happening, and we are going to the High Court to say "Please go to the magistrate and tell him to commit this case now," ' he declared.

It was against this backlog of complaint that my father got up and pointed out that it was sixteen months since he had first appeared before this court. He had lost count of how many times the prosecution had said they were not yet ready to proceed, despite previous assurances. 'Once again, the latest timescale is designed solely to suit the prosecution, who want to await the New Criminal Justice Act which they have decided, all along, provides the committal process that suits them. I should like to remind the court of Article 6(2) of the European Convention on Human Rights which states: "Everyone charged with a criminal offence shall be presumed innocent until proved guilty according to law." I am entirely innocent of these charges, and when this case finally comes to trial, I shall prove my innocence. However, there are many people who wonder whether it is possible for me to have a fair trial, given the scale of prejudice against me, which still continues.'

He went on: 'May I remind all concerned that I was neither the chairman of the company at the time, nor the board director for finance, City or legal affairs. Also that I am suing Guinness for wrongful dismissal.

'Article 6(3) of the Convention states: "Everyone has the right to have adequate facilities for the preparation of his defence." In these proceedings, with the thousands of pages of complex legal and financial documentation that have been served on me, there is a total inequality of resources. The Crown's resources are unlimited and my co-defendants, men of the City, can call upon vast legal expertise, and the funds to pay for it. I have been denied all assistance, and until I get legal aid of a scale that enables me to have the same degree of resources as the prosecution and my co-defendants, I cannot prepare my case. Sir, I feel very strongly that the oppressive manner in which this case is being conducted against me is a gross violation of the basic human rights to which I am entitled.' The magistrate once again merely bowed to the prosecution request for a further remand.

The next day the press carried many reports of Ernest's comments, with dramatic photographs of him brandishing his copy of the European Convention of Human Rights. The *Daily Telegraph* headlined its story 'Saunders demands swift justice', *The Times* called it 'Saunders' human rights protest over trial delay', and the *Guardian* reported: 'Saunders: How can I get a fair trial?' The *Telegraph* went further in its City Comment column: 'As Rumpole might say, justice delayed is justice denied.'

By October 17, Ernest's appeal for the civil proceedings to be stayed had reached the Court of Appeal. State legal aid was now paying his costs, and he was represented by Robert Webb QC. Guinness were as usual represented by David Oliver QC. But the three judges were not persuaded that continuing with the civil proceedings could prejudice Ernest's criminal trial. He was outraged that common-sense had still not prevailed. However, at last the court had castigated Guinness for their oppressive action. 'Guinness request is harassment of Saunders,' Raymond Hughes wrote in the *Financial Times*. He quoted Lord Justice Dillon as saying that Guinness's request for further and better particulars of Ernest's defence to the £5.2 million civil action was 'vexatious, harassing and oppressive'.

The next week my father received a copy of a letter written by the Rev. Oscar Muspratt, vicar of Penn, to Sir Norman Macfarlane. It read as follows:

Dear Sir Norman,
As the Vicar of Penn where the Saunders family lived, I was extremely disturbed to read the comments made in the Court of Appeal on Monday 17 September concerning your continued harassment of the Saunders family.

I cannot understand your motives in continuing to persecute Mr Saunders, who did so much for your Company, and whom you have now ruined in health and reputation, and who is relying on legal aid to defend himself in any case, against allegations that are totally unproven.

I have seen at first hand the mental damage done to his family by your vindictive action and I must ask you to let me know why your lawyers continue in this way, and what you can possibly hope to achieve, as the man has no money.

So far as Guinness is concerned on the other hand, it must be costing your shareholders a fortune to continue to pursue him.

I am shocked to learn that you are apparently even making it difficult for his dyslexic younger son to stay at school, and receive the special tuition he needs.

Can this be the sort of attitude we should expect from the Head of one of Britain's largest companies?'

I look forward to hearing from you.

Yours sincerely,

Ernest was later to learn that the vicar received a perfunctory reply.

On November 28 all the defendants returned to Bow Street. The Criminal Justice Act was now on the statute books, and transfer direct to the Crown Court could take place. Elizabeth Gloster, for the prosecution, told the court that there would be a series of pre-trial reviews before the case was eventually tried. At this point Mayhew's lawyer jumped up to request that bail conditions should be dropped for him as he was a partner in the firm of Cazenove & Co., stockbrokers to Her Majesty the Queen, and the subject of bail was a source of embarrassment for the partners. I could see Ernest about to get to his feet. He told me afterwards that he was so horrified at the arrogance of the request that he would have opposed it himself if necessary. Spens's lawyers followed suit, but they were both slapped down by Sir David Hopkin, the Chief Metropolitan Magistrate.

Ernest then asked the court what 'transfer' and 'pre-trial review' meant, what were the procedures involved and what risk there was to him. He made the point that, after all, he was only a layman without representation, and the court should not merely assume that he understood what was going on.

Gloster then got up to say that Mr Saunders could of course make a legal aid application there and then. Ernest did as bid, but Hopkin promptly refused. It was like something out of Punch and Judy.

Ernest spoke to the media massed outside on the steps of the court. He said: 'By their endless delaying tactics the prosecution have finally got their easy route to the Old Bailey. We may now be moving to a new courtroom, but my determination to vindicate myself will never change. I am innocent of all charges against me. I have been totally disadvantaged. I have no means to defend myself. Nevertheless I intend to prove my innocence. I am asking the media and the public to continue to help in this matter: to follow the process leading to the trial, and the progress of the trial itself – to see that justice is done. I will prove my innocence. But I demand a fair trial, not a show trial. Fair trial or show trial? Which is it to be for me? British justice is on trial here too, before a worldwide audience.'

His question of fair trial or show trial caught the imagination of the public and was shown on every television news bulletin throughout the evening. The morning press continued the theme.

Cynics might say that whoever was pulling the strings behind the scenes had finally been made to feel uneasy about the situation. But whatever the reason, the legal aid machinery suddenly sprang into action. A High Court hearing of the issues raised by Ernest's criminal legal aid application was so hastily convened on December 12 that Ernest's barrister was not even informed what was going to happen. At the end of the hearing Mr Justice Henry was in no doubt that Ernest should receive legal aid.

The question still unresolved was whether that order would grant Ernest the appropriate resources to match those of the Crown prosecutors and of his co-defendants. 'The battle must be fought on a level pitch,' David Mellor, our local MP, told him.

EPILOGUE

In 1981 my father was propelled from relative obscurity into what became the full glare of the public eye, and for one reason only – he was asked to join a venerable but badly managed British company. Until he had committed himself he did not realise quite how badly it had been managed, but he conscientiously set about restoring its fortunes. Over the next five years he revitalised Guinness, increasing its value on the stock market from £90 million to £3 billion by superb management and major strategic acquisitions. Thanks to Ernest the company is now in fabulous shape with a much admired portfolio of quality brands. Along the way he made a lot of people rich, though not himself. He also inevitably made enemies, though not among those who really knew him.

No one outside the family can accurately gauge the incredible cost to Ernest himself and to our family of his dedication to Guinness, and his hard work on behalf of the stockholders. To turn a company round from near penury to world-ranking status in such a short time meant that unpalatable decisions had to be taken. Ernest was never universally liked, but lack of popularity could never justify the appalling treatment he has suffered from his former employer, who so ungratefully dismissed him without compensation in January 1987.

Since then our whole family has been hounded and harassed by a public campaign. And my father's suffering has been aggravated by the slow, relentless grinding of the legal process. We do now have a roof over our heads, and a front door that we can close. Instead of avoiding him, people now come up to my father in the street and urge him on. A number of prominent business schools have invited him to speak and he has shared his experiences of management and also the risks involved in holding the top job. We are picking up the pieces of our lives, but we are conscious that my father's greatest ordeals still lie ahead, and we no longer have any illusions that decency and fair play can be taken for granted. They have to be fought for with every bit as much resolve as my father once fought for Guinness when it was on its knees.

The public must be made fully aware of the issues of justice, human rights and fundamental fairness that are at stake, if only to prepare others for what they may face.

For the first four months of 1989, after criminal legal aid had been granted by Mr Justice Henry, Landau and Landau worked diligently on Ernest's behalf. Norman Turner was acutely aware of the exceptional complexity of the case, its overlap between commercial and criminal law, the huge resources of the Serious Fraud Office and the ability of Ernest's co-defendants to pay for top legal representation. He was adamant that to have a fair trial Ernest should have access to equal resources, and began a stream of correspondence with the legal aid authorities to try to secure the necessary funding.

In April the Serious Fraud Office wrote to the defendants with a proposal to split the criminal proceedings into two trials with three defendants plus Ernest in each. Ernest would be on trial twice.

Having reached an impasse in his negotiations with legal aid authorities, Norman Turner wrote the following letter:

Dear Ernest,

I am writing with great regret to advise you that our current negotiations with the Legal Aid Authorities have not resulted in our achieving the commitment that we require to provide you with the quality of defence that you need in the complex, large and unique case that you face.

You are aware that in the Serious Fraud Office you are dealing with a newly formed Prosecution organisation that has a seemingly limitless budget and needs to prove itself; indeed you might say it is a prosecutor in search of a victim.

Your Co-Defendants are men of considerable personal wealth who can afford the very best legal advice and representation. You have had to resort to Legal Aid having exhausted your personal savings. However, the grant of Legal Aid does not, as is popularly believed, mean that you have in any way the parity of facilities of either your Co-Defendants or, indeed, the Prosecution. . . .

We are a small firm, but we will not do a second class job. I have no intention of compromising on the quality of the defence work you need, and therefore my partners and I have reluctantly been forced to the conclusion that unless there is a change in the immediate future in the attitude of the Legal Aid authorities regarding adequate funding we will regrettably be unable to continue to represent you....

Your present position is this: you have yet to be brought to trial, but in the meantime you have been financially ruined, previously refused Legal Aid to defend yourself on four occasions and over many months and suffered prolonged delays by the Prosecution until it suited them to proceed. Now you have been granted Legal Aid, and there is great and increasing pressure on you to be ready for an early trial. Nevertheless you have the right to a fair trial and to the resources and time to prepare your defence properly. Regrettably the response of the Court to funding, after consultation with the Lord Chancellor's Department, is that they cannot provide the confirmation of adequate remuneration for my firm without which we have so far been unable to embark on the great bulk of the preparation for trial. I suspect that the Lord Chancellor's Department has not been permitted by its political masters to treat you as an exceptional case and to deviate from the Government's policy of cutting back on Legal Aid to the community....

Apart from the question of your entitlement to a proper quality of defence, the Serious Fraud Office have given notice that they wish to subject you to the ultimate disadvantage. They propose that you are to be not just the focus of one trial, but that you, and you alone, should have to endure two separate trials effectively on the same issues. In human terms alone this is a monstrous suggestion, and I have no doubt that all right thinking people will see it in this way. However, it is vital that you make it clear that you will not be prepared to accept such an outrageous suggestion which is entirely aimed, in my view, at placing you in such a state of real as well as legal prejudice that the Prosecution will have the very best chance of winning your conviction.

I have been concerned for some time with the tendency of recent legislation to benefit the Prosecution at the expense of the Defendant, a move which is contradictory to the basic principles of British law. This case accordingly involves matters of public importance that go way beyond the technical charges that are the subject of so much documentation. They involve issues of principle linking justice, politics and human rights. Against this background your position as the key Defendant must be seen to demand a properly funded legal team with the full facilities to do the job: it does not look as if you are intended to get this....

> Yours sincerely,
> Norman Turner

The press reaction to the news that Ernest now faced the prospect of two trials was unanimous. The *Mail on Sunday* called it 'Double

Jeopardy' and a 'gross denial of natural justice'. The *Sunday Express* called it 'the law that has no justice'. Lord Rees-Mogg wrote a leader in the *Independent* entitled 'Why the Guinness case is fast becoming a scandal of justice'. At a time when Lord Mackay's legal reforms filled the headlines and prime-time television, Ernest's case emerged as a real-life illustration to which people could relate of the inadequacies of the legal aid system. Lord Rees-Mogg summed up why Ernest's case was relevant to everyone: 'If Ernest Saunders – with all his experience – cannot operate the legal aid system so as to secure himself a proper defence, what chance do the weaker and less capable defendants have, who may also be involved in complex affairs, and are equally entitled to the presumption of innocence?'

On Thursday 27 April my father and I travelled by tube to Southwark Crown Court on the South Bank next to London Bridge for a preparatory hearing where the defendants would be asked to plead 'guilty' or 'not guilty'. Without Gerald Ronson, who was due to appear the next day, Ernest, Anthony Parnes, Roger Seelig, Sir Jack Lyons, Lord Spens and David Mayhew filed into the dock of the modern courtroom complete with swivel chairs and glass partitions. Sitting in front of them were some 19 wigged barristers and the usual accompaniment of solicitors and clerks.

It took one and a half hours to read out the 65 charges on the indictment. Ernest, on his feet for most of this time, pleaded 'not guilty' to the 49 that were put to him; Parnes pleaded 'not guilty' to 14; Seelig to 20; Lyons to 13; Spens to 5 and Mayhew to 4. Ronson, the court was informed, intended to plead 'not guilty' to 11 charges the following day.

After the pleas were taken, the court was adjourned before Mr Justice Henry proposed to discuss the problem of Ernest's legal representation. After the break the court heard how Landau and Landau would go bankrupt if they continued to provide the required quality of legal representation for Ernest's case and were only funded at the proposed legal aid rates. Landau and Landau advised the court that they would be withdrawing from the case.

Ernest was again without lawyers and seriously considered representing himself, but decided against it. After interviewing several firms, on May 10 Ernest appointed the Manchester Firm Pannone Blackburn as his new solicitors. The issue of two trials was heard by Mr Justice Henry in September 1989. Before the decision could be made public, a ban on all press reporting was imposed.

PRINCIPAL DRAMATIS PERSONAE

FAMILY

Emanuel (Uly) Schleyer(-Saunders)	ES's father
Joanna (Hanni) Schleyer(-Saunders)	ES's mother
Michael David ⎫ Melanie David ⎭	ES's mother's parents
Carole Saunders	ES's wife
Joanna Saunders ⎫ James Saunders ⎬ John Saunders ⎭	ES's children

MARKETING CAREER (1959–1981)

John Treasure	— Marketing Director, JWT
Henry Lazell	— Chairman, Beecham Group
Ron Halstead (now Sir)	— Chairman, Beecham Products
Sir Isaac Wolfson	— Chairman, Great Universal Stores
Leonard Wolfson (now Lord)	— Joint Managing Director, GUS
Pierre Liotard-Vogt	— Chairman, Nestlé S.A.
Dr Arthur Furer	— Managing Director, Nestlé S.A.

GUINNESS BOARD AND PERSONALITIES

N/E = Non-Executive Director

Benjamin Guinness, Earl of Iveagh	— Head of Guinness family Non-executive

	Chairman of Guinness until July 1986 when became President
Viscount Boyd	— N/E Deputy Chairman (until 1986)
Anthony Purssell	— Managing director until EWS appointed (1981)
	— Deputy Chairman (until 1982)
Hon. Jonathan Guinness	— N/E Director (until 1988)
Hon. Finn Guinness	— N/E Director (until 1986)
Edward Guinness	— N/E Director until 1989 Chairman Harp Lager Company
Peter Guinness	— Director (until 1984)
Marquess of Dufferin & Ava	— N/E Director (until 1986)
Christopher Parsons	— N/E Director (until 1984)
Peter Keehan	— N/E Director (until 1986)
Ken Whittaker	— N/E Director (until 1984)
Michael Ogle	— Director (until 1982)
Stanley Darmon	— Director (until 1982)
Michael Hatfield	— Former Managing Director, Guinness Park Royal
Mark Hely-Hutchinson	— Former Managing Director, Guinness Ireland
Tony Spicer	— Group Finance Director (until 1982)
Arthur Furer	— N/E Director (1983–1987)
Olivier Roux	— Controller/Head of Finance (1982–1984). Director of Financial Strategy and Develop-

	ment (1984–1987)
Thomas Ward	— Senior Partner, Ward Lazarus Grow & Cihlar – Washington DC Law Firm. N/E Director (1984–1987)
Vic Steel	— Managing Director, Guinness Brewing Worldwide, (1985–1987)
Brian Baldock	— Managing Director, Guinness Development Division (since 1986)
Shaun Dowling	— Managing Director, Guinness Commercial Division (since 1986)
Sir Norman Macfarlane	— Chairman, Macfarlane Group. N/E Director of Guinness (since 1986). Chairman of Guinness (1987–9)
Sir David Plastow	— Chairman of Vickers. N/E Director of Guinness (since 1986). Deputy Chairman (since 1987)
Sir Ian Maclaurin	— Chairman of Tesco. N/E Director of Guinness (since 1986)
Ian Chapman	— Former Chairman of William Collins. N/E Director of Guinness (since 1986)
Anthony Greener	— Former Managing Director of Dunhill. N/E Director of Guinness (since 1986)
Alan Scrine	— Company Secretary
Chris Davidson	— Guinness in-house P.R. Director

Margaret McGrath — EWS's Secretary (until 1987)

ADVISORS AND PERSONALITIES IN BELL'S BID (June–August 1985)

Bill Bain — Chairman, Bain and Co.

John Theroux — Vice President, Bain U.K.

Anthony Richmond-Watson — Corporate Finance Director, Morgan Grenfell – Merchant Bankers to Guinness

Raymond Miquel — Chairman of Bell's

Henry King — Partner, Denton Hall & Burgin, Solicitors

Brian Basham — PR Advisor, Broad Street Associates

Colin Liddell — Guinness's Scottish PR Advisor, Charles Barker Scotland

Sir Gorden Reece — Consultant to Guinness

Andrew Gifford — Consultant to Guinness, GJW

Angus Grossart — Managing Director, Noble Grossart – Merchant Bankers to Guinness

Sir Jack Lyons — UK Advisor to Bain & Co.

Jennifer Lang — Saatchi and Saatchi (corporate advertising agency to Guinness)

Lord Spens — Corporate Finance Director, Henry Ansbacher & Co. – Merchant Bankers to Bell's

Christopher Reeves — Chief Executive, Morgan Grenfell

Graham Walsh — Head of Corporate Finance, Morgan Grenfell

Bill Young — Consultant, Bain & Co.

Sir Gordon Borrie — Director-General, Office of Fair Trading

Bill Walker — MP for Tayside North

Nicholas Fairbairn — MP for Perth and Kinross

Peter Tyrie — Managing Director, Gleneagles Hotels Group

ADVISORS AND PERSONALITIES IN DISTILLERS BID AND AFTERMATH
(January–September 1986)

Tim Bell	— PR Consultant to Guinness, Lowe Howard Spink
James Gulliver	— Chairman of Argyll Group
Malcom Rifkind	— Secretary of State for Scotland
Charles Fraser	— Chairman of Morgan Grenfell, Scotland
Roger Seelig	— Corporate Finance Director, Morgan Grenfell
John Connell	— Chairman of Distillers
David Connell	— Director of Distillers
Bay Green	— Corporate Finance Director, Kleinwort Benson – Merchant Bankers to Distillers
Sir Nigel Broakes	— Chairman of Trafalgar House. N/E Director of Distillers
Bill Spengler	— Vice Chairman of Distillers
Sir Thomas Risk	— Governor of the Bank of Scotland
Frank Lowe	— Chairman, Lowe Howard Spink – Advertising Agency to Guinness
David Walker	— Director of Bank of England
Sir Godfray LeQuesne	— Chairman, Monopolies and Mergers Commission
Jeremy Lever QC ⎫ John Swift QC ⎬	— Competition policy barristers
Michael Howard ⎫ Geoffrey Pattie ⎬	— Ministers at the DTI
David Mayhew	— Partner in Stockbrokers to Guinness Cazenove & Co.
R. W. 'Tiny' Rowland	— Chief Executive, Lonrho PLC
Gerald Ronson	— Chairman, Heron Corporation
Anthony Parnes	— Stockbroker, Alexanders Laing and Cruickshank
Howard Hughes	— Senior Partner, Price Waterhouse, auditors to Guinness
John Chiene	— Senior Partner, Wood Mackensie, stockbrokers to Guinness
Robin Leigh Pemberton	— Governor of the Bank of England
George Blunden	— Deputy Governor of the Bank of England.

Sir John Nott	— Chairman, Lazard Brothers
Anthony Salz	— Partner, Freshfields, solicitors to Guinness
Rev. Oscar Muspratt	— Vicar of Penn, Buckinghamshire
Robert Maxwell	— Chairman, Mirror Newspaper Group

(October 1986 – present time)

Sir Alex Fletcher	— Former Trade Minister, Consultant to Argyll
Ivan Boesky	— Wall Street arbitrageur
Paul Channon	— Former Secretary of State for Dept. of Trade & Industry
Meshulam Ricklis	— Chairman, Rapid American Corporation (USA)
David Wynne-Morgan	— Chairman, Hill & Knowlton, PR Adviser to Guinness
Sir David Napley	— Senior Partner, Kingsley Napley, solicitors to Guinness
Hugh Peppiatt	— Senior Partner, Freshfields, solicitors of Guinness
Sir Nicholas Browne-Wilkinson	— Vice Chancellor of England
Stephen Ralph	— Partner, Payne Hicks Beach, solicitors to ES
Detective Superintendent Richard Botwright Chief Inspector John Wooton	— Police officers in charge of investigation into Guinness
Norman Turner Gerald Landau	— Partners in Landau and Landau, solicitors to ES
Philip Shepherd	— Barrister
Mr. Justice Hoffman	— Judge of the High Court
John Mathew QC Bruce Laughland QC	— Criminal barristers for ES during 1987–1988
Victor Temple Elizabeth Gloster	— Prosecution barristers
Mr. Justice Henry	— Appointed trial judge

CHRONOLOGY

G = Guinness
DCL = Distillers
MMC = Monopolies & Mergers Commission

1935 October 21	— Ernest Walter Schleyer born Vienna
1938 September	— Schleyer family leave Austria for UK
1942–1948	— ES attends Caldicott Preparatory School, Buckinghamshire
1948–1954	— ES attends St. Paul's School, London. Family change name from Schleyer to Saunders (1948)
1954–1956	— ES in National Service
1956–1959	— ES studies law at Emmanuel College, Cambridge
1959–1961	— ES's first job with 3M, industrial products manufacturer
1961–1964	— ES with J. Walter Thompson, advertising agency. Marries Carole Anne Stephings (1963)
1964–1973	— ES continues marketing career at Beecham Group
1973–1975	— ES with Great Universal Stores, mail-order group
1975–1976	— Saunders family move to Switzerland. ES works for Castolin S.A.
1976–1981	— ES with Nestlé S.A. in Switzerland
1981 October	— ES joins Guinness PLC
1982	— G rationalises business. Pretax profits improve from £41.8m to £50.9m

| 1983 | — Guinnless advertising campaign. Pretax profits rise from £50.9m to £58.8m |

1984

February	— Gulliver researches possible takeover bid for Distillers
June	— G acquire 'Martins' newsagents chain
November	— G purchase 'Champneys' health group
	— G pretax profits rise from £58.8m to £70.4m

1985

January	— G buy 'Natures Best' health products
February	— G buy Neighbourhood Stores UK 7-eleven franchise
March	— G plan Bell's acquisition
May	— Bell's share price jumps 158–183p
June 14	— G bid £330m for Bell
19	— Miquel returns from USA
25	— ES meets Miquel in London
27	— G release offer document
July 12	— Bell's defence document published
14	— Lord Spens complains to Takeover Panel about Morgan Grenfell acting for G
23	— Office of Fair Trading approve G bid
August 2	— G buy R.S. McColl, newsagents chain
5	— Bell's publishes formal defence document
7	— G raise bid to £370m. Tyrie advises Bell's shareholders to accept offer
23	— G win control of Bell's with 70% of shares
September 1	— Argyll and Lazards agree with Takeover Panel that there will be no bid 'at the present time' for DCL
30	— G pretax profits up from £70.4m to £86m
November	— G buy Cranks health food restaurant chain
December 2	— Argyll launch £1.87bn bid for DCL
17	— Argyll publishes formal offer document
23	— G and Bain hold planning meeting to discuss DCL
30	— DCL releases defence document

1986

| January 8 | — ES meets Bay Green of Kleinwort Benson, DCL's bankers |

9 — O.F.T. clears Argyll bid

18 — ES goes to Connell's home

19 — DCL hold all night board meeting and recommend G's bid and payment of G's costs

20 — G launch £2.2bn bid for DCL

27 — Argyll complain to Takeover Panel about cost's agreement. Complaint rejected

February 6 — Argyll issue writ claiming agreement is unlawful under Companies' Act. Argyll raise bid to £2.3bn

13 — G bid referred to Monopolies and Mergers Commission (MMC)

17 — ES sees LeQuesne at MMC

19 — First G bid allowed to lapse. ES wants to stop bidding, but is persuaded to carry on

20 — Second G bid announced – £2.35bn

25 — Argyll apply for judicial review of decision to allow first bid to lapse

27 — G Annual General Meeting (AGM)

March 3 — G release formal offer document

3 — Argyll case thrown out by High Court

14 — G sues Argyll and others over bid advertisements

March 21 — Office of Fair Trading clear second G bid. Argyll raise bid to £2.5 bn

26 — G hold Extraordinary General Meeting to approve increased underwriting

April 15 — G have 32% of DCL

17 — G have 46% of DCL

18 — (Lunchtime) G declare victory. Have 50.7% of DCL

May 18 — Risk, Ward and ES meet in Washington DC

June 12 — G board discusses who should be Chairman of Group

26 — Risk and ES dine at Savoy

July 8 — G board propose ES as Chairman. Iveagh elects for Presidency

10 — Risk meets Iveagh at G head office

11 — ES hosts merger celebration party

13 — *Sunday Times* breaks story that Risk will not be appointed Chairman

14 — G confirm that ES is to become Chairman. ES, Iveagh and Ward go to meeting at the Bank of England

15 — Wood MacKensie resign as brokers to G

August 13 — G announce that 5 new non-executive directors will be appointed

22 — G sends out circular to shareholders explaining why Risk was not appointed

September 8 — Charles Fraser resigns as Chairman of Morgan Grenfell (Scotland)

11 — G hold EGM in London and wins huge majority for new board proposals

November 14 — Boesky plea-bargains in USA. Fined $100m

20 — Scottish MP's table House of Commons motion attacking ES

December 1 — DTI inspectors arrive at G. National Gallery reception in evening

2 — House of Commons Insider Dealing debate

8 — Dinner ES, Macfarlane and Iveagh

9 — Lazards appointed as advisors to G

10 — G 1986 results announced. Pretax profits for 15 months up from £86m to £355m

11 — Schenley (USA) announce they have bought over 5% of G shares

13 — ES and Roux return from New York

18 — G announce $100m investment in Boesky fund

19 — False rumours in press of ES's resignation over Boesky investment

30 — Morgan Grenfell resign as bankers to G. Seelig resigns from Morgan Grenfell

1987

January 4 — ES arrives back from holiday in Switzerland

5 — 'Roux letter' arrives at G head office

6 — G holds board meeting at offices of Kingsley Napley. Roux delivers speech of apology

7 — Executive directors write letters of complaint about Macfarlane.

9 — ES agrees to step aside on full pay with legal fees paid

10 — ES flies to Switzerland to see Furer and then to Ireland to see Iveagh

11 — ES and CAS given weekend's rest at Champney's. Macfarlane appointed acting Chairman at board meeting

12 — Roux resigns from board

13 — ES is admitted to Lister Hospital, Chelsea

14 — ES sacked by G as Chairman and Chief Executive, asked to resign as Director. Tom Ward also asked to resign. Furer resigns.

— G announce £25n. invoices. Macfarlane sends circular to shareholders

20 — Reeves and Walsh resign from Morgan Grenfell

21 — Ronson pays back £5.8m to G

22 — Lord Spens resigns from Henry Ansbacher

23 — Sir Jack Lyons dropped by Bain & Co.

27 — Anthony Parnes dropped by Alexanders Laing and Cruickshank

— Cazenove deny illegal activity

February — ES attends DTI interviews despite poor health

27 — G begin legal action in Jersey over £5.2m MAC payment

March 8 — ES and CAS leave for rest in Switzerland

19 — G issue writs against ES and Tom Ward over £5.2m payment

25 — Mareva injunction granted over ES's assets in UK

April 6 — Rowland meets ES in Geneva

8/15 — ES goes to court to try to get Marera injunction lifted. Vice-Chancellor gives judgement against him

May 5 — Macfarlane writes to G shareholders. ES returns to UK

6 — ES attends DTI interview. Arrested by police. Spends a night in jail

7 — ES appears at Bow Street Magistrates Court charged with 3 offences. Bailed into custody of solicitor

12 — ES released on bail of £500,000

19 — ES's bail varied so he can visit CAS in Switzerland. ES leaves for Switzerland

26 — ES resigns directorship of G

27 — G AGM

June 11 — General Election GB

22 — Saunders family move out of Knoll House

July 7 — ES remanded at Bow Street

17 — G obtain summary judgment against Ward. Order him to repay £5.2m

24 — ES joins Roux as third party to £5.2m claim

28 — ES sues G for wrongful dismissal

August — ES works on DTI submission

September 1 — Remand (Bow Street)

2 — Takeover Panel rule G acting in concert with Bank Leu

October 1 — Parnes arrested in Los Angeles, California

8 — Lyons arrested in London

12 — ES is charged with a further 37 offences. Gerald Ronson is arrested

13 — ES and Ronson appear in court. ES gives press conference at Waldorf Hotel

15 — Roger Seelig is arrested

18 — Boesky jailed for 3 years (USA)

November 3 — Remand (Bow Street)

December — Saunders family homeless

31 — G has record pretax profits – up from £355 to £408m

1988

January — ES moves in with Bowman family. Guinness cut off all funds for living expenses

19 — ES fails to get £5.2m case 'stayed' in the High Court

February — Saunders family denied all living expenses by G

March 10 — Lord Spens arrested

21 — Saunders family win right to draw living expenses again and money is released by court to buy a small house in London

24 — Parnes arrives back in UK

April 6 — Serious Fraud Office Opens (SFO)

7 — David Mayhew arrested

12 — Remand (Bow Street)

May 12 — G AGM

June 1 — Remand (Bow Street)

July 6 — Saunders family move into own house

11 — Remand (Bow Street)

28 — Judicial review SFO request by E

September 26 — Remand (Bow Street)

October 17 — ES takes 'stay' appeal to Court of Appeal

31 — Criminal Justice Act 1988 in force

November 28 — Remand (Bow Street)

December 12/13 — ES's legal aid hearing. Granted Criminal Legal Aid

16 — First pre-trial review Southwark Crown Court

1989

April 27 — Pre-trial review Southwark Crown Court. Landau and Landau withdraw

May 10 — Pannone Blackburn take over ES's case

APPENDIX

THE INDEPENDENT   18 SEPTEMBER 1989

Saunders needs one trial only

A PRE-TRIAL hearing beginning today at the Law Courts in London will decide whether the criminal case arising from the Guinness takeover of Distillers should be heard in one, two or more trials. There are seven defendants, including the former Guinness chairman, Ernest Saunders. The prosecution, on behalf of the Serious Fraud Office, is expected to propose that there should be two trials of four defendants each, consisting respectively of the corporate participants and advisers, with Mr Saunders appearing in both. Two of the Guinness advisers are expected to apply for separate trials; and other defendants believe it is unfair that they should have to sit through parts of the case which have nothing to do with them. Two trials might last for three to six months each; a single trial up to a year.

The Serious Fraud Office doubts whether a jury of sufficient calibre can be found to sit through so long a hearing. That argument would be more convincing if the SFO were not pressing almost 50 charges, many of them inevitably overlapping. If the number is cut, as is possible, the case for separate trials would be weakened. Should Mr Justice Henry none the less decide that two trials would be better than one, to submit the former Guinness chairman to a double ordeal would run counter to natural justice. Only one trial should be needed to establish his guilt or innocence. If he were found guilty at the first trial, he would be unlikely to receive a fair hearing at the second; and a desire to prevent the second jury from being prejudiced would most likely result in undesirably draconian restrictions being imposed on the reporting of the first trial. Finally, the evidence of those appearing in the second trial might be very relevant to judgement of those in the first. The mere idea that Mr Saunders should be tried twice has done much to arouse sympathy for him where little or none previously existed.

The trial, or first trial, is scheduled to begin in January. Also at stake will be the reputation of the infant Serious Fraud Office, whose first big case to come to court this will be. The SFO was set up in 1987 in response to the report of the Roskill Committee on Fraud Trials, which in 1986 concluded that the public "no longer believes that the legal system in England and Wales is capable of bringing the perpetrators of serious frauds expeditiously and effectively to book." Reckon-

ing that the average juror was out of his depth in such cases, it proposed a Fraud Trials Tribunal consisting of a judge and two experienced lay members.

The Government rejected that idea. But it set up the SFO with formidable powers of investigation – and, in the light of its hostility to publication of the Department of Trade report into the House of Fraser affair, of delay. Part of its remit is to present the prosecution case to judge and jurors in slimmed-down and more assimilable form after some preparatory hearings. Fraud cases are notoriously complex, dealing as they do with the borderlines of accepted practice and with defendants who do not seem criminal. The Guinness case will be a test of its ability to show results.

SUNDAY TIMES   10 SEPTEMBER 1989

Saunders' double nightmare

WHILE the rest of us have been enjoying the best summer for years, Ernest Saunders, the former chairman of Guinness, has been wending his way to the offices of his lawyers, spending up to 10 hours a day on his defence. The publication of his son's book in June ended his social ostracism and he is once again a welcome dinner-table guest, but that is only fleeting consolation to a man whose health is fragile, and whose financial situation is parlous.

We are now approaching the third anniversary of that fateful day in December 1986 when the DTI inspectors entered the Guinness premises, but the trial is still months away, not due to start until January or February at the earliest.

I say "trial" but there may be more than one. Tomorrow week the next stage of these tortuous judicial proceedings opens in a dreary courtroom in Southwark, where the prosecution will ask Mr Justice Henry to "split the indictment", and make it two trials, half the defendants to appear in one, half in the other, with Saunders common to both.

One can see the desirability of this from the prosecution's viewpoint. There are 49 charges against Saunders alone and I cannot even count those against the other six. The bulk of them are centred around alleged breaches of Section 151 of the Companies Act (which basically forbids a company from using its own money to support its share prices), but a great edifice of other charges has been added, in what one lawyer friend calls "one of the biggest scattergun approaches I've ever seen from a prosecution".

Having built the edifice, the prosecution now claims that no one jury can reasonably be expected to understand it – hence the request for a split indictment. Apart from the inhumanity of asking Saunders to undergo two long trials in succession, this raises the other fundamental issues. For instance, how does the judge avoid the dangers of a second jury being influenced by the first? Does he impose tight reporting restrictions on trial one – as happened in the later stages of the Postgate/Grob trial causing serious consternation in Fleet Street – and hope that the jury in trial two remains blissfully ignorant of the rumours that will undoubtedly whizz through the City and the press? What happens if a defendant is suddenly and inexplicably absent from his office, and gives his forwarding address as Wormwood Scrubs?

As a layman, let me suggest a Lord Denning-type solution. Instead of the scattergun approach, let the prosecution trim the charges down to a focused smaller number which a single jury can be expected to understand. We could then have one trial, save a lot of public money and behave in a much more humane manner – all at the same time.

SUNDAY TIMES   17 SEPTEMBER 1989

Misjudged trials

MY SUGGESTION last week that the Guinness prosecutors should drastically trim back the number of charges (and have one trial rather than two) struck a nerve among m'learned friends in the legal profession. Most lawyers I know are appalled at the thought of subjecting Ernest Saunders to two trials, possibly lasting six months each.

On Tuesday I had a call from a former judge, a man whose name most of my readers would be familiar with. He has been involved in many a leading fraud case. I thought initially I was in for a ticking off for attacking the judicial process, but quite the contrary. He told me that he, and many of his fellow judges, feel far more strongly than I do about the manner in which fraud cases are increasingly being prosecuted. "It has got utterly and completely out of hand," he said.

In the old days, he said, prosecutions kept fraud charges at a level capable of being understood by juries (and by judges). In the past five or six years, however, he and his colleagues have found prosecutions pressing 30, 40 or even more charges, many of them repetitive; accountants and other experts have been wheeled into courts in ever greater numbers, using terms and introducing concepts that even the lawyers barely understand. And all the time the prosecution piles more charges, including conspiracy, which my friend the judge regards with even greater misgiving. "They forget about the guts of the case – the charges basically should say 'this is the crime, and you did it'."

The 49 charges against Saunders should be cut, he reckons, to comprehensible levels. Splitting the trial into two, with Saunders common to both, would, he says, be a "wicked abuse". I have found no one who disagrees.

SUNDAY TIMES   24 SEPTEMBER 1989

Saunders gag

I WOULD LIKE to bring you the latest news in the case of Regina v Ernest Walter Saunders, but I can't. Section 11 of the Criminal Justice Act 1987 now forbids it, and coupled with a stiff letter from the attorney general's office, it stopped all newspaper reporting of the preliminary hearings last week. Even as I write this, my lawyers are standing at my shoulder.

It may be a long, long time before you read further court reports of Saunders and the other Guinness defendants. One wonders whatever happened to Lord Denning's famous principles of open justice and freedom of the press? As he said: "It is of the first importance that justice should be done openly and in public."

Shocking case of legal torture

ON MONDAY WEEK Mr Ernest Saunders is to learn whether he is to face two trials for his part of what has become known as the Guinness affair.

Whether Mr Saunders will be found innocent or guilty does not concern us here. What should be a matter of public concern, however, is that a man is being put through what can only be described as a form of legal torture.

The prosecution say that he should face no fewer than 69 charges – and that, they say, justifies having two trials.

That's outrageous and unnecessary.

Mr Saunders has already had to wait an unconscionably long time for his case actually to be heard. To expect him to sit in court day after day, week after week and month after month on two separate occasions is to add a quite unacceptable degree of suffering to a man already brought quite extraordinarily low by events which have overwhelmed him.

Two trials for Saunders would shame the British legal system.

INDEX

Bestselling Non-Fiction

☐	Complete Hip and Thigh Diet	Rosemary Conley	£2.99
☐	Staying off the Beaten Track	Elizabeth Gundrey	£6.99
☐	Raw Energy: Recipes	Leslie Kenton	£3.99
☐	The PM System	Dr J A Muir Gray	£5.99
☐	Women Who Love Too Much	Robin Norwood	£3.50
☐	Letters From Women Who Love Too Much	Robin Norwood	£3.50
☐	Fat is a Feminist Issue	Susie Orbach	£2.99
☐	Callanetics	Callan Pinckney	£6.99
☐	Elvis and Me	Priscilla Presley	£3.50
☐	Love, Medicine and Miracles	Bernie Siegel	£3.50
☐	Communion	Whitley Strieber	£3.50
☐	Trump: The Art of the Deal	Donald Trump	£3.99

Prices and other details are liable to change

ARROW BOOKS, BOOKSERVICE BY POST, PO BOX 29, DOUGLAS, ISLE OF MAN, BRITISH ISLES

NAME...

ADDRESS..

....

....

Please enclose a cheque or postal order made out to Arrow Books Ltd. for the amount due and allow the following for postage and packing.

U.K. CUSTOMERS: Please allow 22p per book to a maximum of £3.00.

B.F.P.O. & EIRE: Please allow 22p per book to a maximum of £3.00.

OVERSEAS CUSTOMERS: Please allow 22p per book.

Whilst every effort is made to keep prices low it is sometimes necessary to increase cover prices at short notice. Arrow Books reserve the right to show new retail prices on covers which may differ from those previously advertised in the text or elsewhere.

Bestselling War Fiction and Non-Fiction

☐ Bat 21	William C Anderson	£2.50
☐ Royal Navy and the Falklands War	David Brown	£8.99
☐ The Cocaine Wars	Paul Eddy	£3.99
☐ China Seas	John Harris	£3.99
☐ Passage to Mutiny	Alexander Kent	£3.50
☐ Colours Aloft	Alexander Kent	£2.99
☐ The Hour of the Lily	John Kruse	£3.50
☐ The Bombers	Norman Longmate	£4.99
☐ Convoy	Dudley Pope	£3.50
☐ Winged Escort	Douglas Reeman	£2.99
☐ Typhoon Pilot	Desmond Scott	£2.99
☐ The Spoils of War	Douglas Scott	£2.99
☐ Johnny Gurkha	E D Smith	£2.95
☐ Duel in the Dark	Peter Townsend	£3.95

Prices and other details are liable to change

ARROW BOOKS, BOOKSERVICE BY POST, PO BOX 29, DOUGLAS, ISLE OF MAN, BRITISH ISLES

NAME...

ADDRESS...

....

....

Please enclose a cheque or postal order made out to Arrow Books Ltd. for the amount due and allow the following for postage and packing.

U.K. CUSTOMERS: Please allow 22p per book to a maximum of £3.00.

B.F.P.O. & EIRE: Please allow 22p per book to a maximum of £3.00.

OVERSEAS CUSTOMERS: Please allow 22p per book.

Whilst every effort is made to keep prices low it is sometimes necessary to increase cover prices at short notice. Arrow Books reserve the right to show new retail prices on covers which may differ from those previously advertised in the text or elsewhere.

A Selection of Arrow Books

☐ No Enemy But Time	Evelyn Anthony	£2.95
☐ The Lilac Bus	Maeve Binchy	£2.99
☐ Rates of Exchange	Malcolm Bradbury	£3.50
☐ Prime Time	Joan Collins	£3.50
☐ Rosemary Conley's Complete Hip and Thigh Diet	Rosemary Conley	£2.99
☐ Staying Off the Beaten Track	Elizabeth Gundrey	£6.99
☐ Duncton Wood	William Horwood	£4.50
☐ Duncton Quest	William Horwood	£4.50
☐ A World Apart	Marie Joseph	£3.50
☐ Erin's Child	Sheelagh Kelly	£3.99
☐ Colours Aloft	Alexander Kent	£2.99
☐ Gondar	Nicholas Luard	£4.50
☐ The Ladies of Missalonghi	Colleen McCullough	£2.50
☐ The Veiled One	Ruth Rendell	£3.50
☐ Sarum	Edward Rutherfurd	£4.99
☐ Communion	Whitley Strieber	£3.99

Prices and other details are liable to change

ARROW BOOKS, BOOKSERVICE BY POST, PO BOX 29, DOUGLAS, ISLE OF MAN, BRITISH ISLES

NAME...

ADDRESS...

....

....

Please enclose a cheque or postal order made out to Arrow Books Ltd. for the amount due and allow the following for postage and packing.

U.K. CUSTOMERS: Please allow 22p per book to a maximum of £3.00.

B.F.P.O. & EIRE: Please allow 22p per book to a maximum of £3.00.

OVERSEAS CUSTOMERS: Please allow 22p per book.

Whilst every effort is made to keep prices low it is sometimes necessary to increase cover prices at short notice. Arrow Books reserve the right to show new retail prices on covers which may differ from those previously advertised in the text or elsewhere.

Bestselling General Fiction

☐ No Enemy But Time	Evelyn Anthony	£2.95
☐ Skydancer	Geoffrey Archer	£3.50
☐ The Sisters	Pat Booth	£3.50
☐ Captives of Time	Malcolm Bosse	£2.99
☐ Saudi	Laurie Devine	£2.95
☐ Duncton Wood	William Horwood	£4.50
☐ Aztec	Gary Jennings	£3.95
☐ A World Apart	Marie Joseph	£3.50
☐ The Ladies of Missalonghi	Colleen McCullough	£2.50
☐ Lily Golightly	Pamela Oldfield	£3.50
☐ Sarum	Edward Rutherfurd	£4.99
☐ Communion	Whitley Strieber	£3.99

Prices and other details are liable to change

ARROW BOOKS, BOOKSERVICE BY POST, PO BOX 29, DOUGLAS, ISLE
OF MAN, BRITISH ISLES

NAME..

ADDRESS..

....

....

Please enclose a cheque or postal order made out to Arrow Books Ltd. for the amount
due and allow the following for postage and packing.

U.K. CUSTOMERS: Please allow 22p per book to a maximum of £3.00.

B.F.P.O. & EIRE: Please allow 22p per book to a maximum of £3.00.

OVERSEAS CUSTOMERS: Please allow 22p per book.

Whilst every effort is made to keep prices low it is sometimes necessary to increase cover
prices at short notice. Arrow Books reserve the right to show new retail prices on covers
which may differ from those previously advertised in the text or elsewhere.